UNDERGROUND OVERGROUND

A PASSENGER'S HISTORY OF THE TUBE

ANDREW MARTIN

P

PROFILE BC

This paperback edition published in 2013

First published in Great Britain in 2012 by
PROFILE BOOKS LTD
3A Exmouth House
Pine Street
London ECIR OJH
www.profilebooks.com

'The Burial of the Dead' taken from *The Waste Land* © Estate of T.S. Eliot
and reprinted by permission of Faber and Faber Ltd

3 5 7 9 10 8 6 4 2

Designed by Geoff Green Book Design, Cambridge
Typeset in Jenson by MacGuru Ltd
info@macguru.org.uk

Printed and bound in Great Britain by
CPI Group (UK) Ltd, Croydon CRO 4YY

A CIP catalogue record for this book is available from the British Library.

ISBN 978 1 84668 478 4
eISBN 978 1 84765 807 4

MIX
Paper from
responsible sources
FSC® C020471

'A jaunty history, studded with little observational gems ...
he can occasionally stop you in your tracks with a well-turned
phrase' *Sunday Times*

'Seeing Martin puzzle his way through the history is half the
fun, as are his lively interlocutors ... the language is beautiful'
Financial Times

'A highly engaging journey through the history and geography
of the tube.' *Independent*

'An excellent 'passengers history' of the network ... entertaining'
Spectator

'Deeply pleasurable ... Martin has all the history at his finger-
tips ... *Underground, Overground* is the book to take with you
next time you find yourself stuck in a deep tunnel' *Prospect*

'This engaging and witty social history of the London
underground is guaranteed to beguile' *Observer*

'Hugely entertaining ... gives us all the lore and myths ...
Underground, Overground captures the same zest, zaniness and
sense of marvel shown in BBC Two series *The Tube*.' *The Times*

'I missed my stop on three separate occasions while engrossed
in this readable and very funny history' *Country Life*

'So dense with fascinating facts that a Londoner can dip into
it at almost any point and get a new insight to enrich their
experience of the city ... a fine tribute' *Time Out*

'Martin's witty tome is as entertaining as its subject is
frustrating.' *Word*

'Finally, a note on the writing. It's beautiful. It's just really
elegant, effortless, perfect prose.' *Baroque in Hackney*

'Mr Martin clearly know his onions, and loves the Underground, and enjoys telling others why. His enthusiasm is infectious ... recommended as an enjoyable read' *Underground News*

'Plenty of fun' *Evening Standard*

'Compelling social history' *Choice*

'I would strongly endorse Martin's book as the stop to get on at' Will Self, *Guardian*

ANDREW MARTIN is a journalist and novelist resident in North London. He qualified as a barrister but turned to journalism after winning the *Spectator* Young Writer of the Year Award. He has written for most British newspapers, and contributes regularly to the *Guardian* and *Independent*. He is the author of ten novels (all published by Faber), including eight in the 'Jim Stringer' series of historical thrillers based around railways. The first of these was *The Necropolis Railway*. The latest, *The Somme Stations*, won the Crime Writers' Association Ellis Peters Award for historical crime fiction. Two other titles in the series were shortlisted for this award, and in 2008, the series was shortlisted for the CWA Body in the Library Award. He broadcasts regularly, and has written and presented TV documentaries.

A NOTE ON THE TITLE

On London Underground, there are the cut-and-cover lines running just below the surface, and the Tubes properly so-called, which are on average about 40 feet down. But 'Tube' is now used as shorthand for the whole network, not least by London Underground itself, as in 'Upgrading Your Tube'; and it is used to mean the whole network in the title of this book. It tends to be older Londoners who hold on to the distinction. A friend of mine was visiting his mother who lives about 500 yards from Parsons Green station on the District, which is a cut-and-cover line. At the end of the evening she said, 'How are you getting back?' He said, 'Oh, on the Tube', and she looked at him absolutely blankly. '*What* Tube?' she said. 'There *is* no Tube here.' To her and to all other sticklers for the distinction I apologise, and I offer in mitigation the fact that my title *does* take note of the paradox that seems to embody the overall perversity of the Underground: 55 per cent of it is on the surface.

CONTENTS

CHAPTER THREE: THE METROPOLITAN AND ITS ASSOCIATES

CHAPTER FOUR: THE EXPANSION OF THE METROPOLITAN AND THE EXPANSION OF THE DISTRICT – AND A PAUSE FOR THOUGHT

CHAPTER FIVE: DEEPER

CHAPTER SIX: THREE MORE TUBES

CHAPTER SEVEN: ENTER YERKES

'DAD, I'M OFF TO LONDON'

I have always been keen on the London Underground, even though I was born in Yorkshire. I was like Richard Larch in *A Man from the North* (1898), by Arnold Bennett: 'There grows in the North Country a certain kind of youth of whom it may be said that he is born to be a Londoner. The metropolis, and everything that pertains to it, that comes down from it, that goes up into it, has for him an imperious fascination.'

My father worked on British Rail, and I had free first-class train travel on the national rail network in the form of a Privilege Pass. I also had free travel on the London Underground, which seemed almost indecent, given that my dad did not work for the Underground and that I came from 250 miles north of London. If at all bored in York, I'd say, 'Dad, I'm off to London', and I'd collect up my Priv Pass and a handful of the privilege Underground tickets that were usually lying about the house. (Whereas normal Underground tickets in the Seventies were made of green card, the privilege tickets were green and white card – special, you see.) 'Well, don't lose your Pass, or I'll get sacked,' my dad would say.

London wore me out. But then I had a very exhausting method of traversing the city, which involved pinballing about from one public street map to another. In theory you could work out your route by pressing buttons that illuminated little light bulbs, but the 'You Are Here' part had always been carefully vandalised, and without that you might have been anywhere. So I'd take the Tube, because the Tube map I could understand. But precisely because it is schematic rather than geographically accurate, with the central area magnified for clarity – so that the distance between Archway and Highgate on the Northern Line, which is about a mile, is shown as being less than the distance between Leicester Square and Covent Garden on the Piccadilly Line, which is about 800 feet – I would take journeys I didn't need to take, for example *from* Leicester Square to Covent Garden, which is the shortest trip possible on the Underground. 'When in doubt take the Underground', urged an early Underground poster showing a bewildered little bowler-hatted man with an illuminated 'Underground' sign behind him. That little man was me.

The Underground was my ally in London. I was the son of a railwayman, and what was the Underground but an incredibly high concentration of railways? Also it offered a key to the city ... so maybe I *wouldn't* get off at Leicester Square. I might stay on all the way to Manor House, where I would step out and have a walk around, always keeping Manor House station in sight, just as Doctor Who keeps the Tardis in sprinting range when he lands on a new and possibly dangerous planet. I would travel to a place on the slightest of motivations, to find things out. Was there a Manor House at Manor House? (No, only a pub called The Manor House.) Was there a hill at Gants Hill? No; that would be almost as naive as expecting a hill at *Dollis* Hill. (There isn't even an apostrophe at Gants Hill, a deficiency it shares with Parsons Green but not

Earl's Court. But by way of compensation, there is a beautiful Underground station.)

In my boyhood, the system was not what it had been in the triumphalist inter-way heyday, and nor was it like the spruce, sparkling (if badly overcrowded), upgraded Underground of today. In the Seventies the system was run-down and demoralised. Road transport was the future; the Underground was being 'managed for decline', and the system was filthier even than the streets above. You were not to lean against the station walls, or that was your rally jacket ruined. In most of the stations about a quarter of the tiles would be broken. Sometimes the station name was meant to be spelled out by tiles, and Londoners' toleration of the position at, say, Covent Garden – rendered for years as something like 'COV—T G—DEN' – implied an impressive broad-mindedness on their part.

You could actually see the atmosphere in the stations: it was sooty, particulate. There is an Underground poster from the late Thirties by Austin Cooper that advertised something as unmysterious as 'Cheap Return Tickets' but did so with an abstract image: a lonely searchlight trying to penetrate a jaundiced miasma. That was the Underground of my boyhood: a marvel of engineering but also a dream space, in which people of all classes and races would float past you, with the strange buoyancy of a passing carriage. In the case of the people in your own carriage (or 'car', since the Underground is riddled with American railway terminology), you could look at them directly, or you could look at their reflections in the windows, and they would be sunk in their own dreams; all this under electric light, so that it always seemed – as it always still *seems* – to be evening on the Tube, which is my favourite time of day. The trains then still had smoking carriages, and I would sit in these because their passengers seemed the friendliest – and I would *smoke* in the smoking carriage, because it seemed the done thing.

The trains also had guards: a Gothic-looking priesthood, with their ill-fitting black uniforms and black DMs. They carried covetable, riveted black leather holdalls that contained the big key that unlocked the control panel by which they opened and closed the doors, and billy-cans they used for making tea at 'tea points' (basically kettles secreted behind panels in the station walls). I liked the way they would close their own guard's door after they'd pressed the button to close all the other doors, and they would then hang out of the carriage as it sped along to the tunnel headwall. They did this just for the hell of it, I thought. The guards were pale men, possibly as a result of spending too much time underground. Like most Londoners, they were slightly disreputable-looking, and intimidatingly self-contained. It was impossible, I reasoned, to be more of a Londoner than a Tube guard, since they actually operated the city. In the Seventies the guards did not command public address systems, but they would sometimes – when they could be bothered – bawl out their catchphrase 'Mind The Doors', and I couldn't believe they weren't doing it in a spirit of irony or, more likely, sarcasm. The idea that such a vast populace could be suborned by such a gnomic phrase ... it didn't make any sense, unless perhaps the passengers were in on the joke. (In the incredibly boring Underground horror film *Death Line*, from 1971, a dying cannibal who inhabits an abandoned tunnel somewhere near Russell Square station can speak no words of English except for a distorted version of 'Mind The Doors', which he has picked up, parrot fashion, from having heard it so many times.)

If I found the Tube trains morbidly fascinating, I had a simpler enthusiasm for the escalators. Everyone likes going on escalators as far as I know. It feels like a free ride, and the longer they are, the better. The only escalator in York was at Marks & Spencer's, and people would hesitate for ages before getting on, apparently waiting for the right stair to come rolling along, whereas Londoners would step on while reading a newspaper.

My journeys were given a further spice by fear. A train travelling at a little over 20 miles an hour (the average speed of a Tube train in central London) with tunnel walls one foot away on either side feels much faster than one going at the same speed through fields. Surely the tiny clearance would eventually prove insufficient, and the train would scrape against the wall? Or the tunnel would collapse; or the train would run into another train coming the other way or, failing that, into the back of a slower one going the same way. In short, I considered the idea of trains in subterranean tunnels to be a very daring and audacious one. I was also disturbed by the noises of a Tube train, such as the roaring of the air-brake compressor, which sounds like a roar of defiance from the train. (The train will not go unless there is sufficient pressure to release the brakes, hence the noise.)

I have now lived in London for twenty-five years, during the early part of which I commuted from outlying parts of the city to central newspaper offices, latterly the *London Evening Standard*. After I left the *Standard*, I began writing a column called 'Tube Talk' for the paper's magazine, *ES*. This was in the second half of the Nineties, when the Underground was fitfully emerging from its post-war slump and becoming once more a fit subject for conversation. Every week I would receive a quantity of letters justifying the columnist's epithet 'a bulging postbag' (about six). Cumulatively, I received hundreds of letters in which people got off their chest things that had been bothering them about the Tube for years. Didn't anyone at London Underground know that the announcement, 'This train terminates at Morden via Bank' was ungrammatical, there being no place called 'Morden via Bank'? Why couldn't every third train in the rush hour contain no seats? Why wasn't there a Tube station at Victoria Coach Station? A poet called Roger Tagholm wrote in to say he'd seen

a man carrying a surfboard down the escalator at Tottenham
Court Road. ('Now *that* was weird.') Tagholm himself had pub-
lished a series of poetic parodies with Underground themes.
One was called *The Rubaiyat of Totteridge and Whetstone*; his
take on *The Waste Land*, which included the lines 'On Moorgate
Station/ I can connect/Nothing with nothing.' An exasperated
woman informed me that, for a year, there had been a sign at
Kentish Town reading, 'Warning, Keep Clear, Grille May Be
Dirty', and when I mentioned this in print, the staff at Kentish
Town kindly sent me the sign, but whether they cleaned the
grille I don't know.

TRANSPORT FOR LONDON ... AND VICE VERSA

In a novel by Dorothy Whipple called *High Wages*, which was published in 1930 but set in the Edwardian period, young Jane Carter arrives at Euston station from the fictional Lancastrian town of Tidsley. It is her first visit to London. She steps onto the Euston Road and takes in the scene. 'Not beautiful certainly, but how exciting! What cars, what buses, what bicycles, what horses – and what was that running with a roar under a grating?'

The roar under the grating was the Metropolitan Railway, currently trading – in somewhat reduced circumstances – as the Metropolitan *Line* of the London Underground. The stretch of the railway that ran under the Euston Road opened 150 years ago, in January 1863. It went from Paddington Bishop's Road station, now called Paddington, to Farringdon Street station, now called Farringdon. It was the first urban underground railway in the world (there had been long underground stretches of main-line railways, also railways in mines), but the Metropolitan was very nearly the only outfit ever to use steam trains on a subterranean railway (it was also done in Glasgow), so its project was only half-modern, and the tunnels under the Euston Road were badly polluted until 1905, when the Met began to be electrified.

By 'grating', Dorothy Whipple refers to the grilles along the middle of the road that were installed in 1871 and 1872 for ventilation, the Metropolitan having given up pretending it didn't have an air quality problem. There were a dozen, each 28 feet long by 2 foot 6, and in *London's Metropolitan Railway* (1986) Alan A. Jackson has this to say about them:

> The author's father, who worked at the Railway Clearing House in Eversholt (then Seymour) Street, Euston, used to recall that these grilles afforded a lunchtime diversion for the younger clerks, whose custom was to keep them under close surveillance. The reason for this was that should any lady be unwise enough to stand over them whilst a train was passing below, the force of the blast would raise her skirts in a satisfyingly revealing fashion.

If you stand over those grates today and crouch down (risking the malevolent stares of passing cabbies), you will see a black baffle plate littered with cigarette ends. You will eventually hear a rising roar from below, and you'll feel the warm updraft as the train runs beneath your feet. If you were also enveloped in steam, you'd also have the beginnings of a ghost story, but then London is full of black holes that take you back into the Underground past. Some of these are *on* the Underground, some are not. One is on the *Overground*: the railway called the London Overground, I mean. The under-river tunnel on that line between Wapping and Rotherhithe is pitch black when viewed from the trains that traverse it, but if it were to be illuminated, passengers would see that they were in what resembles the undercroft of a Gothic cathedral. That was the first of the deep-level Tubes ... *in a way*, and it was once incorporated into a Tube line ... *of sorts*.

Or you could say the Tubes were more truly portended by what lies beneath a certain brick turret near the Tower of London that is ignored daily by thousands of visitors to the Tower. We will soon be lifting up that booth, so to speak, and looking into the momentous tunnel beneath. I take a perverse pleasure in seeing people streaming past it, or in watching City commuters ignoring the stone company crest of the City & South London Railway on the outside of Moorgate station. The simple motif on the crest says it all: trains in tunnels under a wavy river. Don't the passing crowds know how important was the work of that railway? It built what became the Bank branch of the Northern Line, and I suppose that most Northern Line users do try to ignore the Tube, or they see it as incidental penance of their life in London, but if it weren't for the Tube, they probably wouldn't be in London. In fact, there wouldn't be a London for them to be in – not one like the present city anyway.

You might object to the moles under the lawn, but what if the moles actually planted the lawn in the first place? In the interwar period, the Underground would reach out more dramatically, horrifically some would say – The Thing That Crawled Out of the Ground! – to make the vast commuter city of today. It did so partly to solve successive crises of unemployment and partly, and somewhat less nobly, to acquire more passengers. Since we, the passengers thus acquired, are stuck with the Tube, I say why not understand it? The Northern Line commuter who reads this book will learn why the Northern is not so much a line as a network (and a right dog's dinner into the bargain); they will learn why it had the first suicide pits under its tracks (it's because of the Depression rather than anything depress*ing* about the line); and they will find out about London Underground's ultimate answer to those who complain persistently about the Northern.

Turning to Central Line users, I say: Do you know about your glamorous line's association with the West End shops? Do you know why so many of the station interiors are coloured white? Do you know about the personage known as Sonia that it foisted on London?

The Central is my own favourite line. I lived on it for years, and appreciated its high train frequency in the rush hour. The other day I was at Marble Arch in the peak, and I saw a young boy rushing onto the platform in the company of a man who was probably his grandfather (well, I *hope* it was). As the train came in, the boy exclaimed delightedly, 'Just in time!' He probably didn't know that another would be along in ninety seconds. It is amazing that trains should be manifested so frequently, like a conjurer pulling endless rabbits out of a hat – and this book will explain some of the technical and operational wonders of the system. For example, it features an account of Underground electricity written *by* somebody who can't change a plug (me), *for* people who can't change a plug.

The London Underground is the oldest Metro in the world. It has 250 miles of track and 287 stations. At the time of writing, 1.1 billion passenger journeys are made on the Underground every year, the highest figure ever recorded, and more people use the Tube than the rest of the national rail network. You can push these superlatives of scale only so far. Shanghai has more track; the Paris Metro and the New York Subway have more stations. The Paris and Moscow metros are busier. But because the London Underground was never properly planned but just sort of sprawled, and because it was built over the course of 140 years, it is far more revealing of the history and character of the city it serves than any of the above systems. And at the risk of sounding like the compiler of a book of Underground curiosities (this book, I stress, is a full history, albeit one without footnotes and thickets of technical data), I might also mention that it is by far the weirdest of the world's metros. Quite a lot of Londoners know about the dummy houses in Leinster Gardens, Bayswater, which were built to screen a cutting of the Metropolitan Line. But I believe I am the first person to write about what the people who live alongside those façades make of them – or indeed whether they have in fact noticed that they are not real houses.

The Underground is also full of gaps, some of them literal. I refer to the notorious gaps between the trains and the platforms, and we will be meeting a man who can name them all. These gave rise to the 'Mind The Gap' announcements – which, incidentally, will bring us to another story set in Bayswater, this one involving Michael Winner, and a somewhat presumptuous voice-over man. But some of the gaps are more widely defined as mysterious lacunae, both big and small. When I lived out east on the Central Line, there was a Ladies but no Gents at Leytonstone station. At Roding Valley there was a sign saying 'Waiting Room' but no actual waiting room. Our Underground generally begs a lot of questions. Why is there no Tube at Crouch End, or in much of south London? Why is there a Mill Hill East but no Mill Hill West? Why are the Metropolitan Line tunnels between Baker Street and Finchley Road so much smaller than the other tunnels on that line? And why do the westbound Piccadilly and southbound Victoria Line platforms at Finsbury Park occupy spaces much *bigger* than the other platforms on those lines?

With understanding may come appreciation. This book does not intend to make rail enthusiasts of its readers, although we will be meeting the modellers of the Underground, the people (all right then, the *men*) who voluntarily attend lectures on the subject or who try to visit every station within a twenty-four-hour period, following arcane rules that proscribe, for example, the use of Spacehoppers when transferring at street level between termini. We will be asking why the red trains of 1938 were so popular, and why so many men and women want to own bags made of a certain District Line seat moquette. But the wider point is that much of the Underground is beautiful, and I don't just mean the countrified surface stations, many of which have valanced canopies, well-tended flower beds, un-vandalised benches and actual smiling *staff* – all the elements that draw amateur photographers to the branch line stations on the 'big' railways. The Underground somehow doesn't count in the lexicon of railway romance. It seems that less is more: that it is better to have one or two trains a day than to have one every few minutes.

But it is not hard to tune into the romance of the Underground. Look at the towering arcaded walls of the brick ravines through which the Metropolitan runs, with the backs of houses tottering above. The appeal of the cut-and-cover lines is in the sense of being backstage, or down in the basement, of operating covertly. The deep-level Tubes, too, have a glamour, or at least an anti-glamour. There are the constricted, cash-strapped halts of the Victoria Line, which are like so many bodged 1960s' bathrooms; and there are the palatial stations of the Jubilee Line extension, which were built in direct reaction against those bathrooms. But the best Tube stations are those jewel-like ones in the middle of town, on the Bakerloo, Piccadilly and Northern Charing Cross branches, and we will be hearing about the young man called Leslie Green, who worked himself into an early grave in order to create a unique scheme of coloured tiles for the platforms of each – schemes that have been carefully restored in the least talked-about part of the current Tube Upgrade.

And then there is Frank Pick, who, like many of the very best people, came from York, and spent most of his working life as an Underground executive trying to rationalise a city that he had found confusing and overwhelming on boyhood visits from the north. He is the man behind the Underground roundel, the most brilliant and elemental logo since the Christian cross.

Frank Pick: one of the two most important men on the twentieth century Underground. He was a fastidious, sometimes cranky individual (the ink in that pen is green), but with a great sense of style. He used the Underground to rationalise a city he'd found confusing on boyhood visits from the north. But he also oversaw the expansion of the Underground, and in so doing, he admitted that he had made London more bewildering still.

When seen illuminated outside a Tube station located alongside one of the approach roads to London (for example, Hillingdon, when returning to the city from the west), it kindles in me a surge of uncomplicated affection for a city that usually arouses more mixed emotions. It was also on Frank Pick's watch that the diagrammatic Underground map was introduced – that comfort blanket for Londoners, which reassures them that their city makes sense, even though in fact it doesn't, precisely because of the expansion caused by the system that the map depicts.

Frank Pick failed in his mission to rationalise London, as he admitted, and in having promoted the expansion of the Underground, which in turn caused the expansion of the city, he realised he had created a monster which he tried to contain by the imposition of the Green Belt. He goes down as a martyr to the Underground, one of a series of men (and one woman: Mrs Thatcher) whose plans for it did not quite work out as they had intended, and who came to see that it acts more like a wilful organism than a machine to be regulated. I am attached to this idea of the Underground martyrs. It suits my notion of the Tube as something essentially melancholic. The roundel is, to me, a setting rather than a rising sun, and if the carriages rattling through the dark tunnels are akin to any fairground ride, it is the ghost trains, their anxious occupants wondering what they've got themselves into and sitting braced against the shocks to come. (I venture to suggest, by the way, that this book features the only frightening Underground ghost story.)

But if that sounds too negative, I ought to mention that you are about to read a book by a person who regards a Tube journey as an end in itself, someone who takes a Tube train for the same reason as other people go to the theatre: to look at people, to see a spectacle – the oppressive brick arch over Baker Street's oldest platform, say, or the river when viewed from a District train blamelessly rocking its way towards salubrious Wimbledon on a summer's afternoon. Or I'll drift out east on the Central, hoping to experience the proprietorial feeling of being the very last person on the train as it lumbers into Epping; or I'll deliberately take the last train to High Barnet, because I like seeing it 'flagged away' from each successive platform by a guard holding a torch that shines a green beam towards the driver. (Don't blame me for the terminology by the way; I suppose a green flag was once used.) The last train provides a ribald cabaret every night of the week for the cost of a ticket – with a special, X-rated performance on Saturdays – and if I do go right to the very end of the line, I feel a sense of gratitude for the hard work of the driver, as he paternalistically walks along the carriages, and knocks on the windows to wake any sleeping drunks. But in my experience people normally do wake up in time for their stop. It's programmed into them. They unconsciously know the sequence of lurches and jolts that bring them to their 'home' station. Many of the significant events in their lives – job interviews, first dates, last dates – will be framed by two Tube rides. The Underground trains course through their bloodstreams, so to speak, and I feel an atavistic connection with that last train; I experience a kind of pang as it is shunted into the depot to join its sleeping brethren. But it is now time to ride the very *first* train, and to meet the man who brought it about.

CHAPTER ONE

THE WORLD OF CHARLES PEARSON

THE GADFLY

The first stretch of the Metropolitan – Paddington to Farringdon (1863) – was the world's first urban underground railway. It was built to make money, but had been originally conceived with a philanthropic motive, as a means of improving the lives of the London poor, by a man called Charles Pearson.

Pearson (1793–1862) wasn't an engineer or a town planner. He was a solicitor, and this seems to have annoyed the *Railway Magazine*, which, reflecting on Pearson in 1905, said, 'At first blush, there does not seem to be much connection between railways and lawyers.' Another perplexing thing about Pearson is that he was both politically radical and the Solicitor to the Corporation of London, the body that runs the City, which was no more known for progressive politics in Victorian times than it is today.

He was the son of an upholsterer and feather merchant of St Clement's Lane, London. The one photograph that survives of him shows a burly, harassed-looking figure sitting at an untidy desk. He was perpetually busy; it was hard to keep up with him. In an article called 'The Solicitor and the Underground' in the Law Society's Gazette of 1953, a certain D. Heap suggested that Pearson 'felt passionately about whatever cause was for the uppermost in his mind', while the *Oxford Dictionary of National Biography* calls him a 'gadfly'.

Pearson campaigned for the right of Jews to hold public office, and for the abolition of capital punishment. We can see the hand of Pearson on the north side of Christopher Wren's Monument to the Great Fire of London in Monument Street in the City. The inscription written there had blamed the fire on 'Popish frenzy', which was *not* forensically accurate. The website of the Monument states that this slur was deleted in 1830; it is not stated that the deletion was the result of a campaign by Pearson.

He got his job with the City Corporation in 1839, when his advocacy of an Underground railway to serve the City began properly. You might say that he brought about the Metropolitan in the same way that Winston Churchill was said by Clement Attlee to have won the Second World War: by 'talking about it'. And if he hadn't talked about it, and if he hadn't brought it about, then London might never have had an Underground because, as Christian Wolmar writes in *The Subterranean Railway*, 'the advent of the motor car in the late nineteenth century, followed quickly by electric railways and the motor bus, could have resulted in the bypassing of the underground railways as a solution to city traffic problems given the expense and disruption of their construction as happened in most cities in the US.'

PEARSON'S LONDON

In the middle third of the nineteenth century, when Charles Pearson was campaigning for what would become the Metropolitan Railway, London was changing more than at any time before or since. A map of 1845 shows the city extending east not much beyond the City, to the south not much beyond Camberwell, with Clapham as a distinct village. It extended west not much beyond Kensington and Paddington, with Hammersmith as a distinct village, and to the north not much beyond the New Road – which ran from Paddington to a little way north of the City – with pretty Hackney as a separate village.

A map of 1900, by contrast, shows a London more than twice the size of the 1845 city. All the places mentioned above as being separate villages had been comfortably absorbed. London in 1900 extended to Stratford and Woolwich in the east, to Sydenham and Streatham in the south. Associated with this expansion were three factors, all intermingled. First, growing prosperity: London was rising to its ascendancy as a capital of empire and greatest city in the world. Second, growing population: 1 million in 1800; 2.5 million in 1850; 6.5 million in 1900. The third factor was the coming of the railways.

The first railway terminus in London was south of the river, at London Bridge, which was opened by the London & Greenwich Railway in 1836. The station was – and is – approached by viaduct, and the humble properties beneath were 'cleared'. That is to say that the poor were evicted, and their homes demolished. 'London Bridge station' sounds like a pretty solid phenomenon, but it would be constantly knocked down and rebuilt, as other companies muscled in on what had been started by the London & Greenwich. During the 1840s, the South Eastern Railway would begin running into London Bridge, as would the London & Croydon, and the London & Brighton (which would amalgamate in 1845 to become the London Brighton & South Coast Railway). Property was cheaper in south London than in north London, which harboured both the commercial centre of the capital – the City – and the mansions of the West End. It was cheaper to build both railways and suburbs to the south, and commuting – which Charles Pearson called 'oscillating' – began between the village of Greenwich and London Bridge. (The term 'commuting' is from America, and did not become established in Britain until the 1940s.)

The Corporation of London did not like railways, and was against having them within the boundaries of the City. Railways were a threat to property. In 1836, when the London & Greenwich began operations, the Corporation was refusing permission for the Commercial Railway to build a terminus within the City, mainly on the grounds that it would only add to traffic congestion. But the Corporation then relented, and in 1840 the London & Blackwall Railway, as the Commercial had become, opened a line from the docks into Fenchurch Street station. This is not the present Fenchurch Street station, but it was *on* Fenchurch Street, which was – and is – within the City of London. So here was a station that had broken through. The line into Fenchurch Street grew in the 1850s, and in 1866 the London & Blackwall was absorbed into the Great Eastern railway, whose cheap train fares would be responsible for the bulging out of north-east London.

In between the London & Greenwich and the London & Blackwall, two other railways, more typical of their time, arrived in London. The first was the London & Birmingham, which launched Euston station in July 1837. In 1838 it celebrated its arrival with a stone giant arch (strictly speaking, a propylaeum), which was demolished in 1962. The London & Birmingham did not, at this point, cater for commuters. It did not create an inner London passenger station north of its Euston terminus (the first stop after Euston was at Harrow); instead, it built a giant goods yard, its main interest being the carriage from south to north of freight and passengers – or rather, from *north* to *south*, because the L&B emanated from Birmingham, and the early railways generally uncoiled from the north, and were funded by northern industrial wealth.

Charles Dickens wrote about the coming of the L&B in

Dombey and Son. He describes its effects on the 'frowzy fields and cow-houses, and dunghills, dustheaps, and ditches and gardens and summer houses' of 1830s' Camden, which he called Staggs's Gardens. (A 'Stag' was a railway speculator.)

> Houses were knocked down; streets broken through and stopped; deep pits and trenches dug in the ground; enormous heaps of earth and clay thrown up … There were a hundred thousand shapes and substances of incompleteness, wildly mingled out of their places, upside down, burrowing in the earth, aspiring in the air, mouldering in the water, and unintelligible as any dream … In short, the yet unfinished and unopened railway was in progress.

He described this railway as 'defiant of all obstacles', but it pulled up sharply enough on the New Road, stopping short of the grand estates of the West End, whose landlords were not about to have their elegant streets and squares invaded by so many coke-dusted Gradgrinds from the north. So the Great Northern visited all its chaos and destruction on the people who were the traditional recipients of that kind of thing: the poor.

The second 'inter-city' railway rolled into the suburban village of Paddington. The Great Western opened a Paddington station in 1838, a wooden terminus to the north of the present station, which would arrive in 1853. As with Euston, the site was bounded to the south by high-class property: a no-go zone for railways.

Paddington was at the western end of the New Road, so there were two main-line stations on that road. Two more will be along shortly, and we might now imagine ominous tremors along its length as the road surface prepares to erupt, because Charles Pearson would come to the audacious conclusion that the answer to London's problems lay beneath it.

His interest in railways is not the quality that marks Pearson out. Everyone was interested in railways. Over a thousand miles of them opened between 1837 and 1845, most of what would become the national network. They caused a social, economic and psychological revolution that perhaps exceeded the one caused in our own day by the coming of the internet. (Imagine the Information Superhighway as an actual physical structure.) The disparate time zones of Britain were unified under 'railway time' – as Dickens famously observed in *Dombey*: 'It was as if the sun itself had given in.' In 1847 *Punch* magazine stated that 'How many miles will become how many minutes', and that was absolutely correct. (Passengers on the Underground do not know how many miles they've travelled, only how long it has taken.)

In the face of the railways, a romantic fatalism developed. John Martin painted canvases of the Ancient World elided with industry, a genre called the 'apocalyptic sublime'. His painting of *The Last Judgement* (1853) features a scene of Biblical angst taking place under a blood-red midnight sun. Approaching in the background is *a train*. Whether it is heading for heaven or hell at the parting of the ways is not clear, but it is coming on very purposefully indeed.

Mere governments were certainly not going to stand in their way. You needed an Act of Parliament to build a railway, but that wasn't very hard to obtain if you could give the appearance of adequately funded competence. There was some guiding legislation; Parliamentary committees would issue recommendations, but British governments would not fund, still less plan, railways. 'Having observed this policy in action,' notes the *Oxford Companion to British Railway History*, 'countries on the European mainland adopted others of an entirely different kind.' Why were Victorian governments so attached to *laissez-faire*? In his book on British railways *Eleven Minutes Late* (2009), Matthew Engel blames the French Revolution: *that* was what happened when the state got involved in the operation of society. Stephen Joseph, the director of the Campaign for Better Transport, says, 'It may be because we never maintained a standing army. So there was no sense of the tactical importance of transport.'

What marked Charles Pearson out was that he was not *intimidated* by railways. He saw the good and the bad in them, and how they could be used for humane purposes. For example, they might be used to cure a problem they had exacerbated, namely slum-living.

Pearson's London was what we now call central London, and much of it was slums. Today most of us wouldn't say no to a *pied à terre* in Clerkenwell, but in 1850 it was a slum. Drury Lane? A slum. Seven Dials and Covent Garden? Holborn and Finsbury? Slums. The new railways were of no help to the residents of these places, and they had made life worse for the poor who happened to be in their way. In *Landlords to London*, Simon Jenkins observes: 'By the end of the century, it is estimated that over 100,000 people had been uprooted from their homes by the coming of the railways ... Railway building in London simply crowded neighbouring slum properties even more densely and forced up their rents.'

Pearson saw an answer in 'oscillation'. He noted that the poor were keen on Sunday railway excursions to the country, and commuting was getting under way; it is just that the poor couldn't afford to take part. The merchants of the City were moving out to places such as Camberwell, Kensington, Islington, Mile End or salubrious and newly suburbanised Hackney. They might travel by coach and horses or by train. Thomas Briggs, a senior bank clerk in the City, lived in Hackney, and on 9 July 1864 he was returning there by train from Fenchurch Street after a Saturday spent at work when he was bludgeoned to death in a first-class carriage, probably by a young German tailor called Franz Müller. (Let's hope it *was* Müller, because he was hanged for it.) And so Briggs was an all-round pioneer: an early commuter and the very first victim of a railway murder. For the slightly less well-off, moving to the slightly cheaper houses of, say, Fulham or Brixton, the new fleets of horse-drawn omnibuses would come into play, but there was a problem on the roads. Victorian Londoners did not speak of 'traffic jams' – that term came from America after the First World War. They spoke rather of traffic 'locks' or 'blocks', and their prevalence would be one reason why Pearson began to direct his thoughts underground.

THE NEW ROAD (AND THE NEW TRAFFIC)

The New Road – and we might now imagine a more violent quaking along its length, as its moment of truth approaches – had been built in 1757. In 1857 it was decided it was no longer new, and it was renamed, along most of its length, the Euston Road, while the stretches to the west and east became Marylebone Road and Pentonville Road.

It ran from Paddington to the City, which may sound familiar. Crossrail, the underground express line that is supposed to be opening in 2017, will also connect those two places. The definitive London commute is from west London to the City in the east, and in his novel *Keep the Aspidistra Flying* (1936) George Orwell invoked 'the strap-hanging army that swings eastward in the morning, westward at night, in the carriages of the Underground'. The other important west–east route was along Oxford Street, but that was packed with expensive property, and the original purpose of the New Road was to allow cattle to be driven from the fields west of London to Smithfield Market on the western edge of the City without going along Oxford Street, which was becoming known for its smart shops. (Cattle *had* been herded along Oxford Street, creating the unwelcome possibility of a bull entering retail premises – a china shop, for example.) In *The Bus We Loved* (2005) Travis Elborough describes the New

Road as 'London's first by-pass … a kind of perimeter fence, a *here be yokels* boundary line between the burgeoning town and the country'. Elborough was interested in the New Road because in 1829 it became what is taken to be London's first bus route. A bluff coachmaker and ex-naval man called George Shillibeer operated the service. It ran from the Yorkshire Stingo Tavern to the Bank of England from 4 July 1829. ('Stingo' means strong beer; the tavern was located in dusty Chapel Street, off the Marylebone Road, not far from where the Edgware Road Metropolitan station would be built thirty years later.)

Shillibeer's bus was a sort of unprecedented barn on wheels. It was not a Hackney carriage, and it was not a stagecoach. Hackney carriages were the forerunners of taxis. They were for individual travel. Short stages – meaning short-hop stagecoaches, as opposed to the inter-city ones that Dick Turpin robbed – carried about a dozen passengers, half of them sitting on the roof, whereas omnibus passengers numbered twenty, and were all inside. Short stages you had to book in advance, whereas the omnibus was a turn-up-and-go service. You loitered along the route and waited for the bus to come along. You climbed up from the back end and paid the fare to the conductor. Free periodicals were available inside, so the *Metro* newspaper available on the Underground today is not the brash innovation you might think.

The omnibus arose from the demands of a rising population – the rising population of *France* in the first instance, since that's where the concept came from, and Shillibeer had been involved in making the early French vehicles. It was an idea whose time had come. Even so, Shillibeer's bus was banished to the margins of London, as main-line trains and trams would be. Hackneys and some short stages were allowed to run in 'the Stones', as the central London parishes were known. The omnibus was not allowed to run there, but the New Road was just beyond the limits of the Stones. A single fare was a shilling. That was

George Shillibeer, who introduced the bus (below) to London. It was obviously a good idea, because he was soon overwhelmed with competition and put out of business.

SHILLIBEER'S OMNIBUS.

A New Carriage, on the Parisian Mode, for the Conveyance of Inside Passengers from PADDINGTON to the BANK.
Established by G.Shillibeer, Coach Builder &c., N.12 Bury St.' Bloomsbury Square.

cheaper than a Hackney or a short stage, but still expensive. A pint of beer at the time cost 2d., and you would soon be able to travel back and forth for a whole week on the Metropolitan Line for a shilling.

In 1832 omnibuses were allowed into the central streets, and by the end of that year 800 were operating in London. In 1834 Shillibeer was driven off the New Road by the competition and set up a bus service from Greenwich to the West End – just in time to be put out of business by the above-mentioned London & Greenwich Railway. He did time in the Fleet Prison for debt; he then applied to the Treasury for the post of Inspector of Omnibus Duties, a position for which you'd have thought he was well qualified, having *invented* omnibuses. But he was turned down, and so became an undertaker. It is possible that Shillibeer's bathetic end is the reason that buses did not become universally known as 'Shillibeers'. Some operators *had* called their buses Shillibeers. Shillibeer himself had wanted to call his own buses 'Economists', but that lacked a certain sparkle, even by the standards of 1829. Omnibuses, by the way, are so called because of a shop in Nantes, France, where, in 1828, an early bus stopped alongside a shop owned by a Monsieur Omnes. What he sold is not recorded, but whatever it was, he sold it under the slogan 'Omnes Omnibus', meaning 'all for all'.

The standard single fare settled at 6d. – three pints of beer. The later omnibuses were drawn by two horses, whereas Shillibeer's original had used three. Omnibuses were usually crowded, and in January 1836 *The Times* published a list of rules that would make them more bearable; this is quoted in Volume 1 of *A History of London Transport* (1963), by T. C. Barker and Michael Robbins.

Omnibus Law, rule number one: Keep your feet off the seats.

Rule two: Do not impose on the conductor the necessity of finding you change. He is not a banker.

…

Rule number 5: Sit with your limbs straight, and do not with your legs describe an angle of 45, thereby occupying the room of two people.

By the 1840s, there was the 'omnibus nuisance' on the central streets of London.

There was also a Hackney carriage nuisance, a private carriage nuisance, a cart-and-wagon nuisance and horse-and-rider nuisance. In *London: The Biography* (2000) Peter Ackroyd quotes a work called *Memories of London in the 1840s*, which speaks of a London sound, 'as if all the noises of all the wheels of all the carriages were mingled and ground together into one subdued, hoarse, moaning hum'. Again, the early railways only fanned the flames. They brought more goods and more people into the city – to stay for good, or to depart at the end of the day.

As Pearson well knew, the roads in and around the City were particularly narrow and labyrinthine, therefore liable to clogging. The City was built to a medieval street pattern that remains. Those gold-paved lanes were sacred, but the approaches could be altered. In the 1840s, Oxford Street was extended towards the City through some slums by means of the bleak New Oxford Street. The Fleet Valley (thronged with the rookeries of the poor) made a north–south barrier that would be cleared by the building of Farringdon Road. A little later the baleful, and balefully named, Holborn Viaduct – which looks designed for midnight suicide bids – would traverse this from west to east. It is a fact that all the streets designed to relieve Victorian traffic jams are dead streets. Ask yourself: have you ever had a good time on any of the above-mentioned roads? Or on that blackened runnel called Queen Victoria Street? Or on grey, monumental Kingsway, which is on a scale to suggest a triumphal procession, but with the reason for the celebration forgotten? (It was opened in 1905, to relieve narrow Drury Lane and even narrower Chancery Lane.) To see the streets that these bold thoroughfares replaced, I recommend *Lost London, 1870–1945* (2009), by Philip Davies, with its ghostly photographs of sagging, timber-framed houses. It is the London of Dickens, who had nothing to say about the coming of the Metropolitan Railway, even though he lived for seven years after its opening, and to whom accordingly we now say goodbye.

The density of the traffic was one of the reasons why, as Pearson would say before a Parliamentary Commission in 1846, 'A poor man is chained to the spot. He has not leisure to walk and he has not money to ride to a distance from his work.'

By his railway, Pearson would free the poor man.

PEARSON'S PLAN A AND PEARSON'S PLAN B

Pearson's first idea, set out in 1839, was for a railway in a wide, covered-over cutting. It would connect a giant half-underground station at Farringdon with stations all over England. It would also connect – at cheap ticket prices – Farringdon with new estates of cottages for artisans and clerks which he said ought to be built 6 miles north of London. The appeal of Farringdon was that this slum-ridden area was being redeveloped by Pearson's new employers, the Corporation of London. This was in conjunction with the transfer of the livestock market at Smithfield (the one to which the cattle had been driven via the china shops of Oxford Street) to uncluttered Islington.

This railway plan may sound dramatic – more Fritz Lang's *Metropolis* than metropolitan railway – but it was conceived at a time when the potentialities of railways seemed infinite. Pearson's railway would be drawn by atmospheric power, a fad of the 1830s and 1840s – a 'rope of air', as the great engineer Robert Stephenson once described the method. Trains were propelled by a piston set in a pipe lying between the rails. The piston was sucked along by stationary pumping engines that created a vacuum. This utopian transport ideal (a smokeless railway!) figured in the more fantastical of the early railway schemes. In the mid-1850s, for instance, Joseph Paxton would propose an atmospheric 'Great Victorian Way' encircling the whole of central London. The trains would run within a 72-foot-wide glass arcade that would also accommodate shops, roads and walkways and pedestrians – all of which suggests that the success Paxton had scored in the building of the Crystal Palace for the Great Exhibition of 1851 had rather gone to his head.

Incidentally, a number of atmospheric railways were built and operated, most of them justifiably obscure. But one became an object of fascination to the more troglodytic sort of Londoner.

In 1863 the Post Office built a driverless underground atmospheric railway for carrying mail from the District Post Office, Eversholt Street, to Euston station; two years later it was extended to the General Post Office in St Martin's Le Grand. The building of the line was symptomatic of the road traffic problem in London at the time. The tracks were 2-foot gauge, the tunnels about 4 feet wide, and the carriages resembled the 'logs' on log flumes seen at amusement parks. The line had the superbly business-like name of the Pneumatic Despatch Railway but was plagued by air leakages and abandoned in 1880. From 1913 the Post Office built an electrical underground railway from Paddington to Whitechapel, serving nine stations at its peak. Like its predecessor, it was driverless, with 2-foot gauge tracks but wider tunnels. Guests could sample the line in a VIP passenger car, decorated with the monograms of British monarchs from George V to Elizabeth II. It closed in 2003, the Post Office, besieged by competitors in communications, unable to justify the cost. In a civilised world it would re-open, relieving the streets of some lorries.

But to return to Joseph Paxon, in spite of his grandiosity, there was nothing inherently eccentric about proposing underground or half-underground railways in the mid-nineteenth century. The Victorians were moles. In the nineteenth century about fifty railway tunnels of more than a mile in length were constructed, compared to three in the twentieth century. The very first proper inter-city railway, the Liverpool–Manchester of 1830, had involved two tunnels under Liverpool, both longer than a mile. According to *The Oxford Companion to British Railway History*, it is cheaper to build a tunnel than a cutting of more than 60-foot depth.

In 1846 a Royal Commission on Metropolitan Termini was set up to establish ground rules for the numerous applications to build railways into London. Pearson put his scheme to the commission in heartfelt terms:

> The passion for a country residence is increasing to an extent that it would be impossible to persons who do not mix much with the poor to know. You cannot find a place where they do not get a broken teapot in which to stuff, as soon as spring comes, some flower or something to give them an idea of green fields and the country.

But the Commission rejected Pearson's plan, and any other that sought to infringe the rights of central London landlords. The Commission recommended against new stations in the West End or the City, and the boundary line to the north would be the New Road. The presumption against railways in central London would remain effective until 1858 (Victoria Station), with one exception, which we will consider shortly. The inadvertent effect of this ruling was the creation of the lines and stations of the London Underground, because these would avoid the ban.

Now to Pearson's Plan B …

In 1851 the Great Northern Railway had reached London and begun operating into a terminus at Maiden Lane, just north of the New Road. In 1854 they moved up to the New Road itself, with the opening of King's Cross station, east of Euston. The railways were alighting on the New Road like birds perching on a branch (the Midland Railway would open St Pancras, between Euston and King's Cross, in 1868), and Pearson took note. Whereas his first scheme had ignored the New Road stations, and simply sought to upstage them with a bigger and better – and madder – station of his own, his second plan tried to co-opt them.

It involved a railway going beneath the New Road and connecting some or all of the main-line termini gathered there and then bending south towards the City (so far, so sensible), where it would conclude (and here his fancifulness broke out again) in another vast half-underground City terminus: a complex involving two stations, one for long-distance and one for local traffic, both with numerous platforms 300 yards long, with a 13-acre goods yard and engine stabling facilities. This time it was proposed the terminus would connect to some more tangible workmen's estates – the north London suburbs being built along the route of the Great Northern Railway.

The Corporation was interested in the idea, because it thought it might lead to the main-line railway companies funding municipal improvements in Farringdon, and in 1852 Pearson deposited his City Terminus Bill in Parliament. It was always doomed. The main-line railway companies might welcome an underground connection that would enable them to run through to the City, but why would they underwrite a vast terminus that would take away their business? Yes, an argument for the great City Terminus would be the amount of road traffic it might spare the city streets. But a stronger argument against was the amount of road traffic it might *create*. Plus, it contravened the ban of 1846.

What was required now was the intervention of some men who were not gadflies.

PEARSON MEETS THE BUSINESSMEN

The logic of Pearson's arguments was accepted, up to a point, by a consortium of businessmen. In August 1854, after Pearson's own scheme had failed in Parliament, the consortium obtained royal assent for what had initially been called the Bayswater, Paddington & Holborn Bridge Railway, and which gradually became the 'North Metropolitan' and finally the Metropolitan Railway.

It would run beneath the New Road from Paddington to King's Cross, there drooping south towards the City, just as Pearson's scheme had done. But there would be no sprawling terminus – instead, a more modest station at Farringdon. The line would connect to the Great Western main line at Paddington, in return for which that company would invest in the Metropolitan. There would also be a connection at King's Cross to the Great Northern main line, in return for which that company would *not* invest in the Metropolitan. (But it would have to pay to use the tracks that would carry its trains through to the City.)

The consortium set about a faltering campaign to raise the million pounds required, a job made harder by the outbreak of the Crimean War in 1854. It should by now be apparent that Charles Pearson was not the sort of man to resent the success of a rival scheme, especially one that might bring the social benefits he had sought by his own proposal. In 1859, when it looked as though the Metropolitan Railway Company would be wound up with no line built, he wrote a pamphlet: *A Twenty Minutes Letter to the Citizens of London in Favour of the Metropolitan Railway and City Station.* Gadfly he may have been, but by this 'letter' he persuaded the Corporation of London to invest £200,000 in the line, a most unusual example of a public body investing in a Victorian railway. The Corporation also sold land in the Fleet Valley cheaply to the Metropolitan. What was its motive? The answer lay in the above-mentioned property development scheme. The corporation had just opened its new cattle market in Islington, and it had plans for clearances in the Fleet Valley that would make way for the new Farringdon Road, and adjacent meat market. It was felt that the Metropolitan Railway would serve the meat market, since it would carry both passengers and freight, and that it would reduce road congestion in the City. In fact, it would do the former but not the latter. Transport begets transport, and the coming of the Met to the City would only attract more of those swarming buses.

CHAPTER TWO

THE METROPOLITAN RAILWAY

THE LINE IS BUILT – AND OPENED

The construction of the first stretch of the Metropolitan Railway began in October 1859, and the line was opened to the public on 10 January 1863. It was built on the cut-and-cover principle. The railway was laid into a shallow grave. The road, mainly the New Road, was dug up, and the tracks were laid down in a brick cutting that was then roofed over, with the road replaced on the top of the roof. For this reason a cut-and-cover railway is in engineering terms technically a bridge (because of the roofing-over) rather than a tunnel. The crown of the tunnel arches are sometimes just inches under the road. The early Underground lines were all built on the cut-and-cover principle, because tunnelling technology was not sufficiently advanced to make deep-level Tubes. (The cut-and-cover lines are the Metropolitan, District, Hammersmith & City, and the Circle, which is not so much a line as a service that uses the tracks of those other lines.)

The first stretch of the Met was built for most of its length beneath the centre of New Road. It was advisable to avoid building an underground railway beneath private houses at the time, because the law would require you to buy those houses. The Met of 1863 was not *entirely* covered over. When it bends south between King's Cross and Farringdon, it is in open cutting. Go to Swinton Street, WC1, five minutes' walk south and east of King's Cross. It's a ghostly street of powdery-looking terraced houses. Where the terrace comes to an end on the south and east side, an 8-foot wall takes over. You know there must be something fascinating beyond that wall because someone's tried to stop you seeing over, and there are shards of glass embedded in the top. However, there is a small step or foothold; find it, and look over the top. Then look down and you'll see filthy pigeons on a brick ledge; look further down to discover the secret of Swinton Street: the tracks of the Metropolitan. Wait for a train, and you will observe that it traverses that crevice with satisfying violence, but not sufficient to disturb the pigeons, which are in league with the line. Go to Swinton Street in the evening, and you're back in the King's Cross of *The Ladykillers*: crepuscular, fumacious, railway-haunted.

Or take an eastbound Met from King's Cross outside the rush hour, when you ought to be able to find a window seat. Again, look up, to see the beautiful brick valley made by the Metropolitan: the towering arcaded walls with brick struts going over. It's like being in the moat of Gormenghast Castle. This is hard-core London, and just before Farringdon station you will be able to glimpse the vast steel pipe that carries what was the Fleet River and is now the Fleet sewer over your head.

The Fleet looks safely contained now, although you never know. It surprises me that no terrorist has made common cause with the surly and embittered Fleet, which, in Peter Ackroyd's words, became 'a river of death' as it sidled through the meanest streets of London en route to the Thames. In *London: The*

Biography Ackroyd describes its progress with melancholy relish. It 'moved around Clerkenwell Hill and touched the stones of the Coldbath Prison; passed Saffron Hill, whose fragrant name concealed some of the worst rookeries in London … Then it flowed down into Chick Lane … the haven of felons and murderers.' The Fleet made its last public appearance in June 1862, when it burst into the Met building works east of King's Cross. There is a famous illustration of the resulting chaos of collapsed brickwork, littered with wooden buttresses heaped as for a giant's game of pick-up-sticks.

The inundation is described in Arnold Bennett's novel *Riceyman Steps*, which was written in 1923, but set in 1919:

> On the Wednesday the pavements sank definitely. The earth quaked. The entire populace fled to survey the scene of horror from safety. The terrific scaffolding and beams were flung like firewood into the air and fell with awful crashes. The populace screamed at the thought of workmen entombed and massacred. A silence! Then the great brick piers, fifty feet in height, moved bodily. The whole bottom of the excavation moved in one mass. A dark and fetid liquid appeared, oozing, rolling, surging, smashing everything in its restless track, and rushed into the mouth of the new tunnel. The crown of the arch of the mighty Fleet sewer had broken.

The central character's uncle tells the story 'with such force and fire' that he has a stroke and dies. The London Underground has been tangling with the buried rivers of London ever since – and with the Thames. What became the Jubilee Line was initially called the Fleet Line, an act of propitiation, perhaps, to this most abused river. When I mention that Fleet pipe at Farringdon, people will tend to say, 'Yes, and it appears again in that great big pipe that goes over the platforms at Sloane Square station', which is very satisfying since it gives me the opportunity to point out that the Fleet would not suddenly veer west at Farringdon in order to make a beeline for Chelsea. The river carried in the pipe at Sloane Square is the Westbourne, and the pipe is said to shake in a rainstorm. Behind one of the innocent-looking doors on the platform at Sloane Square is a horizontal metal grille, beneath which is a pump, working away in the seething tributaries of the Westbourne. But that's nothing compared to Victoria Station, where a million gallons a day are pumped away, most of it from the Tyburn brook. There is a pumping house underneath the station that an Underground press officer once refused to let me see, sadistically adding, 'It resembles the set of *Phantom of the Opera*.' It is possible that the Waterloo & City line is nicknamed 'The Drain' because of the water pumped away, but there are other theories, the line being drain-like in so many ways. At the start of the Second World War floodgates would be installed at the ends of the under-Thames sections of the Bakerloo and the Northern lines to save them from inundation should bombs damage the riverbed.

The other famous image from the Metropolitan before its official opening is a photograph of 'Mr Gladstone at the Private View'. It was taken on 24 May 1862, and it shows Gladstone, Mrs Gladstone and John Fowler, the swaggering and super-rich engineer of the Met, together with other dignitaries and share-holders of the line sitting in two rough contractors' wagons. The photograph reveals that Edgware Road had an arched glass roof, which it would lose soon after opening for the sake of improved ventilation. When I was writing my 'Tube Talk' column, a woman wrote to me praising Edgware Road. 'What you have at Edgware Road is sky.' What you also have is howling wind.

(Most of the cut-and-cover stations had elegant, arched glass roofs, and most have now lost them. The surviving glass roof at Notting Hill Circle and District platforms is the reason you will

Mr (and Mrs) Gladstone are given a preview of the Metropolitan Railway. They are at Edgware Road (which used to have a roof). Gladstone was very involved with railways and thought they were too important to be unregulated. He insisted on cheap trains for the travelling poor, and envisaged railway nationalisation. He lost money on Underground stocks, and his coffin would be carried to Westminster Abbey on the District Railway.

generally feel good while waiting there. John Betjeman's poem 'Monody on the Death of Aldersgate Station' was triggered by the loss of the glass roof – 'Snow falls in the buffet of Aldersgate station' – and its replacement by low-level awnings as a result of repairs in 1955, following war damage. Aldersgate, incidentally, was on the Metropolitan extension beyond Farringdon. It started life in 1865 as 'Aldersgate Street', and is today Barbican.)

In the Gladstone photo, the sitters look too small for their conveyances, and this is because they were sitting in extra-wide – that is, broad-gauge – wagons of the Great Western, which would run along the Met on broad-gauge tracks (7 foot 2 inches between the rails), together with trains using standard-gauge tracks of 4 foot 8½. In the Met's own language, the line ran 'on the mixed-gauge principle', which makes the arrangement sound almost sensible. That broad gauge did not last long, and all Underground trains today run on the standard gauge. But there is a continuing distinction between the *loading* gauge (the size of the trains) of the deep-level Tube trains and the loading gauge of the cut-and-cover trains. The latter are bigger – as big as mainline trains. That's why they're less claustrophobic, and it's why drivers on the cut-and-cover lines refer to the trains driven by their colleagues on the Tubes as 'Hornbys' – toy trains.

The early Underground trains were essentially ordinary steam trains that just happened to be running below the streets in the middle of London. Being ordinary trains on ordinary tracks, they could then continue, having emerged from their tunnels, in the open air, which meant they became much entangled with main-line railways. In May 1898, for example, the funeral train of our Mr Gladstone would be brought from his country estate at Hawarden to Westminster station on the District Line via Willesden Junction. One of his biographers notes, 'Victorians saw no indignity in a coffin for a state funeral arriving by Underground.' But I don't think it would be seemly that a Prime

Minister be brought to his final resting place by a deep-level *Tube* train.

I wonder whether the Grand Old Man, sitting in that wide wagon at Edgware Road, had any premonition of that later Underground event, or of the fact that he would lose £25,000 on Met and District stock in the 1880s. According to H. G. C. Matthew in *Gladstone, 1809–1898* (1997), he took the loss 'fairly equably'. Although Gladstone seems to us high-minded and remote, he was keen on public transport. He once said that the best way to see London is from the top of a bus. In 1900 the *Railway Magazine* ran a feature called 'How Some Celebrities Occupy Their Time When Railway Travelling'. In spite of the present tense, it included dead celebrities, and it noted that Gladstone had occupied himself by translating the odes of Horace. As President of the Board of Trade in the 1840s, he was aware of the dangers of leaving so important a social force as railways unregulated. In fact, he showed himself willing to entertain railway nationalisation, and his Railway Act of 1844 reserved to the state the power to take control of the companies should they behave irresponsibly. Those powers were never used. He also required the operators to run 'Parliamentary Trains' – one each day calling at every station at a fare of not more than a penny per mile for Third Class.

The Metropolitan Railway opened to the public on 10 January 1863. The *Illustrated London News* wrote:

> … it was calculated that more than 30,000 persons were carried over the line in the course of the day. Indeed, the desire to travel by this line on the opening day was more than the directors had provided for; and from nine o'clock in the morning till past midnight it was impossible to obtain a place in the up or Cityward line at any of the mid stations. In the evening the tide turned, and the crush at the

Farringdon-street station was as great as at the doors of a
theatre on the first night of some popular performer.

The line's begetter, Charles Pearson, had died of dropsy on
14 September 1862. He had naturally refused a payment from
the Metropolitan in return for his advocacy of the line, but the
company paid an annuity of £250 to his widow.

The line was an immediate success, and well reviewed. On
30 November 1861 *The Times* had called the proposed railway
'Utopian', adding that even if it could be accomplished, [it] would
certainly never pay'. It described the scheme as 'a subterranean
railway awfully suggestive of dark, noisome tunnels, buried many
fathoms deep beyond the reach of light or life'. But on the opening day *The Times* reported the Metropolitan to be 'the greatest engineering triumph of its day ... ingenious contrivances for
obtaining light and ventilation were particularly commended.'
(Two decades later, however, on 7 October 1884, the paper would
be back to square one, reporting the journey from King's Cross to
Baker Street to be 'a mild form of torture which no person would
undergo if he could help it'.)

WHAT WAS IT LIKE?

The Times objected to the atmosphere, but let's consider first the
physical environment. The line connected the (quite) fresh air
and semi-rural setting of Paddington to the heart of the City at
Farringdon. If you travelled in that direction, you were on the 'up'
line; the opposite direction was the 'down', and if I ever meet anybody who sticks with those terms, I will shake them by the hand.
(Eastbound and westbound came in later, when the Americans
got involved in the Tube.) The up and down lines ran next to
each other in vault-like tunnels, whereas the Tube trains would
occupy their own tunnels. That's why the cut-and-cover lines

are more human than the Tubes. They are more companionable. You can see people going the other way – your perspective is broadened.

No surface building of the original Metropolitan survives. Perhaps this doesn't matter. They were tackily decorous: Italianate, and clad in imitation white stone. In *London's Metropolitan Railway* (1986) Alan A. Jackson calls them 'cheap and nasty'. For the nearest equivalent we are referred to Bayswater, built when the Met pushed south of Paddington in 1868. Most of the stations, as noted earlier, had glass roofs, and the grandest glass-roofed station was the Met's King's Cross, a little way to the east of the main-line station. It was knocked down in 1910, and in the 1940s the whole cut-and-cover operation at King's Cross was swept beneath the main-line station. The glass roofs were elegant, but of particular interest to the Victorians were the brick-roofed stations. The young readers of *Discoveries and Inventions of the Nineteenth Century* (1876), by Robert Routledge, were directed towards Baker Street and Gower Street (now Euston Square), which were 'completely underground', showing 'great boldness and inventiveness of design'. Great Portland Street was originally completely bricked over, but the arch was opened to the sky at the western end, and it remains so today. The boldness has also been lost at Euston Square, where horizontal iron girders now traverse the roof. They penetrate the lateral skylights – brick holes made through the springing of the roof arches – that were a feature of that station, and of Baker Street, where they survive in modified form. Because the streets have been moved around overhead, the apertures no longer necessarily rise up towards daylight, so electric light has been fitted into them to duplicate the effect.

The grandest survivor of the original Metropolitan is Baker Street, which would become the headquarters of the Railway, its spiritual home. But here it is my duty to address an anomaly that must have been vexing the brighter sort of tourist since the late 1980s. Then, an administrative change at London Underground brought the Metropolitan Line under the control of the department running the Hammersmith & City Line. As a result, the purple of the Metropolitan Line ceased to appear on the Tube map west of Baker Street, and the line from there to Paddington was shown as belonging to the Hammersmith & City and the Circle Line only. The operational change this reflects means that today all Metropolitan trains approaching the historical platform at Baker Street from the east are whisked north at the last moment, to proceed along the Metropolitan's north-pointing 'country' branch. There is no longer anything Metropolitan – neither 'Railway' nor 'Line' – running through the beautiful brick-vaulted station that is so liberally decorated with illustrated panels proclaiming 'Metropolitan Railway 1863' and 'The world's first Underground Railway'.

Then again, most people don't notice.

We're not quite done with nitpicking, because I ought also to mention that the first Metropolitan station at Paddington – Paddington (Bishop's Road) – now serves only the Hammersmith & City Line. A new stop – Paddington (Praed Street) – was opened in a cutting under Praed Street when the Metropolitan extended south towards Bayswater in 1868. This now serves the Circle and the District but no longer the Met because, to repeat, *the Met no longer runs west of Baker Street.*

In *London Underground Stations* (1994) David Leboff mentions (with approval, I might add) the 'dull yellow lighting' of the old Met platforms at Baker Street, and the whole of the line seems to have had an ochre-ish tone when opened. The platforms were lit by gas flames in glass globes, and gas burns yellow if there are impurities in the atmosphere. The atmosphere of the Met contained plenty of impurities – very little *but,* as we will see. Today the lights are still in glass globes. They are sodium bulbs, and these too have a tendency to burn yellow with age. And, the electric lighting of today reflects off the same yellowish bricks as the gas lighting of 1863. (Those bricks are made of the London clay excavated when the line was built.)

A romantic friend told me that in 1863 the pendant globes would have swayed as the trains came in. I liked the detail – shadows swaying to left or right as the train approached – but surely the globes would hang from a rigid gas pipe? I consulted Christopher Sugg, a historian of gas, whose great-great-great-grandfather prepared – in 1907 – the first demonstration of street gas lighting in London. He replied: 'The installation was quite rigid, but at some stage the pendant fixtures were provided with a cup-and-ball joint at ceiling or roof level to allow for movement and simplify cleaning by rotating the lamp.' (Result!)

The formerly Metropolitan platforms at Baker Street are the most atmospheric on the Underground, and whereas the Bakerloo and Jubilee Line platforms at Baker Street are decorated with tiles showing motifs related to Sherlock Holmes, they are not needed on the old platforms, whose ambience puts you straight into a Holmes story. When walking in the off-peak over the small wood-panelled footbridge that connects the two original platforms – which itself resembles an old-fashioned railway carriage hoisted above the tracks – I would not be surprised to see a top-hatted man approaching me.

Met carriages were like the main-line carriages of the time. The doors swung open. People could, and did, open them in tunnels, and therefore the tops of the doors were rounded to prevent snagging. The carriages were lit by gas, a relative innovation on trains at the time, which were usually lit either by oil or – in third class – by nothing. Second- or third-class Met compartments had one gas lamp; first class had two. This was, as we will see, a most class-conscious railway, and signs hung along the platforms reading 'Wait Here For First/Second/Third Class'. There were no waiting rooms. They would have been an indictment of the service frequency, of which more in a second; there are still very few waiting rooms on the Underground, and the ones that do exist are usually on the stations inherited from the main-line railways. But there *were* licensed refreshment rooms, provided by those pioneers of station dining Messrs Spiers and Pond. Lee Jackson, who wrote an absorbing thriller set on the early Metropolitan, *A Metropolitan Murder* (2004), alerted me to a book of 1899 called *Inquiries Concerning Female Labour in the Metropolis*, which is written by 'Anon' and describes the conditions in which bar girls worked on the Met. They stood for eleven hours a day, and slept in subterranean rooms. They were allowed to consume 10d. a day in spirits, or teetotal girls could have ginger beer or lemonade. Most of the girls spent the money on stout, 'which is sustaining'. The girls were sometimes followed home to their company lodgings by 'hangers-on' who used the bars as clubs. 'Some of them are "horsey" individuals; not a few are flash mobs men, who go there to discuss business.'

The bar at Baker Street is now a snack shop, part of a chain called Treats. A man working on the ticket gate at Baker Street told me he remembered it as a bar, 'from when I was a kid. There was a sort of narrow ledge all around the walls for you to put your drink on. There were no seats.'

'So it was like a betting shop,' I suggested, 'in that you weren't encouraged to hang around?' 'That's right,' he said, 'but people did.'

In 1933 Spiers and Pond would still be operating fifteen bars at Metropolitan stations. In his book *Underground London* (2005) Stephen Smith mentions two late surviving station bars: 'Pac-Mac's Drinking Den, on the eastbound Metropolitan Line platform of Liverpool Street station, was open for business until 1978, when it became a café called The Piece of Cake. The other bar, The Hole in the Wall, was on the westbound platform at Sloane Square.' That closed in 1985, and is today another Treats.

In 1985 smoking was banned – by the chain-smoking Transport Secretary, Nicholas Ridley – on all partly or wholly subterranean stations, the ban on smoking on trains having been introduced the year before, after a fire at Oxford Circus. And smoking goes with drinking. One woman told me she worked in the City in the early Eighties, and all the hard-drinking traders in her office would stop off at the Sloane Square bar on their way back to the west London suburbs. 'It was like a little community. The barmaid knew all their drinks, and where they lived. I remember her calling out as a train came in, "Tel, it's your Wimbledon!"'

Those not drinking could read the advertising posters. Here is the gloomy novelist George Gissing, from his novel *In the Year of Jubilee*. Jessica Morgan and Samuel Barmby are waiting for a train at King's Cross:

> They stood together upon the platform, among hurrying crowds, in black fumes that poisoned the palate with sulphur. This way and that sped the demon engines, whirling lighted wagons full of people. Shrill whistles, the hiss and roar of steam, the bang, clap, bang of carriage doors, the clatter of feet on wood and stone – all echoed and reverberated from a huge cloudy vault above them. High and low, on every available yard of wall, advertisements clamoured to the eye: theatres, journals, soaps, medicines, concerts, furniture, wines, prayer-meetings – all the produce and refuse of civilisation announced in staring letters, in daubed effigies, base, paltry, grotesque.

The novel was set in 1887, when the Met had fallen from fashion, and written six years later, when it had fallen still further.

It was the start of 120 years and counting of complaining about Underground advertising. In Orwell's *Keep the Aspidistra Flying* the impoverished poet and former advertising copywriter

Gordon Comstock, reflects: '*all* modern commerce is a swindle. Curiously enough, it was the advertisements in the Underground stations that first brought it home to him.' By then the posters in the stations had all been marshalled within borders of standard sizes, which didn't deter the *Daily Mail* from complaining, on 26 November 1957, that 'Out of 200 advertisements running alongside the Piccadilly escalators, 48 show women in underwear.' When I was writing my 'Tube Talk' column, a man sent me a letter complaining about the advertisement of cars on the Underground. Why would the Underground masochistically promote a rival transport mode? The answer, I discovered, was that the adverts on the network must not 'harm the brand', and a car advert per se was not deemed to do that. However, a car advert that said, 'Why are you using this horrible Tube when you could be driving one of our lovely cars?' would not be allowed.

Station stops on the early Met were supposed to last a minute, but would often take less. The trains were going at something less than 20 miles an hour. It doesn't sound much to us, and there is a story of a guard who was on the platform at Paddington when his train pulled away, and so he rushed 'at street level' to catch it up at Edgware Road. But a fast horse-drawn carriage at the time moved at only 10 miles an hour. There was a two-minute train frequency in the rush hour, which is better than the current frequency on the line. Signalling was by the standard 'block' system of the time, which prevents any two trains being on the same track section at once, but this was operated with boldness, with margins shaved. The Metropolitan would prove to have an excellent safety record nonetheless.

BUT COULD YOU BREATHE?

A conventional steam engine emits smoke and steam from its chimney. Smoke is always – and steam can be – detrimental to health and comfort. So Chief Engineer Fowler proposed to build an unconventional engine. Before the opening of the line, he airily told a Commons Select Committee, 'What we propose to do is have no fire.' Isambard Kingdom Brunel, Chief Engineer of the Great Western, languidly backed him up, and I imagine him exhaling smoke from his habitual cheroot as he said, 'If you are going on a short journey, you do not take your dinner with you.'

Fowler designed a locomotive with a *small* fire that would heat firebricks. These in turn would keep the boiler hot. The engine was nicknamed 'Fowler's Ghost' because of the secrecy surrounding it. In 1861 Fowler tested it on the Great Western main line. It went 7½ miles; then it stopped. It seemed they would have to take their dinner with them after all. Sir Daniel Gooch, Locomotive Superintendent of the Great Western, then designed a tank engine that could consume its own steam and smoke, this being diverted into the water tanks at the operation of a lever. Or the exhaust gases could be directed through the chimney in the normal way when the engine came to any suitable aperture.

It says something about the Metropolitan's lack of confidence about these condensing engines that smoking – by human beings – was banned on the line from the outset, whereas it had been allowed on all prior railways. Given that it was happy to run gas-lit steam trains alongside wooden platforms, the Met couldn't say this was on the grounds of the *fire* risk. No, they knew they had an air quality issue. (The smoking ban was overturned in 1874, as a belated result of an amendment to the Railway Regulation Bill of 1868, which required all railways to provide a smoking carriage. In his last speech in the house John Stuart Mill spoke in favour of the amendment.)

Smoke and steam did leak from the engines into the tunnels, both because condensing mechanisms didn't work and because the temptation to fire the engines in the normal way – which immediately creates chimney emissions – was overwhelming.

Why? Because sending the steam into the water tanks eventually made the engine water boil, and the locomotives couldn't work in that case. Secondly, the engine fires needed the draught created by the normal operation of the chimney in order to burn properly – and you need a good fire to keep up the steam pressure.

Soon after opening, trains were shortened so as to put less strain on the engine, and thereby reduce the emissions. In rush hours the passengers left behind on the platforms as a result of this foreshortening were collected by 'expresses' that dashed through the tunnels like men holding their breath, and took fourteen minutes for the 3½ mile end-to-end trip, as against eighteen for the ordinary service. Then the Great Western fell out with the Metropolitan, mainly over the lack of any provision at that point for freight. In August 1863 it quit as train operator and took away its toys (its engines and carriages), although it would continue to send its own trains – badged GWR, rather than Metropolitan – over the line. The Great Northern – connected to the Metropolitan by tunnels under King's Cross, it will be recalled – stepped in and provided carriages and engines that boasted absolutely no condensing facilities, causing an access of the sulphurous fumes that burning coal gives off. In July 1864 the Metropolitan took delivery of some more condensing locomotives: beautiful green, brass-bound tank engines from Beyer, Peacock & Co. of Manchester. These were painted dark green, later 'chocolate' (romantic railway-speak for 'brown'). They carried large headlamps that would bear down on the gloomy platforms. When, sitting in a 'down' carriage, you passed one of these engines on the 'up', you'd have seen the fire glow sliding past in the dark tunnel, since there was no cab.

Those Euston Road ventilation grilles were fitted in 1872, but the Met became increasingly smoky as the Circle service came into operation in the 1880s. In 1896 Mark Twain wrote that:

The engine goes blustering and squittering along, puking smoke cinders in at the window, which someone has opened in pursuance of his right to make the whole cigar box uncomfortable if his comfort requires it; the fog of black smoke smothers the lamp and dims its light, and the double row of jammed people sit there and bark at each other, and the righteous and the unrighteous pray, each after his own fashion.

In 1897 a Board of Trade inquiry looked into the matter. Levels of carbon dioxide and sulphur were found to be high; a chemist of Gower Street testified that he had for years been dispensing 'Metropolitan Mixture' to soothe the coughing fits of regular passengers. On the other hand, a certain John Bell described how his own health problem – quinsy – had been eased by the disinfectant effect of the 'sulphurous acid gas' so freely available on the platforms. John Bell was the General Manager of the Metropolitan Railway. A doctor testified to the effect that the atmosphere on the Metropolitan was 'concentrated fog'. But there was plenty of polluted fog above ground as well. (In the 1920s the Underground Group issued a series of wordy posters entitled 'A Guide to the British Weather'. The first was headed 'No. 1: Fog'. It explained that fog included soot, ashes and sulphur impurities before proceeding to the triumphant punchline: 'There is no fog on the Underground.')

Further air shafts were installed, but 'electrivisation' was coming, and in 1897 everyone knew it. Perhaps there *was* something in the company's persistent contention that the atmosphere could be beneficial, however. At the London Transport Museum a tape loop plays an interview with George Spiller, a fireman on the steam-powered District Railway in the early days: 'We worked ten hour days, eight times around the Circle. In the summer you could hardly breathe going through the tunnels.' He lived to be 102.

Steam engines survived on the cut-and-cover lines until 1971, pulling maintenance wagons at night after the electricity had been switched off. This was three years after the abolition of main-line steam, and people would write letters to the newspapers saying they'd seen, or heard, a ghost train. A recent post on the excellent 'District Dave's London Underground Site' ran as follows:

> In 1968/9 as a callow youth, I moved into digs … in a house with a long garden that backed onto the Met between West Harrow and Rayners Lane. Strange noises woke me in the wee hours of my first night there. Looked out of the window, and saw a ghostly silhouette of a steam loco standing there, complete with eerie glow from the cab. Scared the cr**p out of me, since I had lived in Cornwall for years, and had no idea there was still steam on LT.

The railway author John Scott-Morgan is in regular touch with a man who drove those trains. He, like George Spiller, said the atmosphere was beneficial, and at the time of writing he is ninety-six.

A CLASS-CONSCIOUS RAILWAY

At the time of his death Charles Pearson was campaigning for a workmen's estate to be built a few miles west of Paddington. That didn't happen. He also campaigned for cheap workmen's fares on the Metropolitan, and that did come about. At first, the Metropolitan provided cheap trains voluntarily. Later, a legal requirement to provide workmen's fares would be laid upon the company in return for the right to extend its lines. The early workman's fare was a 3d. return ticket usable in third class on trains departing at 5.30 and 5.40 in the morning. The usual third fare was 5d. return, so the saving was a shilling a week, or a pint of beer every day of the six-day working week. (A first-class return was 9d.)

In a pamphlet of 1865 called *The Shops and Companies of London and the Trades and Manufactories of Great Britain* Henry Mayhew interviewed workmen who had availed themselves of the fare. He presages his account with a eulogy of the Met: 'This subterranean method of locomotion had always struck as being the most thoroughly cockney element of all within the wide region of Cockaigne', which is humour (albeit not of a funny sort), and which reminds us that the tireless chronicler of the London poor had also once been the editor of *Punch*. Early one morning he stood on the platform at Paddington, which was 'a bustle with men, a large number of whom had bass-baskets [wicker baskets] in their hands, or tin flagons, or basins done up in red handkerchiefs. Some few carried large saws under their arms.' It was widely agreed that the 'cheap and early trains' were 'a great benefit to the operative classes'. One man told Mayhew that he lived 'almost in the open country' – in Notting Hill – where he was able to afford two rooms for what one cost in the middle of London. And the railway saved him a 6-mile walk to work.

Mayhew's survey found that 69 per cent of Met travellers went by third class, 20.5 per cent second, 10.5 per cent first. The Met would abolish second class in 1905 at the time of electrification. It would go down to one class in 1941 – by which time it was the Metropolitan *Line* – and its passengers would make a beeline for the ex-first seats, just as third-class passengers had made a beeline for the ex-second seats after 1905, since they had not been physically removed or sabotaged to make them less comfortable. All the *Tubes* had only had one class since their inception – all except one, whose name need not bother us for the moment, but which fell into the ownership of guess which class-conscious company? The Metropolitan.

It may seem that the Met was a snobbish outfit, a betrayer of the egalitarian dreams of Charles Pearson, but in being one of the pioneers of working men's fares the company had helped to bring about a revolution that would allow the working classes to live in London. Cheap trains would supersede Gladstone's well-meant Parliamentary Trains. The acts authorising the subsequent Underground lines would include a stipulation that cheap early morning fares be provided, and the Cheap Trains Act of 1883 would standardise the terms for all railways. The working man's railway par excellence was the Great Eastern, whose cheap fares were responsible for the great bulge of north-east London, and the growth of Walthamstow, Tottenham and the environs.

A couple of years ago I met a woman in a Suffolk pub who was very proud of having just bought an Edwardian house in Leytonstone, east London. I told her that her property was almost certainly built as a result of the Cheap Trains Act. She seemed deflated as, I must admit, was my intention. 'Are you sure it was called the *cheap* trains act?' she asked. 'I mean, as crude as that?' 'I'm afraid it was,' I replied.

Working men's fares began to be abolished from the early 1950s, but there is one wispy, ghostly survival of the scheme on the Underground. For most purposes the morning peak, with its more expensive travel, is defined as 4.30 to 9.30 a.m., but in the case of Oyster Card single fares, the morning peak begins at 6.30. It is the less well-paid jobs that require people to travel before 6.30 (you still see men with their tool bags on the first Tubes of the day), so the generous impulse behind the working men's tickets has not entirely died out.

CHAPTER THREE

THE METROPOLITAN AND ITS ASSOCIATES

THE HAMMERSMITH & CITY AND THE 'EXTENSION RAILWAY'

It was always envisaged, by government and the directors of the Metropolitan, that the railway would expand, and an easterly extension towards Moorgate was authorised even before the opening of the original stretch. In 1864 a Joint Select Committee of both houses of Parliament came out in favour of an 'inner circuit', a loop joining the main line termini to the north with those that were emerging to the south in the early 1860s: Victoria, Charing Cross and Cannon Street. To make this loop, the Met would droop down from Moorgate to Tower Hill at the easterly end, and from Paddington towards Brompton at its westerly end. The base of the arch thus created would be a line running along the north bank of the river built by a separate company, the Metropolitan *District* Railway. The authorising acts were passed in July 1864, and this legislation brought into being what is today the Circle Line ... all of which sounds very simple. In reality, it would be a painful process.

Before we broach the Circle saga, two other extensions of the Met need to be mentioned. The first is the Hammersmith & City Railway – now the western part of the Hammersmith and City *Line*. It was built and jointly funded by the Metropolitan and the Great Western, even as they were arguing over operation of the Metropolitan. It opened in June 1864, running north on 20-foot-high viaducts from the pretty village of Hammersmith via Shepherd's Bush to Latimer Road (where there was a connection to a Kensington station via the West London Railway) before proceeding north and east, to connect with the original westerly terminus of the Metropolitan, at Paddington (Bishop's Road). There it dived underground, eventually enabling its train services to run over, and be entangled with, the easterly extensions of the Metropolitan and the District.

The Hammersmith & City is an annoying railway – an anomaly or distracting complication, like a hair in the gate of a cinema camera. For example, that connection to the West London Railway would allow trains of various operators to run from north to south London in complicated ways. And although built by the Met and Great Western, it was initially owned by a third company: the Hammersmith & City Railway Company, and the line only exists because two of its directors owned land along the route, which they could – and did – sell back to the railway at vast profit.

The line would feature on Underground maps as part of the Metropolitan, and was therefore coloured purple along with the rest of the Met. But in 1989 it became pink ('Why do I got to be Mr Pink?' says Steve Buscemi in *Reservoir Dogs*), the colour denoting a line running from Hammersmith to Barking. From 2008 its original westerly stretch also doubled as part of the Circle service – an 'extension' of the Circle Line, like a piece of Sellotape pulled away from the roll. And one further complication: the original Hammersmith & City Railway was built on the high level.

It has its charm, though. Royal Oak is like a country branch line dropped down amid the main line approaches to Paddington. It's as if two very different train sets got mixed up in the same box. Westbourne Park is also countrified, with valanced canopies and fancy ironwork (which is painted a dingy yellow). West of here, it ascends to its viaduct where, 20 foot off the ground, the Westway seeks to emulate it: two scruffy reprobates shouldering their way through a not very pretty streetscape: the one a railway built by corporate buccaneers, the other a road constructed as part of a discredited plan to girdle London with motorways. A lot of streets and squares, built speculatively with the coming of the Hammersmith & City, failed to go 'up' as expected. Christian Wolmar notes:

> The squares near Ladbroke Grove station ... never managed to attract the kind of people for which they were designed and sank rapidly into multiple occupation, becoming almost as bad as the nearby rookeries of north-west Kensington. It was only with the gentrification process which started a hundred years later, in the 1970s, that these squares started to attract the class for which they had been built.

People who'd been with me at university in the early Eighties were part of that gentrification process, and I associate it with the smell of dope smoke floating through the shabby-genteel house bordering the H & C.

As for Hammersmith itself, that's now a transport hub, but unfortunately cars were invited to the party, so the centre is a roaring roundabout. There are two Underground stations. That serving the District and Piccadilly is on one side of an un-crossable road called Hammersmith Broadway; that serving the Hammersmith & City is on the other side. Whichever exit you emerge from, at whichever station, you are immediately lost.

Before moving on to the Metropolitan's painful encirclement of central London in supposed partnership with the District, there is an emerging north-pointing prong that ought to be noted. In April 1868 a line was constructed north from Baker Street by the Metropolitan & St John's Wood Railway, a subsidiary of the Met that would be incorporated into the parent in 1872. The line went up to Swiss Cottage, occupying for much of the way a single-bore tunnel that only accommodated one train like a deep-level Tube tunnel, even though the line was built on the cut-and-cover principle associated with vault-like tunnels holding two trains. There was barely room to open the outward swinging doors of the Metropolitan carriages, and since there were no corridors connecting the compartments of these carriages, the passenger had just better hope that no prolonged delays occurred within the tunnel – because they would have been prisoners.

In 1872 a second, parallel, single-bore tunnel was built to serve the line, creating the possibility of *two* train loads of passengers being trapped. But these little tunnels, emerging into the open at Finchley Road (reached in 1879) were the start of something big. By the early twentieth century it would be possible to think of them as two mouseholes in the skirting board of a wall separating two great ballrooms. On the south side was the ballroom of central London and the City; to the north, the ballroom of the suburbs that would grow up alongside this rapidly extending projection of the Metropolitan, suburbs made famous in the Twenties as Metroland. The line was known – and still is known to elderly traditionalists – as 'The Extension Railway'.

THE CITY WIDENED

We are about to broach the fraught saga of the Circle Line, but there is another Metropolitan spin-off that comes first, one that has always appealed to me by the baleful beauty of its name: the City Widened Lines or 'The Widened Lines' for short. Its modern legacy is the central core of the Thameslink service, and whereas there are still elderly buffers who speak of 'The Extension Railway' (described above), or call the Circle Line 'The Inner Circle', you will not find many Londoners who speak of Thameslink as 'The City Widened', and if you did find one he'd probably be wearing a bowler hat.

This is a story of north–south connection, and it begins with the fact that late in 1863 the Great Northern Railway completed a subterranean connection from its terminus at King's Cross to the tracks of the Metropolitan enabling the Great Northern to run through to the Met's easterly terminus at Farringdon Street. As mentioned, the Met, in its descent towards the heart of the City, extended in 1865 from Farringdon Street to a station called Moorgate Street (now Moorgate), via Aldersgate Street (now Barbican).

In making this extension, the Metropolitan also built a connection from Farringdon Street towards an overground railway that had just barged its way into the City from Kent. This railway was the London, Chatham & Dover. In 1860 it had obtained an Act permitting an exception to the ban on railways in central London recommended in 1846. The line would traverse a bridge at Blackfriars before running along a viaduct to a station called Ludgate Hill.

In proceeding north from the Thames towards Ludgate Hill station, the line crossed over an iron bridge spanning Ludgate Hill itself (between what is now a Waterstone's and a Santander bank), neatly obliterating any view of St Paul's from Ludgate Circus or Fleet Street. A thousand people had put their names to a petition against the bridge. To add insult to injury, it carried a small thicket of railway signals as well as regular steam trains. There is a Gustave Doré engraving of the street under

Engraving by Gustave Doré of the viaduct that used to run over
Ludgate Hill. In conjunction with the Snow Hill Tunnel, this route
– a spin-off from the Metropolitan Railway – allowed trains to
run from the north to the south of England via central London.
The viaduct was hated when it was built in the mid 1860's, since it
blocked views of St Paul's from the west. But the author of this
book, who recalls the viaduct from its last years (the late 1980s),
liked it.

the bridge. In the jostling throng every Victorian artefact you would expect seemed present: horses, carts, carriages (including a hearse), top hats, slouch hats, canes. The only item missing is a steam engine – until you see one going over the bridge in the background. In *The Imperial Gazetteer of England and Wales* in 1869 a certain J. M. Wilson fumed: 'That viaduct has utterly spoiled one of the finest street views in the metropolis, and is one of the most unsightly objects ever constructed, in any situation, anywhere in the world.' But *I* rather liked it. It was demolished in the late Eighties, and to my mind Ludgate Circus has always looked incomplete without it. But let us follow a London, Chatham & Dover train over that bridge in 1865. On reaching Ludgate Hill it descends into a tunnel and runs north through the new Snow Hill Tunnel to connect with the Metropolitan at Farringdon.

Even though the Met was supposed to be concentrating on building the 'Inner Circle', it had now made itself into a gateway between north and south London. It envisaged profitable demand for use of this gateway by 'guest' railways. The portal offered trains from the north a chance to run through to the south of England or into the heart of the City at Moorgate Street. Trains from the south could run into Ludgate Hill, thus gaining the western part of the City, or head through to the north of England. What trains from the south could *not* do – at first – was branch right to access the Met station at Moorgate Street.

Being accessible from the north, Moorgate Street was an attractive prospect for the Midland Railway, whose terminus at St Pancras opened alongside King's Cross in 1868. The Midland plugged itself into the Met by means of a tunnel under St Pancras. The tunnel started to the north of the station, and involved the excavation of St Pancras churchyard. There were reports of thigh bones and skulls being tossed about as work progressed. A respected architect called Arthur Blomfield was called in to bring some decorum to the site, and his apprentice was Thomas Hardy. In *St Pancras Station* (2007) Simon Bradley writes: 'Hardy's biographers speculate how far this gruesome business may have deepened the writer's tendency to see the skull beneath the skin of life.'

In order to accommodate its paying guests, the Metropolitan doubled the two tracks running between King's Cross and Moorgate Street, these two extra lines running in parallel tunnels or cuttings and coming together at its stations on that stretch. These are the Widened Lines. Just north of Farringdon station, and to the east of Ray Street, there is a wide cutting bounded by another of those brick walls nicely calculated to be just too high for you to see over. So prop your bike against it, and stand on the down-pointing pedal crank. You are looking at the Ray Street Gridiron, a spectacular bridge in a cutting that carries the Metropolitan, the supposed Underground, *over* the Widened Lines (now Thameslink).

In 1871 a junction was created from the southern end of the Snow Hill Tunnel towards the Widened Lines, intersecting with them as they run beneath the meat market at Smithfield, which was new at the time. By this means, trains from the south *were* able to reach Moorgate Street. In 1874 a station was also created at the southern end of the Snow Hill Tunnel: Snow Hill station. It was underneath the new Holborn Viaduct. It was the companion to a station built during the same year at the end of a 300-yard cut-and-cover branch line running from Ludgate Hill to a station giving access to the *roadway* of Holborn Viaduct. This upper station was called, logically enough, Holborn Viaduct. In 1912 its downtrodden companion was renamed, rather demeaningly, Holborn Viaduct Low Level. The upper station was destroyed in the Blitz. The shell of the lower station can still be seen at the southern end of the Snow Hill Tunnel from a Thameslink train.

Anyone standing on the platforms of the Metropolitan at King's Cross, Farringdon, Aldersgate Street or Moorgate would have been diverted by the site of a variety of 'guests'. The Great Northern and the Midland ran commuters into Moorgate and operated services of passengers or goods to the south of England. In the late nineteenth century a service ran from Liverpool to Paris via the Widened Lines and a steamer from Folkestone. (Depart Liverpool 8 a.m.; arrive Paris 10.50 p.m.) But there wasn't much call for that sort of thing. London was too beguiling. People didn't want to travel through it without getting off.

There were goods sidings under Smithfield Market, and condensing steam engines – and later diesels – pulled wagons full of frozen meat from Paddington to there until July 1962. Those sidings now form a subterranean car park between what remains of the market and St Bart's Hospital. Walk down the winding ramp, and as you descend you will see that the walls become arcaded, like the station walls of the old parent company; they become excitingly Metropolitanised.

From the *south*, the main users were the London, Chatham & Dover and the South Eastern Railway, whose chairmen were respectively James Staats Forbes and Edward Watkin, two perennial adversaries whose names are going to crop up in the Circle trauma.

The operations of the Widened Lines, as viewed from the Met platforms, must have seemed archaic after 1905, when the Metropolitan began to be electrified: all those filthy guest engines trying their best – sort of – to stifle their emissions, and passenger carriages still lit by oil. (Steam would survive on the Widened Lines until 1962.) In 1916 the Snow Hill Tunnel was closed to passenger trains, so those from the south terminated at Holborn Viaduct, and those from the north could only go as far as Moorgate.

In 1971 the Snow Hill Tunnel was closed entirely. In 1988 it was re-opened for the purpose of running trains from Bedford to Brighton. In 1990 City Thameslink station was opened, a sprawling underground complex taking the place of Holborn Viaduct and Ludgate Hill stations. 'It's very *Blade Runner*,' a PR for the station told me shortly after the opening. She also said that Thameslink trains were deliberately garish, so as to lure drivers stuck on the M1, which runs alongside the line around Radlett. But I don't think the overcrowded Thameslink service could handle any more passengers today. As for garishness, what I like about the Widened Lines in their previous incarnation is the absence of that quality. Surely it was never summer on the Widened Lines. It was dark mornings and dark evenings; damp worsted, bowler hats, tightly furled umbrellas, smoke fumes and steam, cigarettes and a stiff whisky in the Holborn Viaduct Hotel – and more of those every day for the bowler-hatted commuter who has reached the limit of his promotion, a man who might, in his cups, lament: 'The City has not widened sufficiently for *my* liking.'

TOWARDS LEINSTER GARDENS

By 1876, an expensive eleven years after it had opened Moorgate Street, the Met had crawled under the City streets to Aldgate, via Bishopsgate (which would be renamed Liverpool Street in 1909, after the overground station to which it was adjacent), en route to meet the District Railway at Tower Hill. We have been concentrating on the City because that was the initial target for builders of both overground and underground railways, who were like artists going over and over the same piece of canvas. But we now look at the Met's *westerly* gropings. These began from the new, south-westerly pointing annexe at Paddington – Paddington (Praed Street). From there the Met marched on Bayswater, Notting Hill Gate, High Street Kensington and Gloucester Road before effecting its rendezvous with the District at South Kensington in December 1868.

In building this stretch, the Metropolitan intersected at right angles the broadly west–east pattern of the streets, rather than running along beneath the road, as it had done under the Euston Road. This meant the purchase of many properties, and to save money some stretches were more cut than cover. Railway canyons were thereby created in the streets, and one such canyon abuts Leinster Gardens, Queensway W2. This is a street of elegant stucco terraced houses, two of which (numbers 23 and 24) straddled the mouth of the canyon. They wouldn't have been pleasant to live in, so they were knocked down and replaced with fake houses, about 5 feet thick, with painted-on black windows. The impulse was partly aesthetic – to maintain the harmony of the street – and partly practical: the engines would be able to release steam and smoke behind the façade, like a man putting his hand over his mouth when he coughs.

So began 150 years of practical jokes, with coal merchants sending young apprentices to deliver coal to the façades, or letters addressed to Mr N. O. Body, 24 Leinster Gardens. (There is no letterbox.) In the late Nineties I visited Leinster Gardens for my 'Tube Talk' column. The dummies are sandwiched between two hotels, the Henry VIII and the Blakemore. I walked into the Blakemore and volunteered my sympathy to the duty manager for the way he must be constantly pestered with questions about the pretend houses next door. 'Ah yes,' he said, and smiled vaguely for a while before adding, 'What do you mean?' I then went into the Henry VIII and had the same conversation with the duty manager there. Within ten minutes, staff members from each hotel were standing in front of numbers 23 and 24 and saying to each other, 'But we thought they were part of *your* hotel.' Only the maintenance man at the Henry VIII knew the score, and he took me to room 501, on the top floor of the hotel, and then along a narrow balcony enabling us to look down on the narrow façades, which taper to a thickness of about 2 feet at the top, and down on the trains (District and Circle today) rumbling along between arcaded walls with girders across. No guest, of course, has ever remarked on the strangeness of the view.

London Underground is responsible for maintaining the façades, which are regularly repainted, the grey-black of the stone 'windows' capturing perfectly the effect of closed net curtains. On the ground floor the paint conceals two genuine panes of glass, and, squinting through these, I saw a tiny booth-like room containing a chair and a clock stopped at ten to ten. I asked what this was for, and a spokesman said he'd come back to me, which he eventually did.

'Nobody knows,' he said.

THE METROPOLITAN DISTRICT: THE RATHER UNINTERESTING RAILWAY

It is time to meet the Met's partner in the arranged marriage of the Inner Circle: the Metropolitan District Railway – the District for short. It made its début on Christmas Eve 1868 (South Kensington to Westminster).

In his book *London's Historic Railway Stations* (1971) John Betjeman speaks of 'the rather uninteresting District Railway, which brought Ealing, Richmond and Wimbledon to London'. Certainly it rates the fewest index entries of any line in David Welsh's book *Underground Writing* (2009), a survey of literature about the system. Under 'popular culture', the Wikipedia entry on the line has 'Sheffield band Milburn wrote a song called "The District Line", which refers to London', and, as if *that* weren't enough, 'Canadian guitarist Pat Travers wrote a song called "Life in London", which mentions the District Line.' Also cited is the fictional Underground station in *EastEnders*, Walford East. That's meant to be on the District, a fictional counterpart to Bromley-by-Bow. It is odd that the District should thus be associated with east London because its early expansion beyond central London was all to the more prosperous west, with Earl's Court the hub of tentacles reaching into Fulham, Putney, Wimbledon, Kensington, Kew and Richmond.

The District seems complacently salubrious. It is green on the Tube map, an inoffensive colour. It has not one but two bridge crossings of the Thames, which seems greedy when you think that no other line has even one. It is generally associated with pleasure. Its earliest maps – and it was a pioneer of Underground maps – boasted of the proximity of the Royal Albert Hall to South Kensington station (although it's not *that* near). Its first push into west London coincided with the passing of the Bank Holiday Act of 1871, which made Boxing Day, Easter Monday, Whit Monday and August Monday days off. The District went to Putney to take advantage of Boat Race traffic, and it would capitalise on the shows and exhibitions held at Earl's Court and Olympia. Earl's Court was at first an outdoor complex incorporating an arena, and from 1887 it was the London home of Buffalo Bill's Wild West Show. On the opening day in May 28,000 people came to see this spectacle. 'The Underground Railway was besieged and taken by force', wrote the *Daily Telegraph*. (In his book *Buffalo Bill's British Wild West* (2001) Alan Gallop features a picture of some of Bill's buffaloes grazing at Earl's Court under the caption 'Give me a home where the buffaloes roam ...') In 1894 a Ferris wheel was erected there. I have a painting showing the District station, Baron's Court, at twilight with the big wheel illuminated in the background. It was painted by Alan Wright on 16 June 1906.

(Frivolity is often the motive behind the building of railways. The Metropolitan itself was supposed to be open in time to funnel people from the Euston Road railway termini towards the Second Great Exhibition of 1862. It was a year late. And while the Jubilee Line Extension was not built to serve the Millennium

Dome, it was finished quickly in 1999 in order to take people to the Millennial Party that was held there; and the prospect of the Olympics has spurred the development of railways in east London.)

A well set-up, bourgeois Victorian railway then ... except that right from the start the District was broke, and the reaching out to west London and commuters, and the chasing after exhibitions and pleasure trips, were a desperate attempt to pull in revenue in support of its main task: the building of the base of the cursed Inner Circle. This was to be built beneath property considerably more desirable and expensive than even those in the District's suburbs, and the costs of way leaves, of compensation, underpinning and outright purchases would prove crippling. That Christmas Eve opening in 1868 from South Kensington to Westminster? Desperation. The District was hoping for a big Christmas Day traffic.

That first stretch incorporated Sloane Square (where the Westbourne river had to be captured and inserted into its pipe), Victoria (there would be no profitable connection to the main line station until a subway was built in 1878) and St James's Park. It cost £3 million, absorbing all the debenture and share capital the company had taken up. Investors were now warier of Underground railways. They had seen that the Metropolitan was bringing in lower returns, having broached its City extensions. But the newly established Metropolitan Board of Works (the first London-wide authority) pressed the District to continue with the next part of the plan – Westminster to Blackfriars – so that the building of the railway could go in tandem with the construction of the new Thames Embankment and the sewer it incorporated. The District Railway staggered into Blackfriars in May 1870. This stretch incorporated Embankment (called Charing Cross on opening) and Temple station, which had to have a very modestly proportioned station building on the insistence of the Duke of Norfolk, who owned the land on which it was built, and where the trains under the glass roof of the station were not allowed to blow their whistles, at the insistence of the barristers in the nearby Inns of Court. The District may seem to have been unfairly burdened with travails, but it should be remembered that many other railway companies had wanted to build central London railways, and it was widely anticipated that a completed Circle Line would bring huge profits. Widely, but wrongly.

HOW NOT TO DRAW A PERFECT CIRCLE

Initially, the District operated shuttle services along its own line, using the rolling stock of the Metropolitan because, according to the agreement between the companies, the District would build stations and lines but not operate trains. It was not happy with this arrangement, and in 1870 the District broke away from the Metropolitan, a decision associated with the arrival as Managing Director of James Staats Forbes, already mentioned as General Manager of the London, Chatham & Dover Railway.

The District ordered its own engines and carriages, and so now it was a proper railway. It asserted its independence by creating its own platforms at the stations it was supposed to share with the Metropolitan, namely those where the railways converged in the south-west corner of the not yet circular Circle: High Street Kensington, Gloucester Road and South Kensington. It also built its own connection between High Street Kensington and Gloucester Road, duplicating the Metropolitan's line around that corner, which was already known as the 'Cromwell Curve'. The District's duplication – which would allow it to save money (it would not have to pay to use the Metropolitan's tracks here) – would be used intermittently and cause a number of legal disputes. It too was sometimes known as the 'Cromwell Curve', so the whole matter is confusing. A couple of years ago my wife and

I were out with another couple in a pub. The women were talking schools, and I leaned across to ask the other man (a trainspotter, albeit of a sophisticated sort), 'What can you tell me about the Cromwell Curve?' He smiled seraphically for a while, saying, 'You know, I think I'll settle for just being asked the question.'

It's possible that Arthur Conan Doyle was also interested in the Cromwell Curve. In the Sherlock Holmes story *The Bruce-Partington Plans*, which was written in 1908 but set in 1895, the body of Arthur Cadogan West, a civil servant, is dropped onto the top of an Underground train somewhere west of Aldgate, where the body is discovered. Holmes surmises that it must have been lowered onto the carriage at a place where trains pause and the carriages roofs are accessible. Holmes has a 'vague memory' that a west London street called Caulfield Gardens overlooks an Underground cutting, where the trains stop because of an intersection with another railway. To summarise the thousands of words of internet speculation about the whereabouts of the fictional Caulfield Gardens ... it has been suggested that what Conan Doyle – as opposed to Holmes – vaguely had in mind was the junction of the Cromwell Curve with the line carrying District trains west of Gloucester Road. (The story, by the way, contains this superb message sent from Holmes to Watson: 'Am dining at Goldini's Restaurant, Gloucester Road. Please come at once and join me there. Bring with you a jemmy, a dark lantern, a chisel and a revolver.')

In July 1871 the District crawled a bit nearer to the Metropolitan in the south-*eastern* corner, progressing beyond Blackfriars to Mansion House. Now an 'Inner Circle' service began to operate, albeit with a gap between Mansion House and Aldgate. So if you wanted to go from, say, Blackfriars to Farringdon, you could only go the long way round. The trains ran every ten minutes.

In 1872, following a series of financial setbacks, the Met brought in Sir Edward Watkin as chairman. He was also chairman of the Manchester, Sheffield & Lincoln Railway, and of the South Eastern Railway, the latter being the great rival of the London, Chatham & Dover because of territorial disputes in Kent. Staats Forbes, now of the District, had been running the London, Chatham & Dover during these clashes, and the two now imported their rivalry to London.

CLOSING THE CIRCLE

By 1875 the Metropolitan and the District were carrying about 100 million passengers a year on their branches and their unclosed circle. The figure today for the entire Underground network serving a larger city is 1.1 billion, so the number is impressive. But it ought not to surprise us because London, as we've seen, was booming, with rapid population growth creating not only crowded trains but also more traffic 'locks', and congestion on the streets of the City. So the Metropolitan Board of Works pressed again for the completion of the Circle. But the penny was beginning to drop: even a successful railway could be crippled by its capital costs.

The Metropolitan and the District being unwilling to complete the Circle, another group of opportunists set up the Metropolitan Inner Circle Completion Company to do the job. (There was no escaping that word 'Metropolitan'.) This it proposed to do in conjunction with the building of a spur to Whitechapel, connecting with the East London Railway, which ran from New Cross in south-east London to Liverpool Street via Wapping. The Met and the District wanted a piece of this action. As we will see, they had both been spreading out into the western suburbs when they were supposed to be building the Circle – 'playing away' like a couple in a bad marriage. Here was a chance to pick up passengers from the other side of London.

An independent inquiry recommended that the Met and the

District complete the circle, rather than third parties, and, motivated by the prospect of the East London connection, they now did so. In September 1882 the Metropolitan reached the Tower of London, where it opened a station of that name (now Tower Hill). It was made of wood, and built in sixty hours flat, before the District could object to this station being 'bagged' by the Met as part of its own stretch of a completed Circle. A childish move, yes, and carrying the fingerprints of the stroppy Sir Edward Watkin, but it brought Inner Circle completion within sight, and in October 1884 the gap was closed by joint construction of lines between Tower of London and Mansion House.

On 6 October 1884 the Inner Circle came into operational life, using the trains of the Metropolitan and the District and running over tracks that were also cluttered up with pure Metropolitan trains, pure District trains and a variety of other services. Trains on the Circle service were about every ten minutes, as compared with every seven minutes today. Metropolitan trains ran clockwise around the outer line; District ran anti-clockwise on the inner. Yes, that's the inner rail of the *Inner* Circle. Your ticket was stamped with 'O' or 'I', depending on which way you were going. You were supposed to be given a ticket for the shortest route around the circle, but in 1884, when many legal differences arose over the operation of the line, you would very likely be given a ticket for the 'O' or the 'I' depending on whether you'd bought it at a Met or a District ticket office. So if you bought a ticket at Notting Hill Gate (a Met station) to go to Sloane Square (District), you might be sent by the 'O' (twenty-three stops) as against the 'I' (four stops).

The line was trouble when it opened, and it is trouble today. In 1901 the pioneer of electric tramways in America, Frank Sprague, rode around the Inner Circle. He condemned it as 'a travesty on rapid transit'. We've already seen the difficulty of operating steam engines in tunnels, and now the wheels of those heavy engines were wearing out disproportionately from always going clock-wise or anti-clockwise.

The Inner Circle intersected with other lines at flat junctions. That is, other lines cross it on the same level, and there would be more of these junctions as the Underground developed. In the mid-1930s, when Stalin was looking to make a statement with his new Metro, he consulted Underground engineers, who offered advice to the Russian Minister in charge of the Metro project, Nikita Khrushchev. He was severely told: 'Don't have a Circle Line – too many flat junctions.' Moscow did build a circle line, but with *flying* junctions, by which one track goes over another.

On early Underground maps the Inner Circle was not desig-nated, but you could pick it out by looking at how the Metro-politan and District intersected, at which point it would become embarrassingly clear that the Circle was not circular at all. In her novel *King Solomon's Carpet* (1991) Barbara Vine (aka Ruth Ren-dell) suggests a resemblance to a swimming dolphin, 'its snout being Aldgate ... the crown of its head King's Cross, its spine Paddington'. (But for the tail she goes outside the Circle – invok-ing Ealing Broadway.) On Harry Beck's diagrammatised Tube map of 1933 the Circle resembles, as has often been pointed out, a vacuum flask lying on its side with the narrower top end (where the plastic cup would be fixed) pointing east, which does reflect the fact that the circle is *narrower* to the east, which was a reason not to use it for people who wanted to get from, say, Moorgate to Aldgate. It's quicker to walk.

From the 1920s, incidentally, the Metropolitan was usually shown as purple or maroon, the District green. But for much of the 1940s they were *both* coloured green and referred to as the 'Metropolitan and District Lines'. It was during this phase that the Circle was first picked out on the map as a distinct route when, in 1947, it was delineated by a black border around the green route. It became yellow in 1949, when the 'Inner' was dropped. It was the Circle Line from then on. It may not have been circular, but at least it was conceptually simple in actually being a *circuit*. For a while …

BY THE WAY: THE CIRCLE RE-OPENED

Whereas the Northern Line is the villain of the Underground, the Circle Line settled down as its comedy turn, some levity being permissible since it is not usually used for the grimly consequential business of commuting. There has never been any firm conclusion about how to denote direction of travel on the Circle. Sometimes 'via King's Cross' (or wherever) is used, sometimes 'westbound/eastbound', sometimes 'clockwise/anti-clockwise', but a few years ago there was an internal memo advising against the latter, since in these days of digital timepieces, the terms might not be widely understood.

The Circle generated urban myths: the man who died on it and then went round all day; the language school that conducted its classes on Circle trains, the collective daily fare being cheaper than office rental. In April 2010 the *Independent* reported:

London is in talks with the European Organisation for Nuclear Research about the possibility of using the 23km tunnel of the Circle Line to house a new type of particle accelerator similar to the Large Hadron Collider in Geneva. Particle physicists believe the existing tunnel can be adapted to take a small-scale 'atom smasher' alongside the passenger line at a fraction of the cost of building a new tunnel elsewhere in Europe.

(That was on 1 April, by the way.)

Adding to the fun was the fact that the Circle had the worst train frequency of any line, the trouble being that it is not a line but a service, its trains being guests on the Metropolitan, District, Hammersmith & City – and often unwelcome guests, since if a Circle train went slow or broke down, it would block those other lines. There were not enough access points to get trains off the Circle, or indeed on. In the morning its trains would approach the Circle from various points of the compass so as to get an even spread for the commencement of operations. One Underground staffer described this arrangement to me as being 'like the way the Red Arrows converge from different counties for an air display … only more boring'.

In 2008, as part of the Tube Upgrade, London Underground called time on this ribaldry. The Circle Line was unpicked. It's still yellow, it's still called the Circle, but a tail has been tacked on, and this tail shadows the western bit of the Hammersmith & City Line. Circle trains come along it from Hammersmith to Edgware Road. There, after brooding for a while, they go clockwise around the circle, then anti-clockwise, then bugger off back to Hammersmith. A driver running late can now knock off duty at the Hammersmith depot rather than somewhere in the middle of the Circle. The result is a more frequent service between Edgware Road and Hammersmith, a better-regulated Circle Line (albeit with even fewer trains) and a lot more time for everyone at Edgware Road …

Those who live or travel in the north-west corner of central London have always spent a lot of time at Edgware Road. The District Line terminates there. (In 1926 District trains began running from Kensington High Street to Edgware Road, like a green vine growing up the left-hand side of the Circle.) Edgware Road is also a duty change-over point for Hammersmith & City Line trains; and the service on that line is regulated with 'pauses' at Edgware Road. Even when the Circle was whole, I used often to be chucked off its trains at Edgware Road because something had gone wrong. Now – just to make this clear – it is impossible to negotiate the north-west 'corner' of the Circle *without* being chucked off at Edgware Road.

Incidentally, the Edgware Road we are concerned with is not to be confused (although it frequently *is*) with Edgware Road station on the Bakerloo Line, which stands about 500 yards away, or with Edgware station on the Northern Line. Edgware Road (Bakerloo) is a much more straightforward station than its namesake. Its users tend not to have to spend large parts of their *lives* there – they just pass through. It is also warmer, because it is underground. Our Edgware Road is essentially two island platforms surrounded by sidings and set in a cutting that's very good at funnelling icy winds.

But it has its plus points. In the ticket hall stand pink steel tubs containing well-tended plants – a memorial to the six people killed in the station by one of the terrorist attacks on 7 July 2005. It was not the first bomb at Edgware Road, incidentally. Irish-American republicans (or possibly anarchists) placed one in the tunnel just west of the station in the early evening of 30 October 1883. It damaged a passing third-class carriage, and a couple of dozen working-class men were injured, along with two schoolboys who had come up for the day from Clacton-on-Sea. Later on the same evening, the same 'ruffians' or 'revolutionists' detonated a bomb on the District east of Westminster, but no trains were passing at the time.

For years there was another, more eccentric, garden at Edgware Road. It was on the opposite side of the tracks from platform 1: an ornamental pond with an arrangement of garden gnomes around it. A couple of years ago I suddenly noticed that neither gnomes nor pond were there, so I stopped a platform guard at the station, and said, 'Can you tell me about the gnomes?' '*What* gnomes?' he said, testily. He then evidently remembered, and said they'd been put there by a female member of staff, currently off duty. Every Christmas, he fondly recalled, she'd put tinsel on them. 'But what's happened to them?' I impatiently demanded, and he became testy again: 'Not a clue, mate.' I next asked a booking hall attendant, and he said, 'I don't know about the gnomes, but you can't see the pond because it's winter.' Do ponds necessarily disappear in winter? They do at Edgware Road.

CHAPTER FOUR

THE EXPANSION OF THE METROPOLITAN AND THE EXPANSION OF THE DISTRICT – AND A PAUSE FOR THOUGHT

THE EXPANSION OF THE METROPOLITAN

We now turn with relief from the smoky tunnels to the open air, where the Met and the District found it much easier and cheaper to build railways by which passengers could be ensnared and brought into the vortex of the Circle. Before 1890 – before, that is, the opening of the first deep-level Tube – the District had reached what remain its westerly termini at Richmond, Wimbledon and Ealing Broadway. A couple of years later the Metropolitan had reached its own most northerly point, Verney Junction, which was as bucolic as it sounds. (Branches to Uxbridge and Watford would be completed a little later.)

The projection north of the Metropolitan begins with the two

Baker Street mouseholes previously mentioned. In 1868 those lines had reached as far as Swiss Cottage. By 1880 Harrow had been reached, and during the 1880s the push continued, to North Harrow, Pinner, Northwood … In 1892 the Met reached Aylesbury, 40 miles from London. What, the reader might ask, is a so called *metropolitan* railway doing wandering about in the Buckinghamshire countryside?

I will answer with reference to Julian Barnes's novel *Metroland*, published in 1980 but set in 1968. On page 35 the adolescent schoolboy narrator, Christopher, meets 'an elegiac old fugger' on an Underground train at Baker Street. The fugger is a student of Metropolitan history, and he lists the most northerly stations. 'They were all out beyond Aylesbury. Waddeson, Quainton Road, it went, Grandborough, Winslow Road, Verney Junction.' 'If he went on like this,' Christopher reflects, 'I'd cry.' The fugger then explains why the Met operated in such latitudes. 'Can you imagine – they were planning to join up with Northampton and Birmingham. Have a great link through from Yorkshire and Lancashire, through Quainton Road, through London, joining up with the old South Eastern, then through a Channel Tunnel to the Continent. What a line.'

The fugger's account is more or less correct, and this was all the grandiose vision of Sir Edward Watkin, who had promised the Met shareholders that their 'great terminus' (Baker Street) would be connected with 'many important towns'.

The leap to Verney Junction (which is not only 60 miles from Baker Street, but also a mere 8 miles from *Oxford*, for God's sake) came about through the Met's absorption of the Aylesbury & Buckingham Railway. That never went to Buckingham, but it did go to Aylesbury. In fact, it went from there to Verney Junction.

The Met received income from the transportation of manure between London and Verney Junction for the farms round about, thereby gaining some benefit from the horse bus boom that was otherwise entirely detrimental to its interests. It also built a hotel for excursionists at Verney Junction, which became the starting point of the most glamorous ride it would ever be possible to undertake on the Underground. From 1910, to drum up custom, the Metropolitan would operate a luxury Pullman service from Verney Junction to Aldgate. In other words, they attached to the train two special coaches (called *Mayflower* and *Galatea*), which exceeded in plushness the Metropolitan's ordinary first-class compartments. They were essentially restaurants on wheels. There was also a bar in the carriage. When he became mayor of London, Boris Johnson banned drinking on the Underground, but what would he make of City gents being served whisky and water in crystal glasses in the tunnel approaching Baker Street? 'The scheme of decoration of the cars is that of the latter part of the Eighteenth Century, with remarkably artistic effect', observed the *Railway Magazine* in 1910. The window blinds were of green silk. Above each seat was 'an ormolu luggage rack with finely chased ornamentation and panels of brass treillage'. Each of the eight glass-topped tables featured 'a tiny portable electrolier of a very chaste design'.

But the Met hadn't gone to Verney Junction just to give a luxury ride into town for country gentlemen. A little way beyond Quainton Road on that projection the Met built a prong connecting to the Manchester, Sheffield & Lincolnshire Railway. The Met's chairman, Sir Edward Watkin, was also chairman of that company, which duplicated other railways' routes in an inchoate way between Manchester and Grimsby, and generally stumbled about the north. Given that he was also chairman of the other railways – the Met, the South Eastern and the *Chemin de Fer du Nord* – over whose territory he wanted to approach Paris (where he apparently kept a mistress), you might say he was trying to build a railway in the image of himself. It has been said that he was 'frustrated only by the political and financial

Interior of either *Galatea* or *Mayflower*, two luxury coaches (named after winners of the America's Cup yachting race) available on the Metropolitan from 1910. The ambience was eighteenth century, and the routine was to order a whisky and water after a hard day in the City (or possibly before).

problems bound up with constructing a channel tunnel', and I like that word 'only'. In fact, the preliminary borings undertaken in 1881 by his Submarine Railway Company (which can still be seen at the foot of Shakespeare Cliff, Folkestone) were pounced on by the press as likely to facilitate a continental invasion. So that element of the plan was scotched early on.

But in 1897 Watkin did create his trunk line. You can tell it was a marginal latecomer by its name: Great Central Railway. It was basically the Manchester, Sheffield & Lincolnshire Railway with a changed name and connection to London. It came down from the north to Quainton Road, where it ran over and then (after Harrow) parallel to the Metropolitan's line to Finchley Road. Instead of diving underground with the Met at that point, it went into a new cut-and-cover tunnel of its own, running beneath Lord's Cricket Ground.

It emerged from its tunnel – to a rather muted fanfare – at Marylebone station, which opened in 1899. Marylebone station – the only one in London not used by Sherlock Holmes and Dr Watson – is small because it was built on the cheap, tunnelling to the site having proved very expensive. John Betjeman compared it to a branch public library, and it is upstaged by the Grand Central Hotel to the north of it, which was built and operated by a separate company. Not only was Marylebone small but it was also sleepy, because there was never much demand for the Great Central Railway. Its rivals, the Great Northern and the Midland, would do everything they could to stifle its services, and its trains often ran empty. At first, Marylebone had no connection to an Underground line (not even the one owned by the man who built it: the Metropolitan), but in 1907 the Bakerloo Line would open a Tube station underneath Marylebone called Great Central. In 1917 this became Marylebone Tube station, and it's one of my favourites, with pale blue tiles, like an old municipal swimming pool.

Watkin attended the opening of Marylebone station in a bath chair, having recently suffered a stroke. He would die two years later, in 1901. His vision was only half-fulfilled, but his railway remained romantic and different until recent times.

BY THE WAY: THE FATE OF THE GRAND VISION

The 1920s saw the creation of Metroland, the most important social consequence of the Metropolitan's expansion north, and we will be visiting Metroland shortly. But in 1933 the railway, which had tried to become a main line, would suffer the indignity of amalgamation into public ownership as part of London Transport.

In 1936 London Transport ceased operating passenger services beyond Aylesbury, but it contracted the London & North Eastern Railway to operate freight to Verney Junction until 1947, and things remained quite heroic on the north of the curtailed 'Extension' for some years afterwards. Until 1961 the line was electrified only as far as Rickmansworth, where steam locomotives were attached or detached in place of electric ones. In the same year the stations north of Amersham were given over to British Rail. But the Metropolitan Line of today still has more stations outside the M25 than any other line. It has four: Chesham, Amersham, Chalfont and Chorleywood. Its nearest rival in this respect, the Central Line, only has one: Epping, and whereas that is in Zone 6, Amersham and Chesham are in Zone 9, a fantastical concept created especially for them. And until December 2010 the northern stretch of the 'Extension' featured a charming side-show: the Chesham Shuttle.

When the Met first reached Chesham, in 1889, the townsfolk thought the growth of their town would be inexorable as a result. Their industries, all beginning with 'B' (boots, beer, brushes), would boom. The connection was inaugurated with a party on 15 May 1889. When Sir Edward Watkin arrived to take part, the town band played 'See the Conquering Hero Comes'; the bells of St Mary's Church in Chesham pealed joyfully; a seven-course luncheon was served in the goods station. The cry went up, 'At last, we are on the main line!' And so they were – for three years, until the Met decided to carry on to Amersham, leaving Chesham high and dry on a branch. This relegation was not really the cause of the decline of brush-making, which was the town's main industry. That was down to the introduction of nylon bristles. But the people of Chesham moaned about the shuttle: the waiting room at Chalfont & Latimer was too hot, or too cold; there were leaves on the line. And sometimes the drivers of steam locos (until 1961) would forget to couple up to the carriages, pulling away from Chesham with no train behind. But the drivers liked the shuttle. 'It's a lovely turn to work', one of them once told me. 'There are hardly any signals.' Classical music was played over the intercom in the pleasingly solid and simple, green and white waiting room at Chalfont, while its counterpart at Chesham was bedecked with Station Garden of the Year winners' certificates. (Essentially, Chesham has won the Station Garden of the Year competition every single year since its inception.) The line in-between supplies views of farmhouses, deer, sheep, gently rolling hills and the River Chess, and it is almost as strange to see these things from an Underground train as it would be to see the African savannah.

On 12 December 2010 the shuttle ceased operations, and Metropolitan trains began to terminate at both Amersham and Chesham. The chairman of the Chesham Society welcomed the ending of the shuttle. 'I suppose you could say it's reinstating us to what we were originally. We are a main line, and a lot of people travel on it, so I think it's an excellent thing.'

Chesham's return to the main line coincided with the start of the replacement of the 'A' stock Metropolitan carriages with the new 'S' stock. The 'A' stock had been introduced at the time of the electrification beyond Rickmansworth. It is called 'A' stock because it went up to Amersham. (The 'S' in 'S' stock stands for 'sub-surface'.) At the time of writing some of the As are still running, and they are my favourite Underground cars. They are roomy and airy; the seats are transverse benches that you can stretch out and sleep on in the off-peak. The seating configuration is a reminder that the previous carriages were formed of compartments, and so the benches of the A stock – and the luggage racks and coat hooks that they feature – were a means of letting passengers down gently: a humane decompression after the glory years. The new 'S' stocks – which will be coming to all the cut-and-cover lines – demonstrate that the memory of the glory days has faded to the point where there are only a few stubby transverse, two-person benches; the rest of the seats are longitudinal after the modern, space-saving fashion.

Marylebone is these days used for suburban railway services. Chiltern Railways, who operate the trains into the station, describe it as 'civilised', and so it is. I often think I would like to *live* in Marylebone station, which is equipped with a fairly good pub, a W. H. Smith and a Marks & Spencer's food shop. The Grand Central Hotel is now the five-star Landmark London. I bought a glass of white wine there in 2004 (seven quid) and sat in the great marble and glass atrium listening to an Arab gentleman have a mobile phone conversation while toying with a card reading 'To avoid inconveniencing other guests please refrain from using mobile phones in this area.' The station remains connected to the hotel by a glass canopy or *porte-cochère* that was much admired by John Betjeman, but you could stand all day under that canopy and not see anyone walk from station to hotel. Trains – at least, the sort that run into Marylebone – are not expensive enough for guests at the Landmark London. They come by taxi.

THE EXPANSION OF THE DISTRICT

The District would go east from Whitechapel towards Upminster in the early twentieth century, in what would be the last major instance of cut-and-cover in London. But its first push was west of central London, where it both stimulated and took advantage of housing development. As mentioned, the operational base of this push was Earl's Court.

The first Earl's Court station (1871) was a wooden hut in the middle of a market garden. It served a District connection between West Brompton and the West London Railway. It managed to burn down in 1875, and the Earl's Court of today dates from 1878. As David Leboff points out in *London Underground Stations*, it is the giant train shed with its iron and glass roof that gives the station its 'main line railway feel'. Earl's Court also resembles a giant amusement arcade of the District, with the destinations – Richmond, Wimbledon or wherever – announced on the antiquated light-box indicators like the symbols on a fruit machine, in which case an indication of one of the infrequent Kensington (Olympia) trains has long been akin to three cherries coming up. These old indicators show the destination of the next train by the appearance of an illuminated arrow next to the station name. The arrow may indicate that a train is going to Wimbledon, but it gives no clue as to *when*. Now, however, the indicators are supplemented by dot matrix panels that not only say where but also when. Why aren't the old ones removed? Because they, like the whole station, are Grade II listed.

In the 1870s the District pushed west from Earl's Court, reaching Hammersmith in 1874 – much to the fury of the Metropolitan, which, as we have seen, had already arrived there by the Hammersmith & City. (But the Metropolitan would have its revenge, by in turn shadowing the District between Hammersmith and Richmond for a few years.) Riding the District west of Hammersmith, you immediately know something exciting is coming up, because at Ravenscourt Park you are level with the rooftops. As you approach the Thames, you are riding with the ghost of the London & South Western Railway, which built many of the stations used by the District for its westerly push. The clue lies in the valanced – or serrated – white wooden station canopies, which give some of the stops a country branch air.

The bridge over the Thames – Kew Railway Bridge – is between Gunnersbury and Kew Gardens. It was built by the London & South Western Railway, and it is the best of the two river crossings by the District because *you can see over the parapet.* Therefore you have a view, which you do not from the bridge carrying the other branch of the District over the Thames, which we will come to in a moment.

The terminal station, Richmond, is managed by South West Trains, heirs to the London & South Western Railway, and here the District fades into a railway maelstrom, since Richmond is not only on the Waterloo–Reading line but is also the westerly terminus of the London Overground.

The District next stretched out to Ealing Broadway (from where its trains briefly ran to Windsor). It reached Hounslow Barracks in 1884. In his autobiography, *My Early Life* (1930) Winston Churchill wrote: 'I was able to live at home with my mother and go down to Hounslow barracks two or three times a week by the Underground Railway.' It was 1896, and he was a young cavalry officer. (The District service to Hounslow was withdrawn in 1964.)

Meanwhile, in 1880, the District was approaching its second railway crossing, by extending from the West Brompton stub to Fulham, Parsons Green and Putney Bridge. The station at Putney Bridge opened in time for the Oxford–Cambridge Boat Race in March 1880. Fulham was semi-rural at this point. In Arnold Bennett's novel *A Man from the North* Richard Larch returns at about 8 p.m. one Saturday from a visit to his new friend Mr

Aked (and Mr Aked's pretty niece), who lives in Fulham. 'It was necessary to wait for a train at Parson's Green Station. From the elevated platform fields were visible through a gently falling mist.' Save for the porter 'leisurely lighting the station lamps', Richard is alone. Then, 'A signal suddenly shone out in the distance; it might have been a lighthouse seen across unnumbered miles of calm ocean. Rain began to fall.'

The bridge carrying the District from Putney Bridge station to East Putney is not, infuriatingly, called Putney Bridge. That is a road bridge. We are concerned with the Fulham Railway Bridge, which was, rather impressively, built by the District itself, and not the London & South Western. So the District must take responsibility for the fact that the iron girders of the parapet block any view from the trains of a particularly beautiful part of the river. The modern-day managers of the line do seem to attach importance to views *of* the bridge, however, because when they repainted it in the mid-1990s, they called in the local residents, including a friend of mine, to ask their opinion about some colour swatches. A tasteful light green was eventually chosen. The District progressed from East Putney to Wimbledon by piggybacking on a branch line of the London & South Western Railway, and sometimes overground trains still use the branch as a relief route between Wimbledon and Clapham Common. But they don't stop at the Underground stations.

HIATUS

In the 1880s the population of Greater London increased by 870,000; in the 1890s it would increase by nearly a million. Suburbs were growing fast, especially to the west, where they were generated by the District Railway, and to the north-east, generated by the Great Eastern Railway. The money these new suburbanites earned in the City they spent in the West End, which was ceasing to be a territory of mansions, its streets empty out of season'. It was becoming London's playground, a place associated with pleasure, with life itself. In 1900 the average age of death in the East End was thirty, in the West End fifty-five.

One lure was the music halls. By 1880 there were eighty large music halls or variety theatres in London, and most would soon boast of being 'Illuminated throughout by electricity!' The majority were in the West End, especially in The Strand. In the 1890s Harry Castling sang 'Let's All Go Down the Strand', adding, seemingly irrelevantly, 'Have a banana!' In another music hall song Burlington Bertie 'rose at 10.30, walked up the Strand with his gloves on his hand, and walked down again with them off'. Note that the *flâneur* in question rose well after the time of 'the morning peak', and his peregrinations attest to the growing market for London leisure travel.

Meanwhile the shops of the City were being eaten up by offices. You shopped in the West End. Regent Street – the centre of fashion – had been the resort of society in the early eighteenth century, but its shops catered to a more demotic market by the end of the nineteenth. *The London Encyclopaedia* (1983), edited by Ben Weinreb and Christopher Hibbert, quotes one presumably venerable shopkeeper who in 1900 complained, 'One has to do at least five times the volume of business to get the same returns.' The last quarter of the century also saw the rise of the department store. The biggest shops were not at first very central: Harrods was at Knightsbridge, Whiteleys at Bayswater. But it wouldn't be long before Selfridges landed on Oxford Street. By virtue of their size, these shops were the heralds of the twentieth century. They pioneered the large-scale use of glass, they required central heating, and they had electricity, which in Harrods (from 1898) was used to power London's first escalator. Brandy was offered at the top, to calm shoppers down after the sheer exhilaration of the ride. Selfridges wouldn't have an escalator until 1952, but then *it* was famous for its gilded electrical lifts (and lift girls).

Electricity was smart. The mid-1880s had seen the development of the turbine: a new kind of steam-powered generator. It would eventually stop electricity from being an expensive luxury, but that process would be slow in London compared with American cities, partly because of its fractured local government. As late as 1910, only 7 per cent of Londoners had electric light in their homes. In *Children of Light* (2011) Gavin Weightman notes that Americans visiting London 'were surprised to find the streets still lit with gas lamps'.

There was no overall power company for London, so all consumers of electricity had their own private generating stations. This lent exclusivity to its use, and one of the earliest important generating stations in London was the Grosvenor Gallery Power Station, which sounds as likely to have been written up in *Tatler* as *Electrical News*. The gallery was opened in 1885 by Sir Coutts Lindsay, debonair aristocrat and Crimean War hero. He and his wife, Caroline Fitzroy, were sympathetic to the outré painters of the Pre-Raphaelite Brotherhood, and their gallery would provide a showcase for their controversial works – and it would do so as the first London gallery to be lit by electricity.

Coutts Lindsay had power to spare, and was soon supplying 11,000 lamps by wires radiating over the roof-tops of the West End to other opulent premises: clubs, theatres, large houses. The wires being clearly visible, everyone could see who was in the select club. (While electric trams were prospering in America, and soon would do so in the north of England, they would always be kept out of central London because their overhead wires were considered an eyesore. And electric *trains* were only allowed if they were subterranean. But a provision of the Electric Lighting Act of 1882 allowed anyone to transmit their own power as long as they did *not* bury the cables under the road.) In 1887, in what seems an incredible conjunction, the Grosvenor Gallery Power Station became a sub-station of Deptford Power Station.

The Inner Circle – still the only system of rapid transport in central London – involved no electricity, and by 1890 people were starting to notice. In 1896 Mark Twain wrote of the line that 'It goes by no direct course but always away around'; it was 'the invention of Satan himself'. In the same passage Twain also wrote:

> Hacks [horse-drawn vehicles] are but little needed in American cities for any but strangers who cannot find their way by tram-lines. The citizen should be thankful for the high hack rates which have given him the trams; for by consequence he has the cheapest and swiftest city transportation that exists in the world. London travels by omnibus – pleasant, but as deadly slow as a European 'lift'.

London might also have looked old-fashioned even if you'd just come back from the seaside. Magnus Volk's electric railway began running at Brighton in 1883, and Blackpool had electric trams on the front from 1885. The electric tram would come to London in 1901, operated by London United Tramways and running west of Shepherd's Bush.

Meanwhile horses, pulling hackneys, buses or horse-drawn trams (booming, but confined to the suburbs as their electrical brethren would be), had London to themselves. The buses took short-distance passengers from the Underground lines, especially from the District, as it approached the City, and the receipts of the new railway actually declined in the early 1890s over this stretch. This looks like a case of history going backwards, but, as Barker and Robbins write: 'It was so much easier and more pleasant to jump on a passing omnibus in the Strand than to make one's way down to a smoky tunnel under the Embankment.' It was also cheaper, as a result of an omnibus price war between the London General Omnibus Company and the London Road Car Company.

The traffic blocks of the mid-century had been alleviated for a while by the Underground railways, but in the late century the horse buses were passing through Piccadilly Circus at the rate of ten a minute, and it was more like eleven a minute at Bank.

Something had to be done. Again.

CHAPTER FIVE

DEEPER

BRUNEL'S TUNNEL

The deep-level Tubes required the invention of a tunnelling machine and a means of propelling trains through those tunnels that would not choke the passengers. The answer to the latter was electricity, and we have seen how electric traction had become established by the late nineteenth century. The answer to the first problem would be the tunnelling *shield* – that is, a way of allowing men to dig while protecting them from the earth above. The invention of the shield would be triggered by the challenge of digging tunnels under the River Thames, because you couldn't create *those* by cut-and-cover.

The first shield was developed by Marc Isambard Brunel. He preferred his second forename – who wouldn't? – but was known as Marc to distinguish himself from his more famous son, the above-mentioned Isambard Kingdom Brunel. Marc Brunel would use his tunnelling shield to build the Thames Tunnel, connecting the two banks of the booming docks. It would eventually be the centrepiece of a Tube line of sorts, before becoming a differently branded railway altogether. A ride through the tunnel on that line today takes thirty seconds, and nothing can be seen of it, which is a shame because it took eighteen years to build and is considered beautiful.

Marc Brunel was a royalist refugee from revolutionary France. He specialised in ideas that were ahead of their time – of which he seems to have had about one a week – and he had a gift for making those around him seem churlish and reactionary in comparison to his own far-sightedness. In 1799 he designed a machine to make pulley blocks for the British Navy ... who turned out not to be good payers. He then set up a boot-making factory in Battersea, in which scarred and mangled war veterans oversaw what has been called the first system of mass production in the world. It supplied the British Army during the Napoleonic Wars, and the Duke of Wellington considered Brunel's boots to have played a large part in the British victories. As Robert Hulse, director of the Brunel Museum at Rotherhithe says, 'It was a Frenchman who beat Napoleon', but demand for the boots fell sharply after the Battle of Waterloo, and Brunel was imprisoned for debt in 1821. (By the way, Brunel's army boots are not to be confused with Wellington boots. *Those* foppish articles came from the Duke of Wellington's boot-maker in St James's.) From prison Brunel corresponded with his friend Tsar Alexander I of Russia, for whom he'd been hoping to build a bridge over the River Neva in St Petersburg. The Russians would eventually decide to go under the river, but not before Brunel had shown the way, by building the first sub-aqueous tunnel in the world.

The Thames Tunnel Company raised money from investors who included the Duke of Wellington, and in 1825 Brunel began in typically novel and entertaining style by building a brick cylinder with walls 3 yards thick at Rotherhithe, on the south bank of the Thames. The idea was that it would sink into the ground under its own weight. It did sink – a few inches every day – and

Londoners with nothing much else 'on' would come to watch it do so.

The earth was excavated from the sunken cylinder; the shield was inserted into it, and the tunnelling began, the target being Wapping, on the opposite bank. The shield was an iron honeycomb containing thirty-six cells within which men dug the wall of mud before them. It is said that Brunel got the idea for a tunnelling shield when he was at Chatham docks making his pulley blocks. There he observed the burrowing through wood of *Teredo navalis*, the ship worm. According to Robert Hulse, 'It's half worm, half mollusc, and there are more dead men at the bottom of the sea as a result of those things than all the naval battles put together. They're the reason you had copper-bottomed ships.' The outer edges of the shield supported the tunnel as the men worked, and these edges were the equivalent of the shell of the ship worm. The men stabbing away at the mud with their shovels and picks were the equivalent of its teeth. Every few feet the shield was thrust forward by hydraulic jacks, and bricklayers (working *quickly*, mind you) lined the tunnel behind it, just as the *Teredo navalis* lined *its* tunnels with its own excreta. Unlike the circular shields that built the Tubes, Brunel's shield was rectangular and would make a vault shape when the top corners were rounded off. (Tubes are circular because that is the shape of the shields that built them. Brunel's rectangular shield allowed more room for men to dig. A circle is stronger than a vault, but a vault is more pleasing to the eye.)

The Tubes would be dug through impermeable London clay, an ideal medium for tunnelling, but there was as much gravel as clay under the Thames, and the workings kept being breached by toxic river water. In 1826 Marc fell ill through overwork so Isambard took over, and he was given three assistants. One died more or less immediately; another fell ill and would be left blind in one eye. The first major flood of the workings occurred in May

1827, and Marc Brunel wrote, 'We have been honoured with a visitation of Father Thames', a generous observation given what Father Thames was full of. (The tunnel was dug before the making of the Bazalgette sewers, by which the effluent of London was diverted from the river.) Work restarted early in 1828, but then there was another flood, in which Isambard was swept to the top of the shaft by the surge of water, and a further six men died. In August 1828 the money ran out. With the tunnel about 600 feet long, digging stopped and Isambard went off to build the Clifton Suspension Bridge.

In 1834 Marc Brunel raised enough money to restart digging. This included one of those rare Victorian government grants for an infrastructure project: a £250,000 loan from the Treasury, equivalent to about £250 million today. After further floods and a few fires caused by methane and hydrogen sulphide gas, the tunnel was completed in March 1843, and the major civil engineering feat of its time was opened as … a walkway and tourist attraction. The tourists descended by stairs. There was no money left to create the sloping roadways at either end that would have allowed horse-drawn wagons to use the tunnel, and the Treasury didn't want to know. According to Robert Hulse, the depressing rationale was as follows: 'The main thing was to finish the tunnel. *Not* to have finished it would have been a national embarrassment, but it didn't matter so much what it was used for once it *was* finished.' So a bazaar was opened in the Tunnel, selling tat, and not even useful tat: coffee cans, snuff boxes, commemorative pictures of the tunnel. There were also prostitutes.

I learned about the Brunel tunnel while standing in the Rotherhithe shaft – or *caisson* – during London Open House Weekend. The shaft is now fitted with a concrete floor built above the level of the beginning of the tunnel. The *caisson* is 50 feet in diameter, 40 feet deep, entirely roofed over. It stands just outside the Brunel Museum and is its proud Exhibit A. The original staircase has been demolished, but on what the Brunel Museum exuberantly calls 'high days and holidays' the shaft is opened to visitors, who climb through a kind of trapdoor near the top before descending on a scaffolding staircase to hear a talk by Mr Hulse. Everyone entering the *caisson* was warned to turn back if they were prone to feeling claustrophobic, which only spurred me on. I am prone to claustrophobia, but I wanted to test myself, as did plenty of Victorian men, who would descend the staircase to the bottom of the shaft in a normal and serene manner. They would then clamp their hands on their top hats and leg it from one end of the tunnel to the other, before languidly climbing out of the shaft at the other end, congratulating themselves on having traversed the tunnel before it collapsed or the air ran out.

Actually, the tunnel itself was not as claustrophobic as those that would be dug by the successors to Brunel's shield; and it was much more graceful than those utilitarian drainpipes the Tube lines. Its vault is divided into two elegant arches, themselves divided by an equally elegant series of *transverse* arches. It's very fine, but would it ever be useful? The answer is yes – eventually.

BY THE WAY: THE EAST LONDON LINE

In 1865 an outfit called the East London Railway Company bought the Brunel tunnel for £800,000, and in 1869 they opened a railway through it. The purchase was made on behalf of several railway companies, who would run both passenger and freight trains over the line, and would come to include the Metropolitan and the District.

The line using the tunnel ran at first from New Cross to Wapping. In 1876 it was extended to Shoreditch, then Liverpool Street, the base of the Great Eastern Railway. Between Wapping and Shoreditch, stations were opened at Shadwell and

Whitechapel. In 1884 spurs were built to Aldgate and Tower Hill, tapping into the new Inner Circle, that laborious joint venture of the Metropolitan and the District. It was, as we have seen, the prospect of connecting to the East London Railway via these spurs that motivated the Metropolitan and the District to finish the Inner Circle. A connection to the East London Railway alleviated the sheer boredom of completing the Circle, and it would give them access to … well, to east London. It would also provide them with a river crossing.

The Metropolitan began operating services to New Cross station at the southern end of the East London, where the line met the South Eastern main-line railway, one of several railways besides the Metropolitan of which Watkin was Chairman. The District sent *its* trains into another spur at the same end, where there was a second main-line station, 600 yards from the first and operated by the London Brighton & South Coast Railway but also called New Cross. (Today confusion is lessened somewhat, by the addition of 'Gate' to the name of the latter station.)

The question of which New Cross was which didn't much trouble residents of central London, few of whom saw any need to visit either one, but the East London – electrified in 1913, its stations exotically demarcated with green diamonds – did become quite important for freight, which was carried along the line by the London & North Eastern Railway from 1923. Coal was taken from the north of England to the south via the line, which would also be used to carry military hardware through London en route to the south coast for the D-Day landings, a tunnel being more discreet than a bridge. Otherwise, the East London embarked on its fate as a marginal appendage to the Underground, and I use that word in its loosest sense because the East London is partly on the surface, partly cut-and-cover and partly, in effect (the Brunel tunnel) a deep-level Tube.

In 1933 the East London Railway came under the control of

London Transport, and from then until 1968 it was the same colour as the Metropolitan – purple – on the Underground map. In 1970 it was named on the maps as 'Metropolitan Line – East London Section', and was shown as Metropolitan purple with a white stripe down the middle. It may have looked pretty, but the line in question was tied to the dying 'inner docks'.

In the early 1980s it was allowed to stand on its own two feet as a fully grown, if short and obscure, Tube line: the East London Line. It was connected to Shadwell on the Docklands Light Railway in 1987, but this didn't take it into the mainstream or alter the fact that it was the only Underground line not to penetrate Zone 1. It remained a special, remedial case.

In 1995 the line was closed because the tunnel was leaking, but two hours before work started, English Heritage listed the tunnel Grade II, and negotiations began on how best to conduct the repairs. The line remained closed during these negotiations, which lasted for a year, whereas (as a friend of mine who lived on the line indignantly pointed out) the Congress of Vienna, which completely reorganised Europe after the Napoleonic Wars, took nine months. It was agreed that the dimensions of the tunnel would be preserved and some of the original brickwork would be left exposed at the Rotherhithe end. The work lasted a further year, and the rail replacement bus service became so well established that on its last day bus-spotters came from all over London to say a sad farewell.

I visited the line shortly after it re-opened, noting that the refurbishment had done nothing to eliminate the brackish stink of the Thames at Wapping or the constant sound of rushing water. Standing in that station is like being in the cistern of a great toilet, and you rather dread the flush. There are other anxieties in this, the oldest 'Tube' station. The lady in the ticket office told me that one of her colleagues who worked 'lates' repeatedly heard footsteps approaching the top of the staircase which winds up the original shaft, at which point the footsteps would cease. Because she might be working 'lates' herself one day, I didn't tell her that ten men had died during the building of the tunnel.

The East London Line gained a connection to the Jubilee Line Extension when a new station was added at Canada Water in 1999, but its big break came in 2010, when it was incorporated into the London Overground, a network that rehabilitates some dowdy and obscure suburban lines (most particularly the old North London Railway) to create an orbital railway for the capital. (The Overground has been given a seat at the Underground table. It has the roundel, the Johnston typeface, and it is on the Tube map. The conceptualisation is brilliantly simple, and both the engineering and the aesthetic standards of the revitalised line – once famous for connecting at the slowest possible speed all the most obscure parts of London – are first-class.) In its new capacity the East London even got to keep its Tube Line colour – orange – which it had been given in the early Eighties, since that is also the colour of London Overground. New lift shafts and a modernistic gantry incorporating some sort of high-tech control panel stand within the shaft, creating a clash of genres: Bond film goes Steampunk. From the platforms at Wapping or Rotherhithe you can see the tunnel fleetingly illuminated as the trains approach; it looks so incredibly Victorian that you expect to see Jack the Ripper loitering between the arches.

The platforms at Wapping and Rotherhithe are narrow. Being listed, they can't be widened. They were further smartened up with the arrival of the Overground, and they're decorated with pretty panels depicting the history of the tunnel, but behind them the water still rushes.

Having always been the runt of the Underground litter, and having been incorporated into the system merely as a by-product of the creation of the Inner Circle, the line now plays its part in the realisation of a different dream: a great outer circle, or railway

M25. That's what London Overground will become when the wide arc of the old North London Railway that it incorporates is mirrored by a similar arc to the south, this loop representing the somewhat tardy fulfilment of a plan first recommended by a Parliamentary Select Committee in 1863.

Yes, it was rather bizarre to make a former underground line into part of a network called London Overground, and at Whitechapel the Overground goes *under* the Underground. But let's not spoil our happy ending for the East London Line.

THE TOWER SUBWAY

The next stage of our journey towards the first Tube line takes us to a bit of blustery riverside pavement at Tower Hill and a brick booth that resembles a stray turret from the adjacent Tower of London. Around the top are the words 'London Hydraulic Power Company. Tower Subway Constructed AD 1868' – a fairly perplexing inscription, given that the booth is in suspiciously good condition, and obviously post-dates 1868.

It marks what used to be the public entrance to a cable railway that ran beneath the Thames for a few months in 1894. There was a single carriage on a 2 foot 6 inch gauge track. It was winched along the tunnel by the cable attached to a steam engine, which also powered the lifts. There were not many takers for this claustrophobic ride, and the tunnel suffered the same fate as Brunel's tunnel. It became a walkway; and it ceased to be even that later on in 1894, when the great edifice in whose shadow you stand as you contemplate the turret was opened: Tower Bridge. Why would anyone walk under the river when they could walk over it? In 1926 the booth was built as a monument to the Subway, and an advert for the London Hydraulic Power Company, who installed pipes in the tunnel for the supply of hydraulic power to businesses on either side of the river. Today the tunnel carries optical cables.

What is important about the Tower Subway is the method of its construction.

In 1862 an engineer called Peter William Barlow (whose brother William Henry Barlow built St Pancras station) was sinking cast iron cylinders into London clay in order to create mid-river piers for an entirely different bridge – the Lambeth Suspension Bridge (demolished in 1929). Barlow would swing the process through 90 degrees. He would install iron rings in the process of digging a tunnel, these rings making unnecessary the manically toiling bricklayers who had followed Brunel's Shield. The idea was developed by his assistant James Henry Greathead, a South African by birth, who perfected what became known as the Greathead Shield. With this he engineered the Tower Subway, and it would be used as the basis of all subsequent tunnelling shields.

The first thing about the Greathead Shield was that it was smaller than its name suggested. It wasn't very 'great', I mean. It weighted just over 2 tons – whereas Brunel's giant climbing frame of a shield had weighed 120 tons – and was barely 5 feet long. When I first saw a drawing of one, I was reminded of a stub of pencil or a cigarette butt, and its lightness and manoeuvrability made me think that building a Tube line through compliant clay might not be so difficult after all (and indeed it wasn't, and isn't). The shield was basically an iron sleeve in which – after some preliminary mechanical loosening of the clay – not more than half a dozen men dug. Iron tunnel segments were then assembled within the sleeve, which was jacked forward, cutting into the next lot of clay like a pastry cutter, with the jacks braced against the flanges of the previous tunnel segments. Every time the sleeve was pushed forward, a thin gap remained between the newly assembled tunnel segments and the surrounding clay. Liquid cement was injected into this gap via holes in the segments, further reinforcing the tunnel.

The Greathead tunnelling shield – developed in the 1890's by James
Henry Greathead – enabled the creation of the deep level Tubes.
It is essentially a cylinder within which men or machines can dig.
Iron tunnel rings are also assembled within the shield, which is
gradually pushed forward (pastry-cutter like) by jacks braced
against those rings.

The booth at Tower Hill symbolises the coming of the Tubes, and the peculiar martyrdom of Londoners: they would travel underground, in narrow tunnels lying between about 60 and 200 feet below the surface.

This engineering breakthrough coincided with a psychological urge to burrow deep underground, whether as a function of urban trauma or the need to escape from it. In *Underground Writing* David Welsh identifies this urge in the work of turn-of-the-century novelists. William Delisle Hay's novel *Three Hundred Years Hence* (1881) describes a world 50 feet down – which is about right for a Tube – whose inhabitants use a subway of 'terra-cars'. (Sound familiar?) *The Coming Race* (1871) by Edward Bulwer-Lytton concerns a people called the Vril-ya, who inhabit chambers beneath the earth connected by tunnels and derive their power from an 'all permeating' fluid which they called Vril, and which *we* might call electricity. Welsh focuses particularly on H. G. Wells:

> … there is a descent into the earth at some distant future point in *The Time Machine* (1895); the discovery of a lunar underworld in *The First Men in the Moon* (1901) … All of these subterranean locations suggested that underground railways could be perhaps the first stage in a process of migration beneath the city.

It was geology that facilitated the migration. In 1908 Granville Cunningham, General Manager of the Central London Railway, would write: 'It seems that the beautiful homogenous clay of London had been designed by Nature for the very purpose of having tunnels pierced through it, and it would be a great pity to balk nature in her design.' The London Tubes would be buried in the accommodating London clay, thus circumventing the ban on railways in central London, but there is not so much of that clay in south London, or 'The Surrey Side', as it was euphemistically known in the posher Edwardian guidebooks. That is partly why north London has more Tubes. (Another reason is that the south is better served by main-line trains.)

When I first started visiting London, my dad equipped me with a tattered edition of *The Penguin Guide to London, 1958*. The introduction blithely states:

The Underground Railways of London Transport provide the quickest and easiest method of getting from one part of the Metropolis to another. The seven named lines are connected with each other at many points, and with their numerous branches extend into almost every quarter of London except south of the Thames …

Except *half of London* in other words. Only twenty-six Underground stations lie south of the river, sixteen of them on what is called the *Northern* Line, to the genesis of which we now turn.

THE FIRST TUBE:
THE CITY & SOUTH LONDON RAILWAY

In 1884 Greathead was part of a syndicate that obtained powers for another subway – 'The City of London & Southwark Subway'. The term 'subway' sounded more sophisticated than 'underground railway', which was associated with the sulphurous Metropolitan, and it would be adopted by New York for its own electric metro when work started on that in 1904.

As originally proposed, the line would run from Elephant & Castle to King William Street, just north of London Bridge – in other words from a busy and fully built-up major road junction to the City. It is looked back on as being amusingly dinky.

According to the *Oxford Companion to British Railway History*, 'everything was too small'. But this was the first Tube. It ticked every box: electric power, 'up' and 'down' trains in separate tunnels, electric-lit carriages of a single class with room for standing, and a paying public that flocked into the trains while moaning about them. Like all the Tubes (and the cut-and-cover lines), the popularity of the service would not enable the company to recover its capital costs. Furthermore, it was *called* a Tube by its users, even if the term was not encouraged by the company. 'Tube' was slang, but according to the *Oxford English Dictionary*, one of the first users of the word in a railway context was Queen Victoria, who wrote in her journal in 1868: 'We passed the famous Swily Rocks and saw the works they are making for the tube for the railroad.'

In 1886 digging began with Greathead's shield. Observers were surprised at the two tunnels, but it's cheaper to build two small tunnels than one big one and gives you more flexibility as to routing. It was intended that steam-winched cables would draw the carriages through the tunnels, as with the Tower Subway. But in 1886, with the cables on order, the board changed its mind: 'After much careful consideration, the Directors have come to the conclusion that electrical force … offers the best solution to the difficulty.' Having been behind in the electrical race, London thus jumped into the lead, because this first Tube was also the first important electrical railway in the world.

In 1890 the City of London & Southwark Subway re-christened itself the City & South London Railway, and powers were granted for an extension to the growing suburb of Clapham via the already grown suburbs of Kennington, Oval and Stockwell.

The line opened between Elephant and King William Street on 18 December 1890. On 15 November 1890 *Punch* ran a cartoon in which the figure of Britannia stood between two railways. On one line is a Metropolitan engine, which has the face of an elderly debauchee and is wreathed in choking smoke; the second railway is represented by a dapper, smiling man with a head like a star. He radiates the words 'Electric Railway' and has skates on his feet, perhaps because Greathead – the bringer of modernity, via his tunnelling shield – had once worked on the manufacture of roller skates. The Met train is called 'Old Flame'; the newcomer is 'Young Spark', and he addresses Britannia in rhyme:

> He's just like old Pluto, Persephone's prigger;
> *You'll* follow Apollo the Younger – that's me!
> He's sombre as Styx, and as black as ...

(Actually, I think we'll leave it there.)

The generating station for the City & South London Railway was at Stockwell, and the further the trains went from it, the weaker the voltage. The electric lights in the packed carriages flickered and flared red as the little engines struggled up the incline towards King William Street, but electricity was socially smart, and the generating station would attract sightseers. One was H. G. Wells, who after his visit wrote a short story, *The Lord of the Dynamos*. It features Holroyd, the 'chief attendant of the three dynamos that buzzed and rattled at Camberwell and kept the electric railway going'. The biggest of the dynamos is 'The Lord', and Holroyd's 'Asiatic' assistant, Azuma-Zi, begins to worship it as a god. He sacrifices Holroyd to it by pitching him into its mechanism, and 'The big humming machine had slain its victim without wavering for a second in its heavy beating.' The only sign of the crime having been committed was that 'Seven or eight trains had stopped midway in the stuffy tunnels of the electric railway.'

In *Underground Writing*, David Welsh observes:

> Wells identified an important change from the steam

underground, as the motive power of the tubes is no longer generated from the train itself. The dynamo controls the fate of the tube passengers and, by implication, the life of the city as the circulation of people can be prevented merely by the flick of a switch.

The Underground would eventually be powered by two giant power stations, as we will see, before plugging itself directly into the National Grid. Yes, there are traction sub-stations every two or three miles along every line where the voltage is stepped down, but the average punter doesn't know where they are. Essentially the power source of the Underground is invisible … which might be a matter of blissful unconcern or a cause of anomie. Is the dynamo a liberator for Londoners or an unseen slave driver?

The City & South London was also the first British passenger railway to offer only one class. In *A History of London Transport* Barker and Robbins suggest that 'The idea of a uniform fare was copied from the New York elevated railroad', and here was the start of the American cultural influence on the London Underground that would soon take the form of direct involvement by actual Americans.

The City & South London initially had a flat single fare of 2d., but it was the Central London Railway, opened ten years later, that would be nicknamed 'The Tuppenny Tube' for *its* flat fare of the same amount. The Central was so-called by the *Daily Mail*, which no doubt would have christened the City & South London 'The Tuppenny Tube' had the paper existed in 1890, but it was not founded until 1896, the age of mass media lagging slightly behind the age of mass transit.

The stations on the City & South London were small but pretty, with cupolas to accommodate the winding gear of the small and claustrophobic hydraulic lifts. With these domes the stations looked like little observatories, and you can see the effect at Kennington, the only surviving surface building of the original construction. The tunnels varied between 10 foot 2 and 10 foot 6 in diameter – narrower than all subsequent Tubes, and they would have to be widened in the 1920s.

The carriages were about 26 feet long, 7½ high and just over 6 feet wide – in other words, narrow and low. They featured longitudinal benches, as in Shillibeer's omnibus. Most of the seating on the early Tubes was longitudinal (you sat with your back to the side of the carriage, as on the Waltzer at the fairground) and it is so once again today.

The benches were padded. Each was meant to hold sixteen people, but would often hold twenty, with another twenty standing in the gangway in between. Bear in mind that all this could be happening in the smoking carriage, where most people would have been smoking cigars and pipes rather than cigarettes. There were no straps to hang from, but there were handrails, as in modern Tube trains. Above the benches were narrow slits of window – so narrow that from a distance the carriages looked like goods wagons. The passengers called the carriages 'padded cells', and *Punch* christened the line 'the sardine box railway'.

One of the carriages is now displayed in the London Transport Museum, where it is overseen by an actor wearing the dark double-breasted uniform of a City & South London guard (making him, incidentally, by far the best-dressed man *in* the London Transport Museum). The actor told me that some people experienced claustrophobia when sitting in the carriage even as displayed, with its end-door propped permanently open in the bright and airy museum. 'Quite a fug builds up in there,' he said. He believed that, when the line first opened, clerks heading for the City would get out at the stop just before the river – London Bridge – and walk over the bridge, nonchalantly remarking that they wanted to take a brief constitutional before starting work, when in fact they were scared of going under the river on the train. The railway was more than 100 feet down under the Thames and never less than 45 feet underground along its length.

The actor also told me that the window slits had been clear glass, but the passengers had found the view of the passing tunnel rings disturbing – 'quite stroboscopic, I expect' – so the glass was made opaque, which in turn increased the claustrophobia, and proper widows would be provided on all subsequent Underground trains.

Passengers entered and exited the carriages by means of end-doors. This was partly because the sides were taken up by the continuous bench seats. All the early tubes would use end doors – called bulkhead doors – and these would lead onto small platforms at the carriage ends, where a guard would stand. He would sometimes allow passengers to travel on these platforms, with, on at least one occasion, fatal results, but he would not let them off until the train came to a complete stop in a station, whereupon he would open a lattice gate to the side. For this chap to have controlled entry and exit of passengers from a position *within* the carriage would have taken up too much space, and mid-carriage entry and exit would only become practical with the refinement of automatically controlled sliding air doors which would be pioneered on the Bakerloo in 1920, and rolled out on a large scale in the Standard Tube stock of 1923, at which point Tube trains started to *look* like Tube trains. Station names were written on the dimly lit platform walls, but since there were no carriage windows, guards called out the names.

The railway used the 'Third Rail' system of electrification, like all the early Tubes. (But it would soon be replaced across the network by another system even more exciting – *Fourth* Rail!) The electric locomotives were under-powered and strained to draw the three carriages coupled behind. They looked like two upright pianos with their backs touching. There were two engine men in case one of them fainted or died, the 'dead man's handle' of the later Tubes (a fail-safe device that stops the train if the driver does not maintain manual pressure on a lever) not having been perfected. The engines exerted a magnetic fascination, and in a chapter of *The Railway Lover's Companion* (1963) called 'Tuppenny Tubes', C. Hamilton Ellis wrote that 'In 1892 a passenger fell off a leading car platform, where the conductor took people to "watch the engine" … The unfortunate passenger was cut up in the tunnel and the horrified conductor fled into hiding.' The year before, at Oval, a man had also got his head stuck in the gate of a lift that was ascending. As the lift gate rose towards a girder, it cut his head off. However (and it's a big 'however' as far as that man is concerned), the safety record of the railway would be generally excellent.

In 1890 *Punch* wrote: '[The train is] so packed with people that getting in or out was a regular scrimmage. We entirely endorse the railway company's advertisement that it is "the warmest line in London".' John Betjeman would later recall that the railway 'smelt of feet', and the carriages may have continued to smell of feet after they were taken out of service in the 1920s because some of them found use as changing rooms beside the playing fields of southern England.

The railway followed the streets to avoid having to buy the freeholds of properties. As a result, it found itself pointing east when it arrived at its terminus in King William Street, where the two tunnels were built on top of each other so as to stay within the width of the road. If it had extended from there, it would have ended up in Wapping, and there wasn't much money in going there, as we have just seen. So ten years after it opened, the directors of the railway doubled back, as it were, to the previous station, Borough, for a rethink. From there a new tunnel forged its way to London Bridge (creating an interchange with the main-line station). It then went *underneath* the old tunnel that kinked east towards King William

Street, and progressed to the heart of the City: first to Bank, then to Moorgate, where it arrived in February 1900. By June of that year it had also opened through to Clapham Common via Clapham Road (now Clapham North). The hallmark of the City & South London, remember, was smallness, and to stay within the width of the road those Clapham stations below ground were hardly wider than the two tracks brought in to a single tunnel. Grudgingly aware that it had to accommodate the passengers *somewhere*, narrow island platforms were fitted between the tracks, and today everyone waiting at these stations in rush hour thinks they're going to be jostled into the path of the trains.

The abandoned tunnel between Borough and King William Street was used as an air-raid shelter in the Second World War, and if you stand more or less in the middle of the northbound Northern Line platform at London Bridge today, you can see the old northbound tunnel to King William Street through some ventilation shafts over your head. The old tunnel is now used to ventilate the new one, although its reputation would suggest it didn't have much air to spare.

By the time the City & South London had reached Bank on its crawl north, the Waterloo & City Railway had already got there, and these two would be joined soon after by the Central London Railway and the Great Northern & City Railway (for each of which see below). At Moorgate the City & South London met the Metropolitan and built its headquarters: a handsome brick and Portland stone building that still stands, forming the most impressive part of the modern Moorgate station. It bears the company's arms: a carving of a bridge over water, the two arches of the bridge also resembling Tube tunnels. It shows what the company was about: connecting the City with South London.

In burrowing into the heart of the City, the company had

risked further enormous capital expenditure in order to increase fare revenue, but in spite of high passenger numbers its profitability was not improved. By its arrival at Bank and Moorgate, however, the railway contributed to an important social effect. It would speed up the process by which the City of London was being turned from a place to live and work into a place to work only. In 1851 the resident population of the City was 129,000, many of whom were shopkeepers, tailors, craftsmen and artisans, who 'lived over the shop'. By 1901 the population had shrunk to 27,000. Most of the City was rebuilt as offices over that period, creating a target for the armies of commuters that the Underground would serve. Today a brass plaque marked 'The Heart of the City' stands at the eastern end of Poultry, EC2. It declares, almost boastfully, 'This is the part of London where over 350,000 people work by day, where there are a mere 5,000 residents and caretakers by night.' It had become what Peter Ackroyd calls, in *London: The Biography*, 'a mere counting house'. The biggest counting house in the world, mind you. As Mark Twain wrote in 1896, 'One little wee bunch of houses in London, one little wee spot, is the centre of the globe, the heart of the globe, and the machinery that moves the world is located there. It is called the City.'

On its arrival at Bank, incidentally, the City & South London's directors had threatened to demolish the church of St Mary Woolnoth, but after a public outcry the company built its station in the crypt of the church, the bodies being transferred to the City of London cemetery at Ilford. Therefore St Mary Woolnoth doesn't have a crypt. Or you could say that its crypt is Bank station. Bank station would be rebuilt with the arrival of the Central Line, but it would remain entangled with the underneath of the church, and in the 1980s a photographer friend of mine took a photograph of a blackboard in one of the station passageways, indicating 'EXIT' with a hand-drawn arrow. It

Bank station was hewn by the City & South London Railway out of what had been the crypt of St Mary Woolnoth church. In the late-Eighties, some of the exits were still pretty sepulchral.

points into a very medieval-looking aperture, a way out leading through an unreconstructed part of the old crypt.

The conjunction is almost too good, or bad, to be true, given the connections that have been made between the commuting life and a living death. These famous lines from *The Waste Land* by T. S. Eliot –

> A crowd flowed over London Bridge, so many,
> I had not thought death had undone so many.
> Sighs, short and infrequent, were exhaled
> And each one fixed his eyes before his feet.
> Flowed up the hill and down King William Street,
> To where St Mary Woolnoth kept the hours
> With a dead sound on the final stroke of nine.

– form practically a history of the City & South London Railway, which was fated (or perhaps I should say 'doomed') to become the Bank branch of the Northern Line and which we leave for the moment, before it starts its creep northwards towards Euston (which it would reach in 1907) and south to Morden (1926).

CHAPTER SIX

THREE MORE TUBES

THE DRAIN (THE WATERLOO & CITY RAILWAY)

The apparent success of the City & South London triggered an avalanche of bills for Tube railways, and in 1892 a Joint Select Committee of Parliament set out some ground rules. It was recommended that tunnels should have a minimum diameter of 11 foot 6; also that free way leave under public streets be granted, providing the service should include 'a sufficient number of cheap and convenient trains'. If a railway went under *private* property, the company should 'be allowed to acquire a way leave, instead of purchasing the freehold of the land', subject to compensation for damage. But the early Tubes still tended to follow the public streets in order to save money, hence some tortuous curves.

One of the first of those applicants to be authorised in 1892 was the Waterloo & City Railway. Whereas the history of the London Underground is generally very fiddly, the history of the Waterloo & City is blessedly self-contained and simple. It is today what it always was – a line from Waterloo to Bank whose extreme functionality is reflected in the nickname by which it has always been known: the Drain.

The Drain was built by the London & South Western Railway for a very simple reason: its London terminus, Waterloo, was too far from the City. It was much cheaper to build than the City & South London, being much shorter. It is by far the shortest Tube line, at 1½ miles long, and it has the equally elemental characteristic of being the only one entirely underground. (The Victoria Line is almost entirely underground, except for an overground depot.) How did they get the trains down there? By means of a lift. Just south of Waterloo station, you will see the hole in the ground (normally covered by a grating) where Waterloo & City carriages are raised and lowered before and after being removed by lorry for servicing. Bad weather, therefore, cannot disrupt the metronomic existence of its regular users, but river water does come in, both from the Thames and from its tributary the Walbrook. I have a trainspotter-ish DVD about the line with the usual nasally, number-crunching commentary, but when one of the line engineers shows the presenter the amount of seepage coming in, someone off screen (the cameraman, perhaps) exclaims 'Jesus Christ!' and this hasn't quite been cut out.

This may be why the line is nicknamed 'The Drain', but more likely is the fact that it was built when Tube railways were still a disturbing novelty. In the National Archives at Kew there is a memorandum relating to the opening of the line on which an official of the London & South Western has scrawled, 'Will passengers consent to be squirted through a drainpipe?' Having been so squirted towards Bank, they then had to walk up a long incline to reach the surface. This was created because the Corporation of London wouldn't allow the construction of the building that a lift would have required, and such a building at this spot would have been prohibitively expensive anyway. The slope was always resented, especially on Monday morning, and it was supplemented by the installation of the Underground's first Trav-o-lator – or moving walkway – in 1960.

The Waterloo & City offers the commuting experience distilled to its essence. It goes from the quintessential overground commuter station, Waterloo – the only large terminus in the city with no hotel, such is its dedication to sending people home for the night – to the quintessential Underground commuter's station, Bank: the 'apex of the Underground railway', according to Sigurd Frosterus in his book *London Rhapsody* (1903). There are only those two stations, so that the name of the railway is no longer than a complete list of its destinations, a pleasing state of affairs that would be spoilt if the station at Blackfriars that has occasionally been mooted were ever to be built. At those times when absolutely no commuting occurs – Saturday evening and all Sunday – the line shuts, which is why there is an ominous little dagger next to it on the pocket Tube maps, warning you to 'Check before you travel'.

It is so easy to appear eccentric when using the Waterloo & City. For example, you could try going the opposite way to everyone else. In other words, Bank to Waterloo in the morning peak, Waterloo to Bank in the evening. (Or, when everyone gets off the train at Bank, you could stay on, and go back to Waterloo.) It might be an idea to set yourself up with a flat near Bank and a job near Waterloo. You would more or less always have the train to yourself. But be warned, both sides of the Trav-o-lator, or moving walkway, at Bank run in the same direction – *out* of the station and into the street – in the morning peak. So if you were so mad as to want to descend towards – as opposed to ascend from – the Waterloo & City platforms at Bank in the morning, you would have to use the long slope. I once asked a platform guard at Bank why both tracks of the Travel-o-lator didn't run *towards* the Drain platforms in the evening peak (because they don't; they run alternately then).

He said, 'Because there'd be an almighty bloody pile-up at the barriers, wouldn't there?'

In spite of its being 'The Drain', the tunnels of the line were wider than those of the City & South London. The first trains – which were still in service forty years later – were painted a pretty chocolate and salmon, and had proper windows in spite of there being nothing to see. The carriages had transverse seats, which makes for a narrower gangway and slower loading and unloading; this was perhaps because they were built by a main-line railway company, transverse being the norm on the main-lines. The most significant thing about the trains is that they were a primitive form of Electrical Multiple Unit – an early Brit-ish use of a type of train becoming common in America, and those on the Drain would be of American make.

The *Oxford Companion to British Railway History* says:

Diesel- or electric-powered vehicles are said to be able to operate as multiple units when they can be coupled to others for operation from one driving position as a single train. The driver then has control of power and breaking throughout, so permitting the other driving positions to be left unmanned.

To put it another way, a multiple unit is a set of vehicles that include driving cabs, motors or control units connected to motors, and each of these vehicles also includes passenger seats. Essentially, multiple units – which can be electrical or diesel-powered – are trains consisting of motorised carriages. *There is no locomotive.* It is therefore hard to tell which is the front until they start moving. (When my son, aged three, first saw a Tube train he said, 'It has no face.') Multiple units look unheroic, and their rise has been blamed for the decline of trainspotting. The ones that run below ground are particularly hard to love. They are deliberately un-aerodynamic, their flat front being designed to push air through the tunnels as an aid to ventilation. In *The Subterranean Railway* Christian Wolmar suggests that the Underground lost out to the main-line railways after the Second World War because its 'clean electric powered trains' elicited no sympathy, as opposed to 'the grimy dirty steam engines that were still to be seen throughout the rail network'. The functionality of multiple units might have a subtly lowering effect on the spirits of London commuters, and yet whether on the Underground or on the main-lines coming into the southern termini, they are the pistons that have powered London for over a hundred years.

The original Drain trains were replaced in 1940 with ones offering more standing room. At the time, the Corporation of London was trying to get overcrowding on the line debated in Parliament. The line was passed from the London & South Western Railway, via the Southern Railway, to British Rail, who sold it to London Underground in 1994 for the pleasingly simple sum of £1 – a very fair price, some of its regular users may think. Since the early Nineties the line has used modified Central Line trains, and the Drain has been given its own line colour: a queasy turquoise.

A RED CARPET
(THE CENTRAL LONDON RAILWAY)

My first settled London home was in a rented house in Leytonstone, E11. It was a 1920s' villa with an actual billiard room, although the billiard table was long gone. Not only this, but it was next to mysterious Wanstead Flats, famous for its gloomy fishing ponds and low winter mist; *and* I got to ride on the Central Line, which, as the Central London Railway, was another of the Tubes arising out of the 1892 applications.

The Central was my line. I knew that one of the original promoters, Sir James Henry Tennant, who had made the North

Eastern Railway the most powerful regional railway company in Britain, had his main mansion in York, not far from my dad's house, and the year of the manufacture of the carriages – as given on the door plates – was 1962, the year of my birth. I knew that the Central London Railway (and we'll come to its early history in a minute) became the Central London Line on being taken over by London Transport in 1933; that the name was shortened to Central Line in 1937, and it had become the red line on the Tube map in 1934, having previously been a weak orange. Bakerloo, which *had* been red, became brown. Red suited the Central, and I thought of it as a red carpet rolled out through central London, or an arrow flying steadily along the primary London trunk route: Bayswater, Oxford Street, High Holborn. Its original promoters boasted of its 'extreme directness'.

Every weekday morning I took the line from Leytonstone to Holborn, in order to attend lectures at the Inns of Court School of Law. As I rode into town, I gradually woke up, and as I returned to Leytonstone I often subsided into sleep, lolling against the substantial red armrests. But in 1992 my reveries east of Chancery Lane were interrupted, because a grim event befell the Central. Yes, it was *upgraded*, at a cost of more than £80 million. New trains were introduced. Whereas the 1962 rolling stock had had wooden floors and grey and red seats – a colour scheme pleasingly reminiscent of a coal fire in the later stages of combustion – the 1992 was red and blue. And about a week after the trains came in, all the armrests fell off, or were pulled off by vandals, as had happened in previous years to the armrests on the Bakerloo. London Underground commissioned a feasibility study into whether it might be possible to re-attach armrests and the answer was evidently 'No', because, ten years on, Central Line trains still lack armrests, as do Bakerloo ones.

Without them, it was harder to get to sleep, but there wasn't much question of it anyway, because the 1992 stock were the first

Tube trains to have automated announcements. It was a woman's voice, and a platform guard at Chancery Lane told me Underground staff nicknamed her Sonia, because 'her voice gets Sonia nerves'. Certainly there was an irritating contrast between the way she said 'Bond Street' (all breathy, parvenu excitement) and the way she said 'South Woodford' (no enthusiasm at all).

The new trains were introduced in conjunction with Automatic Train Operation (on the Central, as on the Victoria, the driver does little more than close the doors) and new signalling, but it took months for this to 'bed in', one result being that the new dot matrix indicators on the platforms would read 'Check Destination on Front of Train', which was like spending a fortune on a new watch only to look at the face and see the words 'Ask a policeman'. But now the new signalling *has* bedded in, and the Central is the line that got its upgrade out of the way early. It gives the best train frequency on the network: thirty an hour in the peak. Even Sonia – because she still holds forth – is not so annoying now that all the other lines have their own equivalents. I no longer use the Central every day, but it usually gives no trouble when I do use it. The central stations of the Central have been restored to their original colour scheme – a simple and salubrious white – and it is once again what it always was: the most glamorous of the Tubes.

Well, it was a glamorous syndicate that built it. Handling the engineering side was the Greathead, thirty-one of whose tunnelling shields would be employed simultaneously at the peak of construction. Arrayed behind him were the money men, and the funding of the Central would be a mere footnote in their blue chip lives. They included, besides Sir James Henry Tennant, Sir Ernest Cassel, who lived at Brook House, Park Lane, was a friend of the Prince of Wales and had built railways in China and Mexico, and who, according to the *Dictionary of National Biography*, 'never neglected to keep in contact with the world of influence wherever it was to be found, whether at the card table, the dinner table or at Cannes'. There was also his other good friend Natty Rothschild, and Darius Ogden Mills, President of the Bank of California and of the Edison General Electric Company. The Americans were coming. On the Central, carriages were 'cars', as they are in America, and would come to be on the whole of the London Underground. ('Pass down inside the cars.') It would run 'eastbound' and 'westbound' instead of 'up' and 'down', and there would be leather straps to hang from, as on American commuter trains.

The line, authorised in 1892, was for a railway from Shepherd's Bush to Liverpool Street. Digging began in 1896, and Greathead died soon after. In pursuit of free passage, the Central did its best to follow public roads, so the running tunnels are sometimes almost plaited together rather than side by side, and at St Paul's (which was opened as Post Office), Chancery Lane and Notting Hill Gate the platforms are on top of one another.

The line wriggles its way through the City because the City streets are medieval and not straight, which is why you hear the sharp squealing of wheel rims on track at Bank as the bends are negotiated. At Bank the platform is curved to the extent that not only can you not see one end of it from the other; you can't even see half-way. So there is the most yawning of all gaps between train and platform, and there used to be the greatest, most sonorous 'Mind the Gap' announcement there as well.

The line opened in 1900 from Shepherd's Bush to Bank. (The promised Liverpool Street would not be reached for another twelve years.) The station buildings were of light brown terracotta with the word 'Tube' (they admitted it!) displayed vertically on the flat roof – a tackily expanded façade that gave them a Wild West look. The original style – although not the vertical signage – survives at Holland Park. Once inside the stations, however, there was something graceful and feminine about the line. The single-class carriages were spacious and filled with what looks like an alternation of sofas and armchairs – both transverse and longitudinal, with shaded reading lamps, and padded and evidently *very well-fixed* armrests. Not only were the platforms tiled in white, the tunnels were painted white too – to prettify them, and make them less claustrophobic – and the Central proudly issued a postcard of its tunnel-whitening machine. It and the even vainer Metropolitan would be the main issuers of postcards. (London Transport would stop issuing its own in 1974, but the London Transport Museum continues to produce them.)

Ladies in white dresses were depicted using the line in advertising posters. They showed how it was possible to 'Take the Tuppenny Tube and Avoid All Anxiety'. They were shown buying the tickets in the stations, descending in the lifts and dropping the tickets into a box at the ticket gate, thereby sparing themselves the anxiety of having to retain the ticket on the train. They were shown in dangerously close proximity to smart, top-hatted men, but whereas the men were presumably going to Bank, the women were presumably going shopping at the department stores growing up along Oxford Street, and the Central's nearness to these stores would make the advertising space in its stations the most expensive on the Underground.

Gordon Selfridge had wanted a tunnel connection between the Central station at Bond Street to the basement of his new store, and he wanted Bond Street station to be *called* Selfridges. (In 1932 Herbert Chapman, the dynamic manager of Arsenal, persuaded the Underground Group to rechristen Gillespie Road station on the Piccadilly Line Arsenal after the football club, whose stadium was near by. In 1939, as we shall see, the MCC successfully petitioned London Transport to re-christen St John's Wood station on the Metropolitan Line Lord's. In 2011 I asked Richard Parry, Deputy Managing Director of London Underground, whether I could rename a Tube station, say,

Andrew Martin Place, and he didn't entirely rule it out. After all, there'd been talk of calling Oval 'Foster's Oval' after the sponsors of the cricket ground. 'But it'd be vastly expensive,' he said, 'with all the changes to the maps and the signs. You'd have to put half a million on the table before we started talking.') As it turned out, Mr Selfridge would have to be content with the installation of an in-store booking office supplied by the Central. It issued 5-shilling all-line season tickets for use by female shoppers in the January sales. (In the late 1960s the Central would run extra weekday evening trains for shoppers.)

The *Daily Mail* was a supporter of the Central, and approvingly christened it 'The Tuppenny Tube', a phrase hated by the *Railway Magazine*. In 1907 the Central introduced an additional maximum fare of 3d., and the *Railway Magazine* approved of that: 'The Central London Railway has at length awoken to the fact that "2d. all the way" is not a profitable fare, and has wisely altered its fares introducing a maximum of 3d. The raising of the fare, of course, robs the gutter-title of Tuppenny Tube of its meaning.' It approved of a 3d. fare partly, I suspect, because it made things more complicated. Victorian railways were complicated. If they were not complicated, there would be nothing for the *Railway Magazine* to explain. There was a joke about the flat fare in *Punch*. A yokel up in London for the day buys a ticket on the Central. On being handed it, he says to the clerk, 'But there's no destination stated.' 'That's correct,' says the clerk, 'all our tickets are alike.' 'But,' objects the yokel, 'how will I know where I'm going?' Today London buses have a flat fare, but the Underground covers too wide an area for the policy to be feasible on the network.

There were thirty trains an hour in peak time, twice as many as on the City & South London Railway. The stations, lifts and trains were all brightly lit with electricity, and there was no question of voltage drop from being too far from the source of the power because the Central was the first line long enough to justify the building of sub-stations along the route.

There were just two little problems, the first of which came from the 6-mile length of the line. It smelt. In 1904 the General Manager, Granville C. Cunningham, speculated that this might be 'the smell of the earth', and conceded that there had been objections from 'delicate people'. Electrical fans were installed, then more fans. In 1911 giant fans began blowing ionised air and ozone along the tunnel. 'You were meant to think you were at the seaside,' John Betjeman would recall. 'But you never really did.' The other problem was that the electrical locomotives vibrated, with the result – a Board of Trade inquiry of 1901 found – that the draughtsmen in Cheapside could not draw straight lines. The electrical locomotives were put out to pasture, the carriages were adapted, and Electrical Multiple Unit traction was introduced from 1903.

We will be returning to the Central Line in the 1930s, when it was extended, but first a note about the migraine-inducing complications created by a preliminary, Edwardian expansion at its western end. In 1908 the line was extended to a station called Wood Lane, which was built on a terminal track loop so that trains could turn round and go back the other way, and which served the stadium that had been built for the 1908 Olympics. The station also served the nearby Franco-British trade exhibition held on a site that was called (because of the marble cladding on the exhibition buildings) White City. The stadium itself would later be named White City Stadium. Also in 1908, a station catering to the exhibition was opened close by on the Hammersmith & City Railway, and it was called Wood Lane (Exhibition).

In 1914 the above-mentioned station was closed. But it re-opened intermittently from 1920 under the name Wood Lane (White City). In that year the Central was further extended west to Ealing Broadway. In 1948 Britain again hosted the Olympics at the White City Stadium (Germany was not invited), and the visitors accessed the stadium from a new Central Line station called White City, opened a little to the west of Wood Lane in late 1947. (Wood Lane, with both its original loop and tracks allowing through-running to the stations west of it, was operationally complicated, hence its replacement.) At the same time as White City opened on the Central, Wood Lane (White City) on the Hammersmith & City spluttered back into life with another new name: White City. So now there were two stations called White City. Then, in 2008, a smart new station opened on the Hammersmith & City where its White City station had been.

The name of this new station? Wood Lane.

THE BIG TUBE
(THE GREAT NORTHERN & CITY RAILWAY)

I sometimes catch a train from Highbury & Islington station to Moorgate. As I wait, I am standing on a subterranean platform with Seventies' tiling and the colour scheme of the long-lost Network South-East subdivision of BR. A sign points towards the 'North London Link', which is what the stylishly rebranded London Overground was called a long time ago. The platform I'm on is not branded; it is called Platform 4, but there are no signs of any others. The platform is black; I've never seen a black platform before. I appear to be standing in a Tube tunnel, but there's something wrong, apart from the colour scheme. It's too big.

The train enters the tunnel, and it is definitely not a Tube train. It is a full-size electrical main-line train, and it might well be rain-smeared and filthy, bearing all the battle scars of main-line operation. There is the sense of something that should be outdoors being indoors, like a horse in a living-room. We have entered the dreamlike world of what was officially called the

Great Northern & City Railway, but which would come to be nicknamed, with a mixture of awe and pity, as with the kid at school who has a glandular problem, 'The Big Tube'. And that is how I will refer to it, since its official name is confusingly close to that of the overground railway company that spawned it, namely the Great Northern. It was another of the 1892 authorisations, and it was from the start a line that defied categorisation, although you might pin it down as being somewhere between white elephant and red herring.

The line was conceived by our old friend James Henry Greathead, armed with his amazing tunnelling shield. As authorised by an Act of 1892, the plan was for a line running from the main-line station of the Great Northern Railway at Finsbury Park to Drayton Park, where it would delve underground before running in twin tunnels to Moorgate. Yes, another line aiming for the City.

The idea was to provide an alternative to the congested Widened Lines, which had themselves been intended to ease the congestion on the Metropolitan Line, the aim in both cases being to bring commuters from the north London suburbs into the heart of the City. The particular aim of the Big Tube was to enable commuters from such Great Northern stations as Edgware, High Barnet and Enfield to bypass the parent company's main line station at King's Cross, and to gain direct access to the City in the very trains which they'd boarded at Edgware, High Barnet or Enfield, albeit with different engines attached at Finsbury Park prior to the descent into the tunnel: electrical ones in place of steam-powered. To accommodate these trains, the tunnels of the Big Tube would be 16 foot in diameter, bigger by about a third than the Tube tunnels already built, and for that matter the ones that would be built subsequently.

The Great Northern would build the Big Tube, and guarantee that a certain number of its trains would be run along it to

Moorgate. But there was a delay in raising the money, and by the time work started in 1898 the Great Northern had got into bed with a new Underground partner: the Great Northern & *Strand* Railway, Parliamentary approval for which was given in 1899, and which would achieve fame under a different name as part of the Piccadilly Line. *Its* original proposal was for a Tube line running from Alexandra Palace into Finsbury Park, King's Cross and the West End, thus easing the pressure on the latter two stations, although the idea of connecting Alexandra Palace would be quickly abandoned.

In 1901 the Great Northern cancelled its agreement with the backers of the Big Tube, by which time the latter was half-built, and its big tunnels looked like grandiose folly, since it would now not be allowed running rights into Finsbury Park main-line station. Instead, the Big Tube company was allowed to build a station under the main-line one, so that the line, when it opened in 1904, started as a Tube (albeit a big one) at Finsbury Park. It emerged into the open soon afterwards, then went below ground again at Drayton Park, from where it proceeded to Highbury (later 'Highbury & Islington'), Essex Road and Old Street before finally arriving at Moorgate, where it – a line whose tunnels were far too big – met the City & South London Railway, a line whose tunnels were far too small, and the Metropolitan, a line whose tunnels were at that point still filled with smoke.

At Finsbury Park the Great Northern tried its best to keep secret the presence of its subterranean lodger, like someone who has an embarrassing relative living in the basement. So there were no signs pointing towards the Big Tube platforms, and indeed the platforms of the line remain hard to find today, as already mentioned. But anyone who did find the trains was in for a treat: great mahogany wardrobes of carriages with comfortable transverse seats, clocks and cigarette machines.

The fare for the end-to-end trip was 2d., so it was another

'Tuppenny Tube' of sorts. About 15 million passengers were carried in the first year, a third below expectations. In *Rails through the Clay* (1962), Alan A. Jackson and Desmond F. Croome describe the line's commercial history as 'a sad story'. After an initial contractual dividend was paid, the ordinary shareholders received nothing. The line was a failure, and would be further stifled by the network of electric trams that would grow up around Finsbury Park.

In 1912 it was bought by the Metropolitan, which wanted to extend the line south from Moorgate to Lothbury, and to revive the direct connection to the Great Northern, but these plans met with objections from competitors, and so the Met did its best with the line as it was. The service was improved, and in 1916 the only multi-class seats to be offered on the Tube railways were introduced. Both first and third classes were available, and they lasted until 1934, after London Transport had inherited the line.

In 1939 LT added to the complexity of the Northern Line by making the Big Tube its 'Northern City' branch, with ordinary Tube trains looking too small in the baggy tunnels. As part of the New Works plan of the late 1930s, it was proposed to use the Big Tube as a link between Moorgate and above-ground stations at the north end of the Northern Line. For the Big Tube to be freed from its underground prison in this way, the direct link to the main line at Finsbury Park would have to be finally created, but this plan would be shelved after the war, as we shall see. What happened instead was that the line would be banished altogether from Finsbury Park in 1964, in order that one of its tunnels there could be given to the new Victoria Line. In the general re-adjustment the other was given to the Piccadilly Line, which had first arrived at Finsbury Park in 1906.

Today, if you wait for a southbound Victoria Line train or a westbound Piccadilly Line train at Finsbury Park, you are standing on the old platforms of the Big Tube. In the early Nineties I rented a room in a flat at Finsbury Park, and I would use one or other of those platforms every day. I didn't notice they were too big for the trains that ran in them, even though there's about two feet between the carriage and the tunnel wall there, as against a foot or so in a normal Tube tunnel, but I think I did have a sense of expansiveness and possibility when heading south on the Vic or West on the Picc. Admittedly that could have been because both led to the exciting West End, or it may just have been youth.

Having been kicked out of Finsbury Park, the Big Tube's northern terminus was now Drayton Park. It was in this phase of its existence that the event occurred that has made the history of the line not just baleful and bizarre but also tragic: the Moorgate disaster. On the morning of Friday 28 February 1975 the 8.39 a.m. train from Drayton Park, driven by Leslie Newson, stopped normally at Highbury & Islington, Essex Road and Old Street, but as it approached Platform 9 at Moorgate, the train, which ought to have been going at 15 miles an hour, was travelling at 35 m.p.h., and apparently accelerating. It smashed into the head wall of the 60-foot dead-end tunnel because, as we have seen, the Metropolitan's plans to extend the line south had come to nothing. The tunnel being much bigger than the train, there was room for more mangling to occur than would have happened on a normal Tube. The second carriage was driven under the first, and the third one hit the back of the first. Forty-three people died. At the last moment, driver Newson was seen sitting upright, looking directly ahead, his hands on the controls. He had not lifted his hand from the dead man's handle, an action that would have stopped the train. When his body was retrieved, it was apparent that he had not raised his hands to cover his face. Had he suffered some sort of fit or seizure? The coroner's verdict was accidental death. Laurence Marks, the comedy writer, whose father died in the crash, conducted a journalistic investigation and concluded that the driver had committed suicide, which was emphatically denied by Newson's wife. In 2010 Marks wrote in

the *Daily Mail*, 'Newson didn't want to stop the train. I don't
know why. No one ever will.' It was the worst peacetime disaster
on the Underground.

A friend of mine boarded that train at Drayton Park. She was
a regular on the run to Moorgate, where she was taking a secre-
tarial course. 'I knew *something* was going to happen, and I got
off at Highbury & Islington. I then got on a Victoria Line train,
which took me miles out of my way. I had a sense of physical danger. I don't know how or why – I'm probably a witch.' She knew
Newson by sight. 'I'd see him at Drayton Park, walking from one
end of the train he'd just brought in to the other end to take it
out again. I'd nod to him. He was a cheery, friendly-looking sort
of man.' After the accident she stopped travelling on the Tube for
about fifteen years. She then would venture onto it, but only with
the aid of 'The Way Out' Tube map, which showed the carriages
to board if you wanted to arrive near the exits at any given station. (A recently published little booklet called *Tube Whizzard* is
a refinement of the 'The Way Out' map.) 'I had to minimise my
time on the platforms,' she told me. 'I used to see your column on
the Underground in the *Standard*, but I would immediately turn
over the page. I couldn't bear to read a word of it.'

On 4 October 1975 London Transport transferred the Big
Tube to British Rail. Today the trains of First Capital Connect
withdraw their pantographs from the overhead wires at Drayton
Park and proceed into the tunnel by means of third-rail electrification, which is a method more suitable for tunnel transit. It's a
squalid business really, symptomatic of the blinkered vision, the
make-and-mend, that characterises our railway planning, and
I'm sure it's of little interest to the football fans who crowd bi-
weekly into the Emirates Stadium that now overshadows Drayton Park, but the fact is that the Big Tube has finally reached out
to Hertfordshire with a through connection at Finsbury Park,
which is all it had ever wanted to do.

CHAPTER SEVEN

ENTER YERKES

CHARLES TYSON YERKES:
A GOOD DEAL OF A DREAMER

How to justify naming a chapter after this man? How about this: within the space of five years he electrified the Metropolitan and the District, built the lines that would become the Charing Cross branch of the Northern and the central section of the Piccadilly, and completed what would become the central part of the Bakerloo, a project already under way when he stepped in. He also acquired London United Tramways and fused all the elements together in his Underground Electric Railways of London, the forerunner of London Transport.

Yerkes introduces a welcome note of loucheness to our story, and the only mentions of sex you'll find in most Underground histories are associated with his name. He was twice married and had many affairs. We learn from *Robber Baron* (2006), John Franch's biography of the man, that two sculptures of female nudes flanked the grand staircase of his Fifth Avenue mansion. In the Louis XV room an ornate bed was decorated with 'the likeness of a voluptuous nymph, nude and provocatively posed'. In their *History of London Transport* Barker and Robbins have a fine line in hauteur. When it comes to Yerkes, they introduce him as follows: 'Charles Tyson Yerkes, born 1837, was a stockbroker and banker (once imprisoned) in Philadelphia before he moved to Chicago and became interested in street railways.'

Yerkes, then, was an American, and that ought not to surprise us. American tourists on the Tube seem rather gauche sorts, delightedly photographing each other in front of any old station roundel, but really it's *their* Tube. We have seen that Americans were the pioneers of electric traction, and most of the unfortunate investors in Yerkes schemes would be American. At the turn of the century the balance of trade between Britain and America was shifting in America's favour. There was spare capital in the States, and the cultural and economic colonisation that has been continuing ever since was getting under way. Yerkes had made his first fortune in the purchase and manipulation of municipal franchises for electric trams and elevated railways. In Philadelphia, his repertoire included bribery of officials, blackmail and artificial leverage of stock values. In about 1895 Yerkes said, 'The short-hauls and the people who hang on the straps are the people we make money out of', which usually appears as 'It is the strap-hangers who pay the dividends.' But it was generally the case with Yerkes that nobody received any dividends.

In 1872 there was a fire in Chicago. According to *Rails through the Clay*,

The ensuing financial panic caught Yerkes with his funds spread very thinly in a scheme to enlarge his Philadelphia tramway holdings, and he was forced into bankruptcy. Worse, he was indicted for technical embezzlement because he could not immediately deliver to the city the money he had received from the sale of municipal bonds.

He did nine months in the Eastern State Penitentiary in Philadelphia. He then moved to Chicago, where he built street railways, but the Illinois state legislature was so alarmed by his money-raising schemes that it took over operation of the lines. Refining their disdain, Barker and Robbins note, 'In the end … bribery and corruption failed, even in Chicago.'

So Yerkes came to London in 1898, together with his 24-year-old mistress, the interestingly named Emilie Busbey Grigsby. She was the daughter of a prosperous Kentuckian family which became less prosperous when her father died. Her mother then began running a brothel in Cincinnati, but the young Grigsby would become a coquette of international significance. She liked writers and had made a pitch at Henry James, who unfortunately (for her) was probably gay, insofar as he was anything in that line. Grigsby had written a novel herself, dauntingly entitled *I*, with the subtitle *In Which a Woman Tells the Truth about Herself.*

Yerkes also brought the twentieth century to London. The city, he told the *New York Herald* in July 1900, 'is in crying need of modern transport facilities'. There were plenty of steam trains, but they didn't serve the centre. There were the three Tuppenny Tubes, but two of them were City specialists, and the middle of the largest and fastest-growing city in the world was still full of horses, and full of slums. There was a need, said Yerkes, for the 'labouring classes to get away from densely populated parts into uncrowded localities'. With proper transport, 'People will think nothing of living twenty miles from town.' He sounds like another Charles Pearson, albeit more worldly, and, as with Pearson, the surviving image of Yerkes shows a burly man sitting at an untidy desk. With Yerkes the picture is usually captioned something like 'Yerkes, the cad', and he does have a caddish moustache, but he was apparently softly spoken, with hypnotic eyes and a subtle magnetism. The main difference is that, whereas for Pearson trains were a means to an end – a better life for the masses

– Yerkes was keen on trains per se. He liked speed – driving cars, riding horses – and he was 'a bicycle crank'. He said, 'I hope when I leave the world I shall leave an impress on it, something accomplished, something lasting done', and he chose the building of electric underground railways as his method of achieving it. In 2012, when people tend to make their mark by less laborious means, there is something heroic in this, and soon after he arrived in London, a journalist who knew Yerkes observed that 'although he is a very shrewd man … he is a good deal of a dreamer'.

Yerkes's first move in London was to engage with the promoters of a Tube whose route is evident from the title: the Charing Cross, Euston & Hampstead Railway. Contracts had been drawn up for its construction in 1897, but the promoters lacked the capital to go ahead. In August 1900 Yerkes and his private secretary, a former member of the volunteer Cavalry Regiment, the Rough Riders, were given a tour of the route by members of the syndicate. The legend has it that, high on Hampstead Heath, while his companions looked south pondering the connection to the city 400 feet below, Yerkes looked *north*, towards the further unspoilt fields. 'This settles it,' he is reputed to have said, the implication being that he planned to build houses on those fields in conjunction with his railway. But there are other versions of what was said on Hampstead Heath on that summer's day. In one, Yerkes asks – rather naively, I would have thought – 'Where's London?' On being shown the town smoking away below, he pronounced, 'I'll make this railway.' On 28 September, in a signing ceremony at the Charing Cross Hotel, Yerkes became chairman of the Charing Cross, Euston & Hampstead Railway, having subscribed for one quarter of the capital required to build the line. It is hard to think of that hotel without a Tube line running below it. Well, it soon would be.

In February 1901 Yerkes bought up $3 million worth of District

Railway stock. By the end of 1901 he had, via his Metropolitan District Electric Traction Company, acquired total control of the District and the Charing Cross, Euston & Hampstead, and also the powers granted to the Great Northern & Strand Railway, which – it will be recalled from the sad story of the Big Tube – was the Great Northern Railway's first favoured method of easing commuter blockages at Finsbury Park. Yerkes would join this to the Piccadilly & Brompton Railway to create the Great Northern Piccadilly and Brompton Railway, and you can still see those proud if unwieldy initials, 'GNP & B', written in gilt letters on the front of Holloway Road station. (That's on the Piccadilly Line, which is what the GNP & B would become.)

In 1902 Yerkes also bought from liquidators control of the half-completed Baker Street & Waterloo Railway (which had been authorised between Elephant & Castle and Paddington, and which would become the Bakerloo); progress on which was halted by the crash of a paper edifice called the London and Globe Finance Corporation. At the head of *that* was an extravagant individual who makes Yerkes seem almost demure, and who triggers (for reasons that will be explained) the following eye-catching index entry in Stephen Smith's book *Underground London*: 'Underwater billiard table'.

James Whitaker Wright was not exactly American, but he learned his creative financing there. He had been born in Cheshire and moved to the States at a young age where a made a fortune in gold-mining and acquired a famously beautiful wife, even though he looked like Billy Bunter. On his return to Britain he bought a yacht called *Sybarita* and a Park Lane mansion, and created a vast estate in Surrey: Park Lea. That connoisseur of British mavericks, David McKie, has written of Park Lea:

> Hills were levelled and new hills created ... A vast lake,
> complete with a boathouse commissioned from Lutyens, was

designed as a centrepiece. Beneath it, reached by tunnels, was a smoking room in the form of a subterranean conservatory, so that as they smoked his guests could watch fish, or sometimes even swimmers, disporting themselves overhead.

Or they could play billiards: hence that index entry.

Wright's London Globe & Finance Corporation invested heavily in the Baker Street & Waterloo Railway, enabling tunnelling to begin from a staging in the Thames in 1898. The staging was a platform upstream of Charing Cross Bridge, and from it two shafts were sunk into the riverbed. It sounds bizarre to use the middle of the Thames as a base of operations, but both the City & South London and the Waterloo & City had done the same because it was cheaper to remove spoil by barge than by road. The under-river digging required the use of compressed air, and some workers succumbed to the diver's condition the bends (decompression sickness), requiring a decompression chamber to be built on the works platform. In his pamphlet *Early Tube Railways* (1984) Nigel Pennick takes up the story:

> On August 20th and 21st, blows [or blowouts] occurred which produced waterspouts two and a half feet above the river surface … A competitor in the London Waterman's traditional race for *Doggett's Coat and Badge* got into difficulties in the whirl of water, and complained bitterly that it had caused him to lose.

As that poor chap (I imagine him as an irate Mr Kipps) was floundering in the Thames in consequence of the infant Bakerloo's great fart, Whitaker Wright was floundering in a wider sense. Having made a fortune in American gold-mining, he was now losing one in *Australian* gold-mining, and juggling the shares in his network of holding companies to conceal the shortfall. In late 1900 the London & Globe and twenty-seven other Wright companies went bust, and in 1902 work stopped on the line. Wright's shareholders lobbied for his prosecution, and in January 1904 he was convicted under the Larceny Act. He got seven years.

Wright was shown into an ante-room before being conveyed to prison. Here he handed his watch and chain to a friend who waited with him, saying he wouldn't be needing it where he was going. He was right about that, because he then fell over and died. Wright had taken prussic acid on a visit to the Gentlemen's after sentencing. A fully loaded revolver – his back-up plan – was also found in his pocket.

But now back to Yerkes …

In 1902 he formed the Underground Electric Railways of London company, and the initials UERL were to become familiar to all Londoners. Shares were issued around the world – dodgy shares. In *Underground to Everywhere* (2004) Stephen Halliday writes, 'The capital structure of the company involved a complex hierarchy of shares, certificates, huge commissions to the bankers and other instruments which aroused the suspicion of the financial community.' It also prompted the best sentence in the Barker and Robbins book: 'All this rustling of commercial paper was received rather coolly in London.' A Royal Commission on London Traffic of July 1903 could not understand the detail of the arrangements, and, let's face it, nor can I. At the same time as he was ensnaring investors with what have been called his 'exotic securities', Yerkes was outwitting an even bigger beast in the financial jungle than himself …

John Pierpont Morgan, famous for once having actually bailed out the US government, was planning a new Tube in partnership with London United Tramways. Their electric trams were banned from the centre, and they therefore wanted to expand by going underground. 'The Morgan Tube' would have followed roughly the course of what became the Piccadilly Line. It would go from Hammersmith to Kensington, through the West End to Charing Cross then into the City and north via Tottenham to Southgate, with another prong heading north-eastwards to Waltham Abbey. Morgan's plan came up against Yerkes's schemes and those of other promoters motivated by the early financial success of the Central London Railway (a success that would soon be sharply curtailed by the motor buses). All were to be considered in 1902 by two committees of the House of Lords. The accounts of those deliberations form the densest passages in any long Tube history, but the headlines are as follows.

Yerkes gained approval for the embellishment of the Charing Cross, Euston & Hampstead, and one sees the Northern Line taking ominous shape in the permissions granted for extensions to the original scheme: the southern terminus would be extended in 1914 from Charing Cross to what is now Embankment station. The line would be extended north from Hampstead Heath to Golders Green and from Kentish Town to Archway. (Assent to the junction at Camden from which the Edgware and High Barnet branches would sprout had already been given.)

The Central London Railway had wanted to turn their line into another circle, not an 'inner circle' – that had already been done – but an 'inner*most* circle', and their scheme was rejected in favour of Morgan's more comprehensive plan. But Yerkes torpedoed *that* on discovering a rift between Morgan and his partners in London United Tramways over how the proposed line would be managed. He exploited the rift in order to buy a controlling interest in London United Tramways, so the Morgan scheme collapsed, and Yerkes's own plan to link the Great Northern & Strand with the Piccadilly & Brompton was authorised. From America, Pierpont Morgan sent a telegram to his son, who'd been overseeing the deal: 'Deeply sympathetic with you in your bother over Tubes. Would seem to be the greatest rascality and conspiracy I ever heard of.' And he had heard of a few.

Incidentally, the Morgan Tube (on which it had been intended to run trains throughout the night) would have been a *network*. The Metropolitan and District were really networks as well, and this was a consequence of building Tubes by means of a competitive free-for-all. Each company wanted to expand its territory at the expense of the others. The Northern Line that Yerkes was incubating would also become a network, and one far too complicated for its own good.

The digging of the 'Hampstead Tube' and the 'Piccadilly Tube' would start in 1902. In 1903 the digging of the Baker Street & Waterloo was resumed. Yerkes would not live to see any section of any of these lines opened, but he would see electrification brought to the cut-and-cover lines, and he would build 'The Chelsea Monster'.

TRACTION CURRENT EXPLAINED

Easy to write that heading, less easy if – like me – you can't wire a plug, to deliver the goods.

We begin with a sinister vignette …

A train steams into Aldgate station at four o'clock one afternoon. A lady sits in a first-class compartment, facing the window, 'evidently oblivious of the fact that on this line Aldgate is the terminal station'. She is dead, and it will transpire that she has been murdered. The scenario is from a short story of 1901 by Baroness Orczy, *The Mysterious Death on the Underground Railway*. It features a sage-like character called The Old Man in the Corner (he is always to be found in the corner of an ABC coffee house), who reflects, 'In these days of tubes and motor traction of all kinds, the old-fashioned "best, cheapest and quickest route to the West End" is often deserted, and the good old

Metropolitan Railway carriages cannot at any time be said to be overcrowded.'

Not being electrified, the cut-and-cover lines were coming to seem a picturesque curiosity, and a trigger for nostalgic affection in their older users. In *The Soul of London: A Survey of a Modern City* (1905) Ford Madox Ford wrote:

> I have known a man, dying a long way from London, sigh queerly for a sight of the gush of smoke that, on a platform of the Underground, one may see, escaping in great woolly clots up a circular opening, by a grimy, rusted iron shield, into the dim upper light. He wanted to see it again as others have wished to see once more the Bay of Naples, the olive groves of Catania.

In 1901 the Metropolitan had seemed ready to proceed with electrification by means of overhead wires, but on his arrival at the District, Yerkes favoured a system whereby the power would be provided by two electrified rails – a method tried and tested on the elevated railways of Boston. Board of Trade arbitration favoured this scheme, and what went for the District would have to go for the Met, given the entanglement of the two on the Inner Circle; and in September 1905 the first electric service ran around the Circle. The Tube lines would also eventually adopt this system.

How did it work?

You will have noticed that the Underground tracks seem annoyingly cluttered. There are the two running rails and another two loitering about near by: the power rails, one of which is outside the tracks, the other one in between them. Four rails in all. On the main-line railways running into the southern termini of London things are neater, and there are three rails: the two running rails and one power rail to the side. That system is called third-rail electrification; London Underground has four-rail electrification.

With the third-rail system, the train collects 750 volts from the outer rail. The Underground operates at a lower voltage: 630 volts, and this voltage is split. The outer of the two power rails is at +420 volts; the inner rail is at −210 volts. This splitting is to create a shorter distance to earth (which is zero volts). The main reason for this splitting is to minimise a phenomenon few non-electricians have ever heard of, namely current leakage. If this occurs on the main-line electrified railways, it doesn't really matter. But current leakage in a Tube tunnel can cause electrolysis to occur in steel retaining walls, which in turn causes them to rust; it could also damage the foundations of nearby buildings.

The inner, or negative, rail is also known as the 'current return' rail, because electrical current needs a circuit – a return path to earth, in other words. On the Underground, the non-electrician might be advised to imagine earth as being located in the sub-station from which the power was originally derived, and to where it is – so to speak – sent back by the negative or current return rail. On the main lines the voltage is returned to earth via the carriage bogies (that is, the under-frames and wheels) and the running rails. Any power rail needs to be well insulated from earth, to minimise current leakage, and so the *two* power rails on the Underground sit on curiously genteel and antique-looking porcelain pots.

In addition to this power circuit for traction current, was another electrical system which would provide for an early form of automatic signalling or train protection. A small voltage is fed to the running tracks, and this sets the relevant signal to green. When a train runs onto the track, thus connecting the two rails, a short circuit is created, the current drops out and the signal is switched to red. The system operates in conjunction with a lever on the tracks. If a train should pass a red light, the lever, which is called a tripcock, comes into play. The tripcock releases the air from the train's air-braking system, thus causing the brakes to come on and stopping the train. Annoyingly for people like me who've only just got to grips with this mechanism, it is now being replaced by a more fluid, computerised system of signalling called 'moving block'. By this, the relative positions of trains on tracks is controlled by computer, and instead of a tripcock, a computer will apply the brakes of any train running too close to another one. The installation of moving-block signalling is the main work of the Tube Upgrade currently ongoing. It will allow a greater frequency of trains, and so 'increase capacity'. Moving block will ultimately be used in conjunction with automatically driven trains such as those run – at the time of writing – on the Victoria, Central and Jubilee Lines only. Yes, the trains on those lines do have fully trained drivers sitting in the cabs, but they're not doing much apart from closing the doors, which is why they tend to be sitting with their feet up and picking their noses as they enter the stations.

Now ... How would you go about electrocuting yourself on the Underground lines?

In the terrible horror film *Creep* (2004), a harassed couple (they are being chased, naturally enough, by a flesh-eating zombie) prepare to flee along a Tube tunnel in the small hours of the morning. The woman, evidently unaware that the current is switched off every night after the service stops, asks how to avoid being electrocuted, and the harassed man, also evidently unaware of the fact just mentioned, replies uncertainly, 'Er ... Don't step on *that* rail or that ... Look, don't step on *any* of the rails.' The scene is part of an honourable tradition among creative types of vagueness about Underground electricity.

In *The Man in the Brown Suit* (1926), by Agatha Christie, a man in a heavy overcoat falls onto the rails at Hyde Park Corner Tube station: 'There was a vivid flash from the rails and a crackling

sound.' The man is then lifted off the 'live rail'. A doctor who hap-
pens to be on hand– 'a tall man with a brown beard' (brown-ness
being something of a theme in the book) – examines the body and
pronounces, 'Dead as a doornail. Nothing to be done.' But what is
'the live rail'? Both the power rails are live, as we've just seen. Yes,
there is more voltage in the third rail, the outer one (which is why
it's positioned on the far side of the tracks from the platforms in
Tube stations), and if you touch that you will certainly die as long
as you have some other part of you on one of the running rails,
the other live rail or something else that connects to earth and
enables the current to flow, such as damp track ballast. Keep in
mind that the pigeon who is often seen to stand on the electrified
rails with such insouciance has wings. He has landed on it from
above. He has not *stepped* on it; his legs are not long enough to
allow him to do that, thankfully for him. In electrical terminology he is 'at elevated voltage', but he is not 'carrying current'. By the
same token, any reader who finds himself – as a result of whatever
nightmarish scenario – standing with both feet on an electrified
line should jump off it rather than step down.

In *Railways on the Screen* (1993) John Huntley points out that
in a film of 1941 called *Manhunt*, which features a scene supposedly set on the Piccadilly Line, 'the villain is electrocuted on
the centre (earth return) rail of the system instead of the outer
positive rail'. But is that so remarkable? If you were earthed, you
would probably be killed by that rail as well, even with its weaker
voltage. Most people who jump in front of trains will therefore
be electrocuted twice over besides being cut up by the train. But
I suppose they want to make sure.

We turn next to the question that has been mused over by
every London male while waiting for a train: would you die if
you urinated on an electrified rail? Yes probably, because while
pure water does not conduct electricity, ionised water does, and
that is the category into which urine comes, but you may be saved

by the fact that your stream will be broken into drops, and if the gaps between the drops are big enough you will be insulated. A friend who works for the Underground said the only death-by-urination that he knew of involved a Metropolitan Line driver, who late one night was being given a lift back to the depot by another driver. He leaned out of the cab to relieve himself, and his head struck a signal post.

Another matter ruminated upon by the platform daydreamer: why do you sometimes see sparks under a Tube train? This beautiful little display which as a boy confirmed for me the glamour and danger of London, occurs when there is a break in either of the conductor rails, which may happen as points come up, or the track curves. When a break occurs, the conductor rail slopes downwards away from the collecting shoe, and the sparks represent the electricity reaching poignantly and vainly for its connection, and ionising the air in the process. Why does the train keep moving? Because other rail-shoe connections remain in place along its length. Incidentally, try to avoid saying, 'Oh, the train's making pretty blue sparks!' Say instead that it is 'throwing an arc.'

BY THE WAY: THE CHELSEA MONSTER

In order to power his underground railways Charles Yerkes built a generating station in Lots Road, Fulham. It was opened in 1904 as the largest traction power station in Europe and one of the first to use steam turbines, which have been the only game in town for power stations ever since. The Chelsea Monster, as it became known, was built on a bend of the river that the romantic, but stroppy, artist James McNeill Whistler had often depicted in his 'Nocturnes', and he is said to have remarked that the builders 'ought to be drawn and quartered'. So here were two Americans appropriating a bank of the Thames: Yerkes for industry, Whistler for art.

Lots Road Power Station in Fulham or, as estate agents say,
Chelsea. It opened in 1904, and powered the underground
railways of the American plutocrat, Charles Yerkes. Today, the
Underground is powered from the National Grid. Lots Road was
de-commissioned in 2002, and only two of the four towers remain.
The silent film *Underground* (1928), directed by Anthony Asquith,
features a genuinely gripping chase sequence across its roof.

Yerkes provocatively offered to supply the Metropolitan from Lots Road. But the Met would build its own power station at Neasden (demolished in 1968), and its coal would be brought by rail, whereas Lots Road was supplied by barge. Today buddleia grows out of the Chelsea Monster, and only two of the four 275-foot chimneys survive, so that it looks like a lopsided version of Battersea Power Station, which would be built thirty years later on the opposite side of the river. Lots Road would close in 2002, by which time it ranked as a *small* power station – almost cute. It produced 50 megawatts of power on opening. Today, a medium-sized power station produces 600 megawatts, and a nuclear power station will produce 1,200.

So it had ceased to be monstrous, and we might say the same of Yerkes. He built Tubes to be remembered, but he is not remembered. When he was safely dead, in 1912, Theodore Dreiser began a three-decker novel based on his life. (I've never met anyone who's read it.) There is no blue plaque to Yerkes anywhere in London, perhaps for the simple reason that he lived in hotels when here, so I hope that when Lots Road is redeveloped, there will be some commemoration. It would seem a fitting place, Yerkes having been such a powerhouse himself. But then again, he is also a poignant figure. He goes down as another martyr to the Tube in that – like Charles Pearson, like Watkin of the Met, like Greathead of the tunnelling shield and like Whitaker Wright of the Bakerloo – he died before his vision could be fully realised. The building of the Underground seems like a relay race, in which the competitors expire soon after passing on the baton.

The Yerkes Tubes performed well below expectation in their first years, owing to competition from road transport, especially electric trams. They would be extended in the Twenties and Thirties in an attempt to make them turn a profit, and to create jobs for unemployed Londoners. It was this move that made

London into a true city of commuters, a city of suburbs, and if you think that's a bad thing, you can't really blame Yerkes, who only set the ball rolling.

Yes, his Tube empire may seem like a crass American colonisation of London. It involved guards called conductors after the American fashion, a system of electrification imported from America and American elevators and, from 1909, American escalators; it brought long hours of operating (from five o'clock in the morning to one in the morning), as an approach to the twenty-four-hour operation of many railways in workaholic America; it brought an end to such English gentility as the 'church interval' by which cut-and-cover line trains (and others) did not run between about 11.30 a.m. and 1 p.m. on Sundays. And many of the shareholders in the UERL were American ... but they lost out badly. You might say that what Yerkes brought to London was in effect American aid, an accidental Marshall Plan. As Stephen Halliday writes in *Underground to Everywhere*, 'If Yerkes had been an entirely honest, upright banker, much of the underground system would not have been built.'

Towards the end of his life Yerkes was approached by an astronomer at the University of Chicago, George Ellery Hale, who wanted him to fund a telescope. Fairly typically, Yerkes agreed, on the strict understanding that it would be the biggest telescope in the world. But the sequel also reveals an endearing naivety in his character. Announcing the funding of the telescope, Hale added that Yerkes would in addition be building an observatory to house it. He had not run this past his benefactor beforehand, but it would have been embarrassing for Yerkes to pull out, so the supposedly rapacious capitalist was outwitted by the humbly petitioning academic. The Yerkes Observatory stands at Lake Geneva in Wisconsin, 80 miles north of Chicago, where the winter temperature can be −20° F, cold enough for skies to be quite clear. The floor of the observatory ascends to carry the viewer to the eyepiece. It contains the Yerkes Refractor telescope, 'the last of the great refractors'; it is 62 feet long on a 43-foot-high stand, and is presumably more than adequate for viewing the crater on the moon that, in 1935, the International Astronomical Union named Charles Tyson Yerkes. Fittingly enough, it is on the edge of the Mare Crisium, the Sea of Crises.

If I approach the mouldering Chelsea Monster in the evening, I might see the moon above the surviving chimneys, and I call to mind an Underground advertising poster created in 1938 by Man Ray. It was called *Keeps London Going*, and it showed the Underground roundel adapted so as to resemble a Saturn-like planet benignly orbiting the earth. That's the astronomical Yerkes up there, looking down on London, and to any commuters who do feel he created a mobile prison for them I commend the principles that the man himself laid down for those who would escape a life of drudgery. They are quoted in John Franch's book *Robber Baron*:

1. The worst-fooled man is the man who fools himself.
2. Have one great object in life. Follow it persistently and determinedly. If you divide your energies you will not succeed.
3. Do not look for what you do not wish to find.
4. Have no regrets. Look to the future. The past is gone and cannot be brought back.

YERKES'S BABIES: THE BAKERLOO, THE PICCADILLY, THE CHARING CROSS, EUSTON & HAMPSTEAD

The Baker Street & Waterloo opened from Elephant & Castle to Baker Street in 1906, before progressing in 1907 to Edgware Road station (a different one from the Met's), embracing Marylebone on the way. It would be at Paddington by 1913. Soon after opening, it was officially named what had hitherto been its nickname, the Bakerloo, and the *Railway Magazine* applied its favourite, indeed its only, epithet: it was a 'gutter title'. But you'd have thought the provenance was sufficiently pukka, the name having been invented by no less a personage than Captain G. H. F. Nichols, who wrote a column in the *Evening News* under the byline 'Quex'.

The Great Northern, Piccadilly & Brompton ('Piccadilly' for short) opened in 1906 from Hammersmith to Finsbury Park. The Hampstead Tube opened in 1907 from Charing Cross to Camden Town, where it split to go either west to Golders Green or east to Archway, which was called Highgate, even though it is not in Highgate but at the foot of the hill on which Highgate stands. Hold on to your hat while we follow the history of that station's name. In 1939 an element of honesty crept in when it was re-named Archway (Highgate), but then, in 1941, when a station further north called Highgate (also not in Highgate) opened, there was a reversion towards *dis*honesty when Archway (Highgate) became Highgate (Archway). In 1947, it became Archway.

Between Hampstead and Golders Green another station had been completed, called North End or Bull & Bush. Well, it had been completed at platform level, but no surface building was ever built because, the surrounding country having been unfortunately (from Yerkes's perspective) preserved for the nation, insufficient numbers of commuters would ever use it. Being 221 feet below the Heath, it is the deepest station on the underground. North End or Bull & Bush is also the only closed-down station never to have opened, and you'd think its poignant situation would put a brake on the revels in the Heathside pub called the Bull & Bush after which it was named. (If your train ever stops in the tunnel between Hampstead and Golders Green, you might make out the remnant of a southbound platform.)

I suggest that these Yerkes Tubes are entangled in the minds of most modern Londoners. You are on a deep-level Tube in the centre of the town; the stations are more or less crowded; they are also, if you stop to think about it, attractive. The lines were very civilised in conception. In the early years the lights in the tunnels were kept on, so as to reassure passengers. (Today tunnel lights are *not* kept on, and if you travel in the cab of a Tube train, the stations seem so brilliantly illuminated by contrast that all the passengers seem to be poised on a stage.) Most of the stations have surface buildings. That may not seem like much of a boast, but most of the stations of the Paris Metro do not have surface buildings. There is just an elevator or a staircase set into the pavement, like a challenge presented by a conceptual artist, or like a dream. (This stems from the vanity of Paris. The city authorities considered the city too beautiful to be cluttered with subway station buildings, and it helped that the Metro is a cut-and-cover network, with no need of lift housings.)

The architect of the stations on all the UERL Tube lines was Leslie Green (1875–1908), a delicate-looking man who did everything young, including dying. He'd set up in architectural practice at twenty-two; he became architect to the UERL at twenty-eight, and his early death probably came from overwork – so making him another of our Underground martyrs. He made the Yerkes Tubes assert themselves through four-square, classical buildings containing ticket offices, lifts and an arched mezzanine. These buildings are covered in glazed oxblood tiles that vie with the red of Routemaster buses for being the colour of London. It is not an attractive colour. It's reminiscent of a bruise, or raw liver, or the face of a wino, but then London is not a pretty city. Being glazed, the tiles magnify the effect of rain and shine darkly on a rainy night, with the aid of large and rather funereal shaded lamps, which remind me of the shaded lamps that hang over snooker tables. They would come to be augmented by glass canopies of a midnight blue, on which was written the word UndergrounD, the 'U' and 'D' being exaggerated so as to suggest that the word is progressing from one tunnel to another, and my favourite Leslie Green stations are the ones that still parade this logo: for instance, Russell Square and Chalk Farm.

Altogether the stations offered a subdued welcome, as if to assert that the base note of London life is or ought to be a resigned melancholia. On a rainy evening they seem to proclaim: forget about today; go home to bed and try again tomorrow. The buildings had steel frames, and the roofs were flat, in case anybody wanted to buy the 'air rights' and put an office block on top. In most cases there have been no takers, although Leslie Green stations at Oxford Circus and Camden, for example, have buildings on top. The ticket halls were lined with wood panels and tiles of a relaxing mid-green, with Art Deco stylings that – in spite of the contrast mentioned above – offer an echo of Paris, where Art Nouveau had been rampant in the early twentieth century, and where Leslie Green had trained.

In the absence of trees, gateposts, signal gantries or other signs of 'home' that a traveller on a main line would look for, each platform wall was given a unique design by means of coloured tiles. The names of the stations were often spelled out in these tiles, with charmingly over-exuberant punctuation, hence ': Tufnell: Park:'.

Much of the special patterning was lost in the Seventies, but as part of the current Upgrade, the Yerkes (and other) stations have been restored with a fine feeling for history. So Warren Street is proudly announced as 'EUSTON ROAD', which it hasn't been called since 1907. (But the modern name, written on the roundels, puts you right.) And I sail most days from Archway to Charing Cross through stations decorated in old-fashioned creams, blues and greens … although perhaps my favourite of the restored Yerkes/Green stations is Regent's Park, on the Bakerloo, which is brown, cream, yellow and white – like a chocolate sundae.

The trains on the Yerkes Tubes varied from line to line and were manufactured in various countries, but they were all flat-ended electrical multiple units, with mainly longitudinal seating. They had colourful liveries. On the Bakerloo they were scarlet and cream. It must have been like seeing a stick of rock shooting out of the tunnel at you.

The carriages – or cars – had gated platforms at the end, where 'gatemen' stood and controlled the flow of passengers on and off the trains in the absence of automatic doors. (The Yerkes trains were always crowded in peak times, even though they came into the stations every ninety seconds or so.) When each gateman had secured his doors and gate, he rang a bell, then the conductor rang *his* bell as the signal for the driver to set off. 'This tintinnabulation down the train was a joy to the ear', write Jackson and Croome in *Rails through the Clay*. But passengers wrote letters to *The Times* about the way the gatemen would mangle the station names they shouted out: 'Ampstid' for 'Hampstead' and 'Igit' for 'Highgate'. (Today the automated female announcer infuriates me by saying 'High-gut' and 'Goodge Stree …', with no terminal 't'.) The train staff were at least smartly dressed. They had better be, or they were sacked. They had to keep their double-breasted uniform coats buttoned right up at all times, and so it is just as well that besides passenger flow, there was also air flow, using stair and lift shafts and directed by electrical exhaust fans.

The Yerkes Tubes were more uniform than disparate, and they would not develop their defining individual characteristics until they were extended. Then the Bakerloo would become notable for complications to the north, and entanglement with overground railways, which would serve to highlight the abruptness of its termination to the south: there would never be any advance in that direction beyond Elephant & Castle. The Piccadilly would be not so much extended as over-extended. There are too many stops on it. As for the Charing Cross, Euston & Hampstead, even the 1907 operation was fraught, its trains ominously fitted with destination plates to show whether it was bound for Golders Green, Hampstead or Highgate. The stressful complications would soon be multiplied when it became conjoined with the City & South London, so making the Northern Line.

In spite of being overcrowded in peak times, the cost of building these Tubes cancelled out any savings that occurred from the use of electricity in place of steam. Also, the lines all fell short of their expected passenger targets by about half, mainly because of competition from electric trams – up and running from 1901, as mentioned – and now also petrol-driven buses. In early 1906 Sir George Gibb, formerly General Manager of the North Eastern Railway, became chairman and managing director of the heavily indebted Underground Electric Railways of London. He and Yerkes's banker, Sir Edgar Speyer – a man increasingly indignant at having funded a transport revolution for London with no assistance from the public purse – attempted out of desperation to sell UERL to the London County Council, but nothing came of the scheme.

We should at this point take note of the London County Council (or LCC), which was the democratically elected successor to the Metropolitan Board of Works (which had been a body of appointees) and the forerunner of the Greater London Council. In the two decades after its foundation in 1889 the LCC was run by a progressive grouping and, transport-wise, the Council could be seen as a moral corrective to the UERL. It had disapproved of the financial machinations of Yerkes; it wanted London transport to be run for the benefit of Londoners rather than shareholders, and it operated the largest of the London tram networks, over a Polo-mint shaped territory in central London (since trams were banned from the City and the West End).

Electric trams – those ungainly, boat-like things that so aggrieved the motorist, because they ran down the middle of the roads, and passengers would have to step *into* the roads to get on to them – were for the working classes, and the LCC saw them as a means of extracting the poor from the remaining rookeries of central London. Trams were cheaper than Tubes and buses; the seats were hard; there were 'No Spitting' signs everywhere; the 'top deck of the tram' was notorious as a venue for naughtiness. They carried adverts for the *News of the World*, Bisto or beer ('Drink Worthington Ales'), and their termini were often pubs. A style guide of the 1930s for journalists on the *Daily Express* tried to bring trams upmarket by insisting they be called 'tramcars'. They were transport for the masses in the literal sense that, between the time of their electrification and the early 1920s when buses became more comfortable and commodious, trams carried more passengers than the buses and the Underground combined.

Whereas the Underground generated private owner occupation in the suburbs, the LCC would build subsidised council housing in the 1920s, sometimes following the arrival of the Underground (as at Morden), sometimes not (as at the Downham estate at Catford). But there would eventually be a convergence. The UERL would become London Transport, which would take over the trams of the LCC. The LCC would initiate the campaign for the Green Belt, which the men at the top of London Transport would support. And public transport in London would eventually fall into municipal ownership, albeit under the GLC rather than the LCC.

After their approach to the LCC, Gibb and Speyer moved their fire-fighting to a different front, by re-negotiating with shareholders the imminently due redemption of £7 million pounds' worth of fantastical 'profit-sharing notes' that Yerkes had issued in 1903 against subsequent profits that never materialised. The notes were converted into long-term debt, and the company was saved from bankruptcy. The next task would be to make Tube-use part of the culture of London, and in this connection we will be meeting the double act of Stanley and Pick. But before I introduce our bill-toppers, here is a brief preliminary entertainment ...

BY THE WAY: THE ALDWYCH SHUTTLE

The shuttle services of the Underground have their cult followings, their runtish condition attracting the sympathy vote. We have ridden the Chesham Shuttle at the far end of the Met, and we will be riding the Epping–Ongar at the eastern end of the Central. But the machinations of Yerkes also created the only shuttle to operate in central London. I refer to the Aldwych Shuttle, which briefly gave rise to the glamorous 'Theatre Express'.

The Great Northern & Strand Tube, it will be recalled, was the decongestant for Finsbury Park favoured by the Great Northern main-line railway company. It was originally going to terminate to the south at Holborn, but the LCC was engaged in a programme of slum clearance in order to create the above-mentioned rather blank and pompous thoroughfare called Kingsway and its companion-piece to the south, the Aldwych, which links the Strand to Fleet Street. So the plans for the Tube line changed. It would now encompass Kingsway by terminating south of the new street, somewhere in the vicinity of the Aldwych. When the plan for the line was taken over by Yerkes, he decided to combine it with the proposed Brompton & Piccadilly Circus Railway, by extending the latter from Piccadilly Circus to Holborn. The proposed Aldwych extension was thus left dangling, but the tunnel between Holborn and the Aldwych was dug nonetheless because it was felt that the theatres and new offices around Aldwych would be worth serving, even if the line towards it would be merely a spur to begin with.

Holborn station, incidentally, did not get the Leslie Green treatment because it was to be situated on Kingsway, and the LCC required it to fit in with the look of the new street. Therefore the station is clad in grey Portland stone. The station at Aldwych, which would initially be called Strand, *was* given a full coating of oxblood tiles. It was situated on the south side of the Strand, on the site of the Strand Theatre, and that was a bad omen. Here was a line meant to serve the theatres of the Strand, yet one of those would have to close to make way for it. The theatre closed on 13 May 1905 for building to begin, interrupting the run of a play called *Miss Wingrove*, written by a man with the titillatory name of W. H. Risque. Imagine the irritation of Mr Risque on learning that his play was coming off because the theatre was to be turned into a Tube station. His irritation would surely have been doubled had he known that the only reason the Great Northern, Piccadilly & Brompton had pounced on that particular site was that it had offered the correct alignment for an extension of the spur line to Waterloo – permission for which would soon be *rejected* by Parliament.

The Holborn–Strand link was opened in November 1907, about a year after the rest of the Great Northern, Piccadilly & Brompton had opened. Two-car trains shuttled back and forth in the two tunnels. Whether there were any passengers on those trains is another matter. Aldwych was well served by buses and trams, and the new offices filled up only slowly. If you wanted to go further north than Holborn on the spur, you had to change at Holborn, and people couldn't be bothered. However, a through northbound service to Finsbury Park did operate in the late evenings between 1907 and 1910, and this was the 'Theatre Express'.

It was meant to serve theatre-goers who lived on the main line stops beyond Finsbury Park – say, Enfield. They would change from Underground to main line at Finsbury Park and arrive home at about midnight, looking glamorous in their evening wear and happily clutching their theatre programmes. But there weren't enough culture vultures in places like Enfield to justify the service.

In 1915 Strand station was renamed Aldwych as a result of a pointless little *pas de deux*, by which Charing Cross station on the Hampstead railway was renamed Strand (before reverting to Charing Cross in 1973). In 1918 the shuttle trains were running from the western shuttle platform at Holborn to the eastern one at Aldwych. The station was fading away. In the First World War, National Gallery treasures were stored on the disused platform. In the Thirties the shuttle was down to a one-car service. In 1939 Geoffrey Household set the opening chase sequence in his novel *Rogue Male* – which is a *series* of chase sequences – in Aldwych. The unnamed hero is being pursued by the agents of a fascist power:

> The working at Aldwych is very simple. Just before the shuttle is due, the lift comes down. The departing passengers get into the train; the arriving passengers get into the lift. When the lift goes up and the train leaves, Aldwych station is as deserted as an ancient mine. You can hear the drip of water and the beat of your heart.

The service was suspended altogether in the Second World War, when part of the line became a bomb shelter, and the station was used again for art storage. The Elgin Marbles were transferred from the British Museum to Aldwych, where they, along with hundreds of Londoners, sheltered from the bombs.

After the war the shuttle resumed, but the disused platforms gained an identity crisis, being used for mock-ups of stations on the Victoria Line, the Jubilee Line and the extension to Heathrow of the Piccadilly. Also films were shot on the branch: *Conspirator* (1949), *A Run for Your Money* (1949), *The Clouded Yellow* (1950), *The Gentle Gunman* (1952). The middle two are good, the other two abysmal. *Death Line* (also abysmal) was filmed there in 1972. Meanwhile, the station awaited its shot at the big time. Plans for the link through to Waterloo were revived and died. What became the Jubilee Line was originally going to pass through Aldwych on its way east, but it would terminate at Charing Cross instead (although not for long).

Aldwych station was closed in September 1994, and the Photo-Me booth that had been inside the station was dragged outside, to stand before the shuttered façade so that at least some public service survived on the site. It was very sad, but then again I've been to some excellent parties in the closed-down station. In April 1997 I found myself descending in the gated lift at Aldwych with a vodka and ginger beer in my hand and Janet Street-Porter standing next to me. This was a 'happening', organised by an art group called Artangel. A distorted disembodied voice repeatedly told us to stand clear of the doors, to have our tickets ready for inspection. A man on a gantry in the ventilation shaft played blues on a saxophone while a woman in a white dress paced up and down in front of him. I learned that a Prodigy video had just been shot in the station, and 'part of an episode of *Bramwell MD*', whatever that is. A few months later, Artangel organised another moody installation in Aldwych that was dreamed up – possibly literally – by the art critic John Berger, who in his youth had used the shuttle to get to Holborn Art College (now Central St Martins School of Art). Berger had since abandoned Holborn and rain in favour of the Haute Savoie and blue skies, and the event was supposed to elide – by visual and aural effects – the experience of Tube travel with the experience of being in a certain cave in Chauvet, France, where 70,000-year-old paintings had recently been discovered.

The closed-down station still looks like a Tube station, in its coat of oxblood tiles, and no doubt many baffled tourists every day start hunting for it on the Tube map. But the name it bears is its original one, Strand, the second name Aldwych, which overlay Strand, having been removed. It seems to be going back in time, and it would be good if it became a theatre again, bringing some bright lights to a dull corner of London. Apparently the outline of the proscenium is clear to see in the booking office, if you know where to look. The Strand Theatre could open with a production of *Miss Wingrove*, or I could write a light-hearted Edwardian time-travel play especially for the occasion. It would be called … *Before We Were So Rudely Interrupted.*

CHAPTER EIGHT

EVERYWHERE IN TRAINS

ENTER STANLEY AND PICK

Contemporary Londoners are no more likely to have heard of Stanley and Pick than of Yerkes, but if any two men made London what it is today, it is these two.

Yet they were both from modest backgrounds and were not even Londoners but northerners by birth. Albert Stanley was also American in a way, because his family emigrated from Derbyshire to Detroit in 1880, when he was six, and he began his railway career as an office boy in the Detroit Street Railways Company. (Railways were in his blood, in that his father was a coach painter for Pullman, the luxury-carriage makers.) He was soon *running* the Detroit Street Railways, and then those of New Jersey. His coming to London, and his rise through the ranks of the Underground Electric Railways of London was made possible by the support of the American shareholders, who saw him as one of their own and believed he would look after their interests, about which they were wrong. Stanley became General Manager of UERL in 1907 and managing director in 1910, and one of his first acts was to unite the three Tubes owned by the UERL under one management, which the American shareholders had specifically not wanted to happen, fearing the loss of capital gains (a misplaced fear since their shares were, as Stephen Halliday points out in *Underground to Everywhere*, 'virtually worthless').

Stanley – who became Lord Ashfield in 1920 – was a persuasive, charming man (very keen on women, and vice versa), who wanted to build himself an empire of transport in London. He smoked cigars and wore suits made by Henry Poole of Savile Row, which were known for their 'American cut'; he had a good sense of humour and a knack for publicity. On the evening of 13 May 1924, a baby girl was born on a Bakerloo train. The child was christened – Stanley had the world believe – Thelma Ursula Beatrice Eleanor (think about it), and Stanley agreed to be her godfather, with the proviso that, 'It would not do to encourage this sort of thing, as I am a busy man.' (The disappointing fact of the matter is the child was actually christened Mary Ashfield Eleanor.)

Frank Pick was a much chillier proposition. The son of a Methodist Lincolnshire draper, he grew up in York. After qualifying as a solicitor, he worked under George Gibb of the North Eastern Railway (and subsequently the Underground). The North Eastern was the biggest and most grown-up of the pre-grouping railway companies, being an early electrifier, the first railway to employ graduates, and a pioneer of market research and sophisticated advertising. The fastidious Pick lacked 'the common touch'. He didn't drink; he certainly did not smoke cigars, and when, during the Second World War, he crossed the path of a man who did, the chemistry was terrible, as we will see. For Winston Churchill, Pick was 'the impeccable busman'. He was a workaholic, who communicated by memos written in tiny handwriting – and always in green ink. He joined the UERL in 1906, and in 1912 he sent one of his terrifying green ink missives to Stanley complaining about the ineffectual way the

Underground Group advertised itself, and so Stanley put him in charge of Advertising and Traffic Development.

From then on, Pick devoted himself to rationalising London – a doomed project, but nobody has ever given it such a good go as Pick. On his own boyhood visits to the city from York he'd been fascinated and appalled by the place: 'There was too much of it; it was hopelessly confusing.' Using the highest standards of design, he sought to tidy it up, make it knowable. In a biography of Pick, *The Man Who Built London Transport* (1979), by Christian Barman, he is quoted as writing to a friend during the Great War, 'Another thing that seems to me so stupid is that here in London with unlimited opportunities one takes no advantage of them at all. When I lived in York or Newcastle I was much better able to know what was moving in things than I am now when I am in the middle of it.' Yet he would be responsible for the further expansion of London, to the point where the city once again dismayed him by its size.

In *The Bus We Loved* Travis Elborough writes that Stanley and Pick would have made a good cop show duo: 'Sunday nights ITV1 … Ashfield and Pick: *No Need to Ask a P'liceman*. Bill Nighy is Lord Stanley and Warren Clarke is Frank Pick in Murder on the Metropolitan Line … The Piccadilly Palaver … The Arnos Grove Assassin … Sorry, Mr Man Ray, we'll have to discuss this poster later, they've found another body in Dover Street.' For Elborough, their contrasting natures were 'essentially complementary' and we can see them working a quick one-two as early as 1908. It was Stanley who initiated the action …

On 26 February that year he called a meeting of the managers of the Underground lines, which resulted in the following press release:

The following railways, viz. Baker Street & Waterloo, Central London, Charing Cross, Euston and Hampstead City and

South London, District, Great Northern and City, Great
Northern, Piccadilly and Brompton, and Metropolitan have
agreed to adopt the word 'UNDERGROUND' so that the
Public may become accustomed to associate these lines as a
complete system of Underground railways, and that the word
'UNDERGROUND' may be used by them in connection
therewith, instead of the name of any individual Company, or
abbreviation thereof, or the word 'TUBE'.

Furthermore,

A sign containing the word 'UNDERGROUND' as well as a
large map of the 'Underground' System, to be illuminated at
night, will be placed on the outside of each Station on the
railways enumerated.

As regards the map, this was the beginning of an Aesop-like
fable – 'How the Underground lines got their colours' – because
they were all given a colour, although not the 'right' ones from
today's perspective. It was also the beginning of the path that
would lead to London Transport. The lines had realised that
they had better stop fighting each other, and stick together in
the face of the onslaught from the motor buses that were making
horse buses obsolete.

There would be a system of through-ticketing, and a unifying
slogan – 'Underground to Everywhere … Quickest Way, Cheapest Fare' – this having been suggested (the fact is somehow not
very surprising) by a fourteen-year-old schoolboy called Edwin
Parrington. Revenues began to pick up, modest dividends to
be paid. In 1912 the UERL was able to absorb London's largest
bus company, the London General Omnibus Company. Now it
could use the buses, with their low capital costs, to subsidise the
three Tubes and the District.

Meanwhile bus and tram competition was causing the Central London Railway to flounder after its early success, and as for the City & South London ... that had always floundered. In early 1913 the UERL was able to absorb them both. By now it had also acquired several tram companies and had become known as either the Underground Group or, more sinisterly, The Combine. Of the Underground lines, only the Waterloo & City (which nestled comfortably in the bosom of its main-line parent, the London & South Western Railway), the maverick Metropolitan (which was still determined to make it into the big time on its own) and the Met's strange-looking adopted child, The Big Tube, remained outside the embrace of the Underground Group.

Although Stanley was the political operator while Pick was the aesthete, it was Stanley who made the early running in Underground design. In the conflicting accounts of the evolution of the Underground logo, Stanley is usually credited with being the initiator. He had, perhaps, been impressed by the stark and simple station names on the Paris Metro. He blended these with the wheel imagery of the London General Omnibus Company to create a blue bar with the station name written in white upon it, and a red circle behind. The circle of the 'bull's-eye' was to distinguish the station name from the surrounding advertisements.

This bull's-eye first appeared on District stations from 1908, and Frank Pick would oversee its refinement during the First World War. For him, the bull's-eye was too blob-like. It did not 'hold the eye'. He may have been influenced in his thinking by the logo of the Young Men's Christian Association, which took the form of an inverted red triangle with a bar through it. The graceful thing about that triangle was that it was hollow, except for the bar running through it, and Pick would hollow out the red blob behind Stanley's blue bar.

The purpose of the roundel – as the bull's-eye was coming

to be called – was to carry the names of the stations, and therefore it had to harmonise with the lettering that spelled out those names. This was the beginning of the spread across the network – in station signage and also posters – of a plain and pure typeface designed for the Underground by a refined and venerated calligrapher called Edward Johnston, and officially called Underground Railway Block. In *Just My Type: A Book about Fonts* (2010) Simon Garfield describes Johnston as 'a gaunt, fine-boned man with a full moustache', and there's a picture of him at work with a quill pen that makes him look as other-worldly as a medieval sprite. Pick had wanted a font that would 'belong unmistakably to the times in which we lived', and Garfield writes of what was generally called Johnston Sans that it may be regarded as 'the first "people's typeface", the first to be designed for day-to-day use that was not associated with learning, political manifesto or class, but the need to travel'. The space between the letters is as important as the letters; there's a calmness about this that clashes with the mindset of the typical, flustered commuter, but not in such a way as to constitute a moral reproof; and there is a levity about the typeface. The dot of the 'i' for example, is a diamond. Look at that 'i' when under stress in a Tube station. It's like the wink of an eye.

There is nonetheless a moral *seriousness* about it that suggests a public service rather than a public company, and that was the direction in which the Underground was travelling. At the time when the typeface was being rolled out, Pick was becoming associated with the Design and Industries Association. It (like the Arts and Crafts Movement, to which it was heir) took its cue from John Ruskin's injunction to manufacturers – that they make 'what will educate as it adorns'. From his contact with the Association, Pick distilled the essence of his philosophy, expressed in a lecture in 1916, 'Everything is Made for a Use: The Test of the Goodness of a Thing is its Fitness for Use'. In *The Man Who*

Built London Transport Christian Barman provides a vignette of another disciple of the Design and Industries Association, and a friend of Pick's, Harold Curwen. Curwen had inherited a printing business in Plaistow, east London. In 1915 the government appealed for scrap metal to help the war effort. Curwen gazed at the 'clever, fussy, pretentious Victorian typefaces spread about his composing room floor' and felt a wave of revulsion. He sent away more than 200 founts of type, retaining just one plain one, Caslon Old Face. He became a martyr to his philosophy; one of his main clients, West Ham Corporation Tramways, 'furious to receive their noteheadings set in Caslon … abruptly closed their account'. This was the revolutionary wave that Pick was riding.

PERSUADING PEOPLE TO MAKE JOURNEYS IT HAD NOT OCCURRED TO THEM TO MAKE: THE UNDERGROUND POSTER

We will continue with Pick, and another aspect of his vision of a corporate identity for the Underground: his commissioning of posters. Pick's job was both 'advertising' and 'traffic development'. In fact, he would straddle the worlds of engineering and art: he commissioned both posters that encouraged people to use the Underground lines and also new Underground lines themselves.

The Underground made money from renting poster space to other firms. Posters were the chief advertising medium of the time; they were also the graffiti of the time, the Johnston font being a reaction against their clutter of typefaces. But Pick would claim the poster for art through his work with such eminences as Paul Nash, Graham Sutherland and the American Edward McKnight Kauffer.

The first notable posters commissioned by Pick were by John Hassall (creator of the cherubic, skipping, Jolly Fisherman, who found Skegness 'so bracing'), and they showed an unexpectedly whimsical aspect of Pick's character. One of these, *When in Doubt Take the Underground* (1913), depicts a dazed, Chaplinesque man consulting his watch and looking perplexed. Well, he would look perplexed – he hasn't yet noticed the light of the Underground station sign behind him. The posters that followed over the next thirty years might be read as an exercise in the education of the little man. He would be told about one-off entertainments: Trooping the Colour, Derby Day, the Third Test Match at The Oval, with the nearest stations listed. He would on occasion be bluntly instructed to move to an address on one of the new Underground extensions: for example, *Move to Edgware* (1924). More often, he would be encouraged to live life to the full, especially insofar as this involved travel in the off-peak or at weekends, because the main purpose of the poster campaign was, in the words of Frank Pick, to 'persuade people to make journeys it had not occurred to them to make'. The little man would be peremptorily told, *It's a Bank Holiday, Go Out*. One Pick-commissioned poster of the 1930s showed an oil painting of a raucous West End pub, and I once asked a curator of the London Transport Museum what it had been promoting: 'Oh you know,' he said, 'just ... going to the pub.'

Punch resented this straying of the Underground into extra-curricular areas, and in 1921 it retaliated:

> To the directors of the Underground ... We like looking at your pretty posters. But do you seriously believe that anyone who has not got to go on your wretched railway already will be induced to go on it by seeing a picture – even a picture of a barge labelled BARNES? If you didn't spend so much money on trying to persuade people to go to Barnes you would be able to take me to Charing Cross for a reasonable fare.

But in *Studies in Art, Architecture and Design* (1968) Nikolaus

Pevsner would write of Underground posters that 'no exhibition of modern painting, no lecturing, no school teaching, can have had anything like so wide an effect on the educatable masses.'

He was referring particularly to the posters of 1930–40, which would become increasingly confident and modernistic. They highlighted the technical dynamism of the Underground, using imagery redolent of the Futurists, and much use of the words 'Power' and 'Speed'. The figurative ones also attest to an almost triumphalist confidence by showing an upmarket Underground clientele. In the presence of these glitzy types, our little Chaplin-esque man might have felt ill at ease. For example, *The Playgoer Travels Underground* (1930), by Charles Pears, shows a couple arriving at a restaurant for a late dinner – he in his dinner jacket, she in her fur stole – who look as though they *actually* travel by chauffer-driven car, and the deep bow with which the waiter is greeting them suggests the same. The Underground begins to seem almost decadent, a bad influence. A poster of 1938 by Marc Severin asked the subversive question, 'Why go Home?' Another poster ordered, 'Play between 6 and 12.' The aim in both cases was to stagger the rush hour, but the charm of these productions from our perspective is that they show a London in which people do more than just watch television in the evenings.

The number of self-promoting posters put out by the Underground has declined ever since the war. Colour photography has undermined the poster. The main 'spend' is on digital and radio advertising, and although some of its posters (now commissioned for it by agencies) still aspire to be more than mere adverts, the artistic credibility of London Underground rests with the 'Art on the Underground' programme, which makes parts of stations into what are in effect art galleries for the display of works by 'young and aspiring' artists. I put it to Richard Parry, Deputy Managing Director of the Underground, that being so packed, the system couldn't handle any more passengers, and so didn't

Undergound posters by (clockwork from top left) Verney
L. Danvers, Charles Pears, Mark Laurence and John Hassall.
As commissioned by Frank Pick, they sought to make the
Underground synonymous with London and London synonymous
with pleasure. The equation was all the easier to accept, given that
the posters were works of art in themselves.

advertise for them. 'I think we would be in the business of promoting the right mode choice,' he said, after a longish pause for
thought. 'For instance ... Leicester Square to Covent Garden ...
we might point out that it was quicker to walk.'

THE END OF WALKING
(AND THE EXPANSION OF LONDON)

If Pick and Ashfield began by persuading people to make journeys they didn't strictly have to make, they would – as we shall
see – end their careers having created a much-expanded city
into which millions were locked into a daily commute by rail. As
Punch wrote, in its spasm of reaction against Pick's posters, 'Man
is born free and is everywhere in trains.'

Buses could not cover the distances involved; as for walking, that was becoming passé. In 1846 Charles Pearson had
complained that the poor man was chained to the spot, lacking 'the leisure' to walk. But people still *did* walk across London
at that time, or perhaps it would be more accurate to say that
they trudged. In *London: The Biography* Peter Ackroyd writes:
'Workers walked to the City from Islington and Pentonville,
but now they came in from Deptford and Bermondsey, Hoxton
and Hackney, as well. It has been estimated that, in the 1850s,
200,000 people walked into the City each day.' Ackroyd identifies the last man to have walked every London street as the poet
and historian Thomas Babington Macaulay, who died in 1859.

If anyone walked every street of modern-day London, they'd
probably have a television programme made about them. In
Bleeding London (1997), a novel by Geoff Nicholson, a character
takes three years to walk every street, blackening them out in
his *A to Z* as he goes. I read about this novel in *Walk the Lines*
(2011), by Mark Mason, who did not himself walk every street in
London but conquered his own 'horizontal Everest' by walking

the length of every Underground line. The book conveys a fascination with the Underground, and with the sights that can be
glimpsed by not being on it. For example, 'Round the corner on
Hyde Park Gardens a van bears the logo, "Stephen Fry Plumbing
and Heating Limited".'

The period from 1930 to 1950 was one of continuous suburb-
building. In *London: A History* (2009) Jeremy Black writes: 'The
sprawl was aided by lax planning regulations, as well as the break-
up of estates, in part due to death duties, ... the low price of land,
and the post-war agricultural depression which encouraged
farmers to sell land in order to survive.' The picture is blurred
by the changing definition of Greater London. During the inter-
war period the term meant the area covered by the Metropolitan
Police District, a bigger territory than 'Greater London' as admin-
istered by the Greater London Council, which would succeed the
London County Council in 1965. But by the first measure, the
population of Greater London increased from about 7.5 million
in 1911 to 8.7 million in 1939 which second figure, as Black notes,
represented 'about a fifth of the nation's population'. As the suburbs expanded, the population of the centre contracted by half a
million, partly because the salubrious suburbs became available
with railways to serve them, and partly because office developments pushed up rents. The whole of central London began to
be what the City had already become: a place to enter and depart
from in diurnal rhythm. As Mr Aked observes in *A Man from the
North*, by Arnold Bennett: 'Why, the suburbs are London! It is
alone the concussion of meeting suburbs in the centre of London
that makes the city and the West End interesting.'

A new type of commuter was emerging. Whereas in the late
nineteenth century, he had commuted by steam railway from a
terraced house in a district we would now consider 'inner-city' –
such as Islington, Hackney, Brixton – and had called himself a
'clerk', he was now an 'executive' and came in by electric train from

a semi in Harrow, Hendon, Epsom or Sidcup, his former house having been given over to multiple occupation by poorer people displaced from the central slums. The first type of commuter had been sneered at in *The Diary of a Nobody* (1892), by George and Weedon Grossmith, in the person of Mr Charles Pooter, husband of Carrie, 'After my work in the City, I like to be at home. What's the good of a home if you are never in it? "Home Sweet Home", that's my motto.' But John Betjeman preferred Pooter to the commuters of later years. His poem 'Thoughts on *The Diary of a Nobody*', concludes:

> Dear Charles and Carrie, I am sure,
> Despite that awkward Sunday dinner,
> Your lives were good and more secure
> Than ours at cocktail time in Pinner.

The electrification of the main-line railways to the south of London fuelled this growth, but the Underground was also very complicit, as we are about to see. Where the train lines went, the house builders followed. The cut-and-cover lines had already invaded the countryside; now the Tubes would do the same. Even with the additional fare revenue they brought, these expansions would not have been justified in purely commercial terms, but now the context was more grandiose. Under Frank Pick and Lord Ashfield – as we are now going to have to start calling Albert Stanley – the Underground would become an instrument of social policy. London would counteract economic depression by continuing to manufacture the most important product of all: itself.

The first Tube to invade the countryside would be the Bakerloo. In 1913, as noted, it had arrived at Paddington. By 1915 it had reached Queen's Park, where it emerged from its tunnel to run alongside the newly electrified lines of the London & North

Western Railway, and from early 1917 it shadowed these as far north as Watford Junction. So the Bakerloo went from being 2½ miles long to 14 miles long and – as they say in the shipping forecast – it rather 'lost its identity' at the northern end, having become entangled with a main-line railway. (The Metropolitan would also go to Watford – in 1925.)

The Bakerloo service would be cut back to Stonebridge Park in 1982, before crawling back north towards the present terminus of Harrow & Wealdstone. But enough of this yo-yoing. The point is that by the inter-war years this alliance of Tube and main-line had done its work in helping make north-west London. 'Helping', that is, because another enterprise would be equally important in the same neck of the woods, and in this case Stanley and Pick were not involved.

BY THE WAY: METROLAND

We have seen that the Metropolitan escaped into its Extension Railway, or what it liked to call its 'country branch', by creating those two mouseholes at Baker Street. The aim was to develop suburban traffic beyond the reach of competition from those annoying buses. But there would be an incidental bonus for the Met …

It built its branch in normal railway fashion. That is, the Metropolitan bought the land either by compulsory purchase or by an arrangement with the landowners whereby it might – for the mutual convenience of buyer and seller – buy more than was strictly needed for the route. Railways usually *would* buy more than was needed in order to gain wriggle room – to dodge objections to any given kink of the route. The normal rule is that, after construction of the line, these surplus lands are sold back to the original vendors, so they can profit from the increased values a railway brings (which Frank Pick once estimated as a quadrupling of value). But as Stephen Halliday writes in *Underground to Everywhere*, 'thanks to some strong advocacy in Parliament by the supporters of the Metropolitan Railway, the Acts which had set up the company allowed it to retain such surplus land in its own possession.' Whereas the other lines triggered property development by third parties, the Met became a property developer *itself*, creating settlements that were in turn expanded by third-party developers.

The countryside that would be developed is shown in flickering black-and-white footage taken from a Met train riding along the Extension Railway in 1910. From the perspective of 2012 the landscape is beautiful: trees, thatched roofs, country inns. By Edwardian standards it was nothing special, but on what John Betjeman called 'these mild home county acres' the Metropolitan would create Metroland, a series of Tudorbethan havens for the office toilers of London, destroying the mildness of those acres in the process, of course.

Between 1919 and 1932 a booklet called *Metro-land* was published annually in order to promote the lifestyle and houses of Metroland. (I can't be doing with that hyphen.) They were written with a strangulated lyricism. Metroland was a 'verdant realm' set on 'gentle, flower-decked downs'; houses were 'homesteads' (and they were set on 'estates', at least until the London County Council began to build its own 'estates' for London's poor, thus giving the word a downmarket association). The houses in the booklets were shown with large gardens, demonstrating the influence of the turn-of-the-century Garden City Movement. The railway, with its 'fast and luxurious electric trains', was somewhere distant on the horizon, whereas the vibrations of the trains had cracked Mr Pooter's garden wall in his earlier, more central suburb of Holloway. Actually, most of the Metroland houses were cheap semis, costing about £400 (£20,000 in today's money), but they offered a new way of living: owner occupation.

This was promoted by the Conservative government from 1923 – by means of a subsidy to builders and tax breaks for building societies – in order to meet a housing shortage and alleviate economic depression. The booklet of 1922 included a poem speaking of Metroland as soothing 'town tired nerves, when work-a-day is o'er'. It was a place, 'Where comes no echo of the City's roar'. But that is just what did come, and some writers – especially George Orwell in his novel *Coming Up for Air* (1939) – would denounce the Metropolitan for its destruction of the countryside. Others seemed more interested in the social comedy.

In 1973 John Betjeman's television documentary *Metroland* was first broadcast. It begins, 'Child of the First War, Forgotten by the Second', but the documentary itself would revive the memory of Metroland for the generation that came after. Here was a late-middle-aged man passing on a childhood memory. In *Betjeman* (2006) A. N. Wilson writes, 'If it is true that in death all the scenes of a past life flash past before you, then this television-poem by Betjeman – it is too good to be described as simply a "programme" – took him back through the suburban outskirts of London he had known and loved and love-hated since boyhood.'

Television presenters are supposed to look at the camera, but Betjeman would look sidelong, intriguingly evasive, and the documentary is full of ambivalence. In essence, Betjeman's poetry and prose reveal that he loved the inter-war suburbia of Metroland more than the suburbia it had evolved into by the 1970s, but he loved the countryside more than either. He begins in Neasden, where the cheapest Metroland homes were built. He meets a keen birdwatcher and gives him plenty of rope with which to hang himself. The birdwatcher declares, 'There are something like 400 varieties of house sparrows within a half a mile of my home.' Betjeman's aim is to show us the Seventies' heirs of the 'clerks turned countrymen' who originally bought

into the Metroland vision. In more desirable Pinner, he observes
the residents of quite expansive villas cleaning their cars while
'Crazy Horses' by The Osmonds blares from a transistor. Early
adverts for Metroland mentioned that the properties had 'running at the back of the houses so that a car may be kept', and later
there was 'space so that a garage may be built'. The proximity of
nearby roads was boasted of immediately after mention of the
nearest station – this from a company that regarded the car as
an instrument of leisure rather than as a rival to the train. At still
smarter Moor Park, where there is a famous golf club, Betjeman
swings at a ball and completely misses. With typical archness, he
says, 'One of the joys of Metroland was the nearness of goff to
London' (it was important to leave the 'l' out of golf if you wanted
to advance in inter-war society), and one early map of Metroland
reduced suburban life to its caricature essence, the key indicating
'Metropolitan Railway', 'Roads', 'Golf Courses'.

Metroland developments became smarter and leafier the further they were from central London. Approaching the end of the
line, Betjeman says, 'The houses of Metroland never got as far
as Verney Junction. Grass triumphs, and I must say I'm rather
glad'. Yet he was obviously susceptible to the genuine charm of
the project. There is gentility as well as mock-gentility in the
brochures, innocence as well as mock-innocence in lines such as

Land of love and hope and peace,
Land where all your troubles cease
...
Waft, O waft me there

(from a poem, written by George Robert Simms, in the 1919
brochure). Betjeman was particularly attached to early electricity (the Met was electrified to Rickmansworth by 1925, it will
be recalled). Electricity made everything a treat, and so, from

his poem 'Middlesex': 'Gaily into Ruislip Gardens/Runs the red electric train', or, from 'The Metropolitan Railway', 'Early Electric! With what radiant hope/Men formed this many-branched electrolier'. That poem is subtitled 'Baker Street Station Buffet', and I wonder if it wasn't Baker Street, the 'worn memorial' of Metroland and HQ of the Met, the place where its dreams were plotted, that Betjeman really loved.

Metroland – the documentary – begins in the restaurant of Chiltern Court, the block of luxury flats that has surmounted Baker Street station since 1929. It was a veritable epicentre of Underground-ness. Arnold Bennett and H. G. Wells lived there, as did Underground poster artist E. McKnight Kauffer – and the presenter of *Opportunity Knocks*, Hughie Green, who had a giant model railway in his flat. If you board a Met train about to travel along the 'Extension Railway' from Baker Street into the modern-day Metroland, you may notice a left-behind poster on the platform advertising 'Chiltern Court – London's Newest Restaurant', which is not *quite* true. The Chiltern Court restaurant was a fittingly camp jumping-off point for Metroland. It was a place of pomaded tail-coated waiters, of 'perfect cuisine' and 'faultless service'.

Betjeman sits there at the beginning of his film. 'Are we at the Ritz?' he asks.

No. This is the Chiltern Court Restaurant … Here the wives from Pinner and Ruislip, after a day's shopping at Liberty's or Whiteley's, would sit waiting for their husbands to come up from Cheapside and Mincing Lane. While they waited, they could listen to the strains of the band playing for the *thé dansant* before the train took them home.

A few years later the restaurant closed, and in his book *Betjeman Country* (1983) Frank Delaney transcribes a note he saw written on brown paper and pinned to the shuttered entrance: 'Ann – hope you get to see this message, sorry about wrong directions. The Alsop Arms is on Gloucester Place remember. Hope to see you there later on. Bye for now and love Brian. X.' You can always rely on the Seventies for bathos. What was the Chiltern Court Restaurant has long since been a chain pub, but at least it's a Wetherspoon's chain pub, where the beer's decent, and at least it's called the Metropolitan Bar, and retains the crests of the Metropolitan Railway around the walls.

Metroland was almost the Metropolitan's last adventure before it was absorbed into London Transport, but not quite. In 1932 it built a further extension between Wembley Park and Stanmore ... which proved the wilful Met to be like a bear in a child's storybook, reaching up high for honey from a bees' nest, only to have the whole nest collapse onto him.

The new extension overloaded the tracks into Baker Street. The Metropolitan wanted to construct its own relief line into Baker Street, but since this was a highly built-up area, that line would have had to be in a long tunnel – and an extra-wide one at that, to accommodate the big trains of the Met: an expensive business. Instead, Stanmore would be served – from 1939 – by a new, northern branch of the Bakerloo Line, running mainly on the surface. The Met's own trains would run 'express' from Baker Street to Finchley Road, then to Wembley Park. The stations in between were closed in November 1939 and – in most cases – duplicated on the new Bakerloo branch. But there was no new namesake for the two stations immediately north of Baker Street: Lord's and Marlborough Road. The surface building of the latter was a Chinese restaurant for a long time and is currently hidden behind builders' screens. The former had only been called Lord's – at the suggestion of the MCC – since June 1939. Before that it had been called St John's Wood.

Lord's is sorely missed, especially by cricket fans who object to carrying their picnic hampers and beer cans the half-mile from the new St John's Wood station. If they spent less time consuming picnics and beer, they might find it easier, but still the cry goes up 'Re-open Lord's station!' and it is never quite stilled, even when you point out that the hotel now called the Danubius Regent's Park has been built on top of it. Perhaps if London Underground were to call St John's Wood station Lord's, then the cricket fans might *think* it was nearer. (Some readers may be less concerned with the fate of Lord's and more preoccupied with the fact that, surely, the Bakerloo does not go up to Stanmore. It stopped doing so in 1979, when – in what was becoming a farcical game of pass the parcel – the branch became the northern part of the new Jubilee Line.)

Incidentally, while Betjeman kept his tone light in his *Metroland* documentary, he had, back in 1960, written of an un-named 'High Road' in the main Metroland county, Middlesex:

> Black glass fascias of chain stores, each at a different height
> from its neighbour, looked like rows of shiny galoshes on the
> feet of buildings. Corner shops and supermarkets seemed to
> be covered in coloured plastic, like the goods they sold. All too
> soon the wrappings would be torn off and left to blow about
> municipal rose beds and recreation grounds. Somewhere, if I
> had dared to raise my eyes above the crowded pavement, there
> must have been sky.

CHAPTER NINE

NORTHERN AND PICCADILLY

ANOTHER MONSTER: THE NORTHERN LINE

The railways that would be fused to create the unwieldy Northern Line were the City & South London and the Charing Cross, Euston & Hampstead Railway, known as the 'Hampstead Tube'. The former, it will be recalled, was absorbed in 1913 into the portfolio of the Underground Electric Railways Limited, which had lately finished building the latter from Charing Cross to Camden, where the line bifurcated to Golders Green and Archway.

House builders were following that Golders Green prong with particular avidity because it went into open farmland. The speculators were nominally independent of the railway but may have included among their number some American cronies of Charles Yerkes who shared the epiphany he experienced on his visit to the verdant terrain of Edwardian north London. We don't know exactly what brought on that epiphany, but we can be pretty sure it was something to do with money. Land values at

Golders Green had risen rapidly from the moment the line was proposed, but they did so in a climate of acrimony.

The first controversy was over the effect the line would have on Hampstead Heath, which it passed beneath on its way from Hampstead to Golders Green. Even though the tunnels were to be 200 feet below ground, the Hampstead Heath Protection Society predicted they would loosen tree roots and suck away moisture. The Borough of Hampstead eventually gave permission for the line, providing a station were built between Hampstead and Golders Green, so the railway might serve the Heath by bringing visitors to it. This was Bull & Bush, which, as we have seen, was built but never opened.

The Hampstead Tube had also come up against the social reformer and philanthropist Henrietta Barnett, owner of a weekend cottage on the Heath, and the great matriarch of 'Not in My Backyard'. She counteracted the development of Golders Green by raising funds to buy 80 acres of land to the east of the proposed station, and here the Hampstead Heath Extension was created. On a further 250 acres of land she founded Hampstead Garden Suburb, the rationale being that if the countryside of north London were to be developed, then it would be developed in the right way. 'The Suburb', as it is known to its residents, was a spin-off from the Garden City movement. It was meant to provide homes for all classes – a vision most emphatically not fulfilled, as anyone who tried to open, say, a pub within its boundaries would quickly discover. The Arts and Crafts houses, divided by hedges and not walls, are populated exclusively by the upper middle classes.

It was an anti-Underground development, and indeed most of its houses are a long walk from Golders Green tube station. It seems odd therefore that Frank Pick should have bought a house in the Suburb, except when you recall that his own doctrine of 'Fitness for Purpose' had its roots in the Arts and Crafts

Movement. (He lived on Wildwood Road, where there is a blue plaque, but he is not listed among the notable residents on the Wikipedia page about the suburb, whereas Vanessa Feltz, for example, is.)

Meanwhile, Golders Green was growing fast. Whereas there had been precisely one house – a farmhouse – when the Tube arrived, by the time of the First World War there were 500. In the 1920s Golders Green was promoted by the Underground Group posters – 'A Place of Delightful Prospects' – as looking more like Hampstead Garden Suburb than it actually did. It was a dilute version of the Suburb, with smaller, less cottage-y houses, fewer trees and narrower roads. The trains running from there were always packed, even though there was no option of taking a Bank branch train from Golders Green, because the two components of the Northern Line were not yet integrated. You always had to change at Euston if you wanted to go to the City from Golders Green. That was about to be rectified, and not to help people who needed to get to work, so much as to help people who didn't have a job at all.

In 1921 unemployment rose sharply. This prompted the coalition government of Lloyd George to pass the Trade Facilities Act, by which the Treasury was enabled to provide loans at preferential rates ('cheap money') to subsidise job creation. It was the start of an era of heavy government investment in the Underground, much of it lobbied for by that skilled networker Lord Ashfield, who had made useful contacts while President of the Board of Trade during the First World War.

The first project for which he obtained finance was the joining of the Hampstead Tube to the City & South London, the first connection being made by the burrowing of a line between Camden (bifurcation point of the former) and Euston, terminus of the latter. This junction could be thought of as a pair of scissors opened out. It was designed to enable ease of flow from two northern lines to two southern ones, or vice versa. That sounds (relatively) simple, but if you look at a diagram of the tunnels … it's like an Escher drawing. Follow any one tunnel with your eye, and it immediately goes somewhere you didn't expect, and this over-ambitious entanglement is the reason your train almost always has to wait before entering Camden. The link was opened in April 1924, the too narrow tunnels of the City & South London having been widened to facilitate it.

In 1924 the line to Golders Green was extended to Edgware. In fact, Edgware was already served by a main-line railway – the Great Northern – but it was the coming of the Underground that promoted it from village to suburb (all right then, 'Garden Village'). The extension caused fury in Hampstead, where southbound trains began to arrive fully loaded with the hoi polloi of rapidly growing Edgware, Burnt Oak, Colindale, Hendon, Brent and Golders Green. On the journey to work dignity could not necessarily be maintained. In 1915 Ashfield had declared overcrowding to be 'a permanent feature of the rush hour operation of trains'. It was the price to be paid for the alleviation of congestion on the streets. At the time of writing, overcrowding is worse than ever in the peak hours as a result of the rapidly rising population of the city, and it has been a common feature of the off-peak since the introduction of the Travelcard in 1983.

In 1926 the two parts of the nascent Northern Line were also nipped together to the south, compounding the operation complexity. This was done by means of a link from Charing Cross (now Embankment station) on the Hampstead Tube to Kennington on the City & South London, with a new station – Waterloo – incorporated on the way. An under-river loop had originally been created at Charing Cross-now-Embankment so that it could function as the southern end of the railway. Trains coming into the station would go round this U-bend and head north again. Now the loop became superfluous, but part of it was retained for through-running: hence the extreme curvature of the northbound Northern Line platforms at Embankment. (The abandoned, under-river part of the loop was breached by bombs that fell on the bed of the Thames in the Second World War, but floodgates activated during air raids to protect the Tubes running under the river had come into play, and the line was not flooded.)

In conjunction with these works, the new joint line was extended south beyond Clapham Common to the village (but not for long) of Morden, with six new stations created on the way. (Whereas the stations on the northern extension were in homely, bucolic style so as to fit in with the garden village fantasy, the ones to the south were more distinguished, and we will be meeting their architect, Charles Holden, shortly.)

The extension north beyond Golders Green was above ground except for a tunnel between Hendon and Colindale; the southerly one was below ground. Here was a deep-level Tube reaching far into the south London suburbs, and the tunnel between East Finchley and Morden via *Bank* – that being the long way round – was the longest in the world at 17½ miles, and remained so until the opening of the Channel Tunnel. Why deep-level? Because it ran through territory already built up. Why was it already built up? Because it was served by the main line Southern Railway, which had agreed to the Morden extension as a quid pro quo for the District not proceeding from Wimbledon to Sutton.

In *The Man Who Built London Transport*, Christian Barman writes that, 'The prospect of having to work a double train service starting on a single joint line to diverge on to a pair of lines, and then re-uniting on the other side of London to run on a single line again, was not received with much enthusiasm by the operating men.' There would have to be a great deal of 'weaving in and out of trains', partly because those going to the City would take ninety seconds longer to reach Camden Town than those via the West End. A friend who works for the Paris Metro tells me that the signallers on that thoroughly rational system, involving lines that in almost every case start from point A and finish at point B, with no divergences to points C and D, are in awe of the men who signal the Northern Line. They would appreciate taking on such a challenge themselves, but only for an afternoon or so, by way of a short intellectual game. They wouldn't care to do it day in, day out, for decades. A man who worked for the Underground once told me that if anyone complained persistently about the line, they would be invited to come to the control room at Coburg Street to watch the signallers at work. 'They expect to see a lot of blokes lounging around drinking coffees and having a laugh. When they see the intensity of concentration involved, they usually shut up.'

The joining of the two lines might have been designed to create operating difficulties, and in the Eighties and Nineties, this together with other problems caused by an ageing train fleet caused Dick Murray, transport correspondent of the *Evening Standard*, to begin referring to the Northern as the 'Misery Line', a name that stuck.

The south-pointing extension was, like the developments at the northern end, funded by a Trade Facilities grant designed to counteract unemployment and economic depression, a fact poignantly attested to by the creation of what are commonly called 'suicide pits' beneath the tracks in its stations. Officially, they are called '*anti*-suicide pits', which sounds less like an inducement to kill yourself, but then again, the pessimistic purpose of these trenches between the running rails was to facilitate the removal of dead bodies rather than the saving of lives. Yes, you might fall directly into the pit, the incoming train going above you, but you'd almost certainly encounter one of the two electrified rails on the way. The Morden pits were 1 foot 4 inches deep. The ones that spread across the network in the 1930s were

2 foot deep. They do not exist on the cut-and-cover lines, where the under-frame of the trains is supposed to provide 'greater clearance'.

After an inquest into an Underground suicide in 1921, the Westminster Coroner observed, 'There was something about the roar and rush of the Tube train which was terribly fascinating to a person if he were alone on the platform'. Alone-ness may be an important consideration. Two hundred people try to kill themselves under Tube trains every year, of whom half are successful. The number has not risen commensurate with the great increase in Tube usage of recent years, and my friend Stuart, who works on the Underground, says this is 'because people are embarrassed about doing it in front of a crowd'. He added, hauntingly, 'On a Sunday night back in the late Sixties, it was only you and the driver anywhere east of King's Cross'. In-house at the Underground, they are known as 'one-unders' or 'jumpers'. But in her novel *King Solomon's Carpet* Barbara Vine writes: 'Even those who cannot dive, who would not dream of diving into water, dive, not jump, in front of the oncoming train'. I cannot say whether this is true.

The new, joined-up line we are dealing with continued to be known by its two earlier names, although it was billed as a double act to the extent that posters would advertise 'Charing Cross – For Pleasure; Bank – For Business'. Portmanteau names were suggested: Mordenware, Medgway, Edgmorden, Edgmor. Whichever *Railway Magazine* journalist had described 'Bakerloo' as a 'gutter title' would have been spinning in his grave – providing he were dead, that is. 'Northern Line' was settled on in 1937, when it was being further extended, this time once again in a northerly direction (from Archway).

THE PICCADILLY LINE
(OR THE PICK-ADILLY LINE)

If the extensions to the Northern Line were the work of Ashfield, the roughly contemporaneous extensions to the Piccadilly
were driven through by Frank Pick.

The spur to action was the blockage at Finsbury Park, which – it
will be remembered – was the northern terminus of the Big Tube
and the Piccadilly Line. It was also a station of the Great Northern
main line, and any passenger wanting to proceed north from Finsbury Park had to either go by bus or tram – causing a rush-hour
scrimmage every day as thousands of commuters changed mode
– or use the Great Northern's trains. The company had made sure
of this by an Act of Parliament in 1902 banning Underground
extensions beyond Finsbury Park. By 1923 Frank Pick had risen
to Assistant Managing Director of the Underground Group; the
Great Northern was part of the London & North Eastern Railway; and there was a public campaign against its Finsbury Park
veto. Pick arranged for photographs of the rush-hour scrimmages
to be distributed to the press, and in 1925 the LNER caved in.

Pick began lobbying for an extension of the Piccadilly, and
the funding for this would come not from the Trade Facilities
Act but from equally dour-sounding legislation providing cheap
money for job creation schemes: the Development (Loan Guar-
antees and Grants) Act was passed by the government of Ramsay
MacDonald in 1929, in response to another spike in employ-
ment. It might be objected that most of the unemployment was
in the north of England, but unemployed industrial workers did
migrate to London to work on the extensions, which required
tunnel rings, cabling and concrete produced in the north.

Pick's final plan for the Piccadilly involved an extension northwards to Cockfosters and westwards from Hammersmith beside
the overcrowded District Line stretch towards Hounslow and
Uxbridge, the Piccadilly trains running as expresses between

Hammersmith and Acton Town. The plan would also involve the rebuilding of fifteen Piccadilly stations in central London.

Twenty-two tunnelling shields were used in the construction of the northern extension, which took just three years to build: between 1930 and 1933. It stands in relation to the two suburban branches of the London & North Eastern Railway (to Welwyn and to Hertford) like the middle stump of a cricket wicket, and Pick made the case that it would not therefore steal passengers from those branches. Rather, it would create its own passengers in an area where there was 'an entire absence of development'. The two branch lines are still there (operated by First Capital Connect and National Express East Anglia), and the Piccadilly still runs between them. If you step out of, say, Arnos Grove station and walk about, you can see the Edwardian villas that the big railway brought, and the Thirties semis the Tube brought, although according to the man at the ticket barrier, 'It still felt rural up here until the 1960s. There were lots of gaps between the houses. It was a great place to grow up because you still had bits of fields and trees, and then there were the marshalling yards and goods depots of the railway – I liked all that.' Today the big railway lacks all glamour. New Southgate station is a hellish bunker. The adjacent Victorian Gothic building that used to be the railway hotel now has buddleia growing out of it, and a sign proclaims 'Cars Bought for Cash' ... Whereas Arnos Grove Underground station, with its circular ticket hall, remains elegant, and contains a shrine to the man who designed it, whom we will be meeting in a minute. But first, a verdict on the Piccadilly Line as a railway.

The Pick plan combined expansion with the complete closure of three stations: Brompton Road, Down Street and York Road. Down Street is in Mayfair, and the locals were too posh for the Tube. At York Road, located in the fly-blown territory north of King's Cross, the opposite was the case. All human life is on the Piccadilly; the line is too cluttered with stations, having originated from three railways serving the congested area of central London, and having then been extended. It's unfortunate, therefore, that it should be the line that since 1977 has served Heathrow. When the British Airports Authority first proposed its Heathrow Express service from Paddington in 1988, London Transport responded with its own plan to run Tube trains express to the airport, partly using *District Line* tracks, which would have provided the fastest access by Underground. This ambitious and expensive proposal did not stop the Heathrow Express, which I refuse to use because of the television screen that blares at you the whole way. I stick with the Tube, and, being a north Londoner, any Heathrow flight I take is always preceded by – and often *exceeded* by – an hour and half on the Piccadilly.

HOLDEN

Arnos Grove station was designed by Charles Holden, and a portrait photograph of him is placed behind a window in a now disused ticket booth of the station. The booth was of the type called a passimeter. These stood like islands in the concourses of the inter-war Tube stations, and tickets could be dispensed through windows on either side. The early ones were connected to turnstiles, and a device – the actual passimeter – would count the number of passengers going through. Where they survive, they are not in use for selling tickets because (an indictment of modern London, this) they cannot be made bulletproof. Their function was to speed 'passenger flow' in the efficient and logical stations designed by the man in the photograph.

You can see why Charles Holden appealed to Frank Pick, who as Assistant Managing Director of the Underground group had broadened his artistic interest to include station architecture, and it's for the very same reason you wouldn't have wanted to attempt a night on the town with either of them. Holden,

Arnos Grove station, designed by Charles Holden, with all the
geometrical purity that characterised his work on the inter-war
Piccadilly and Northern Line extensions. This station contains
a small shrine to Holden, including a photograph showing a
forbiddingly puritanical-looking man with small glasses and a
red goatee beard. But he always put the passenger first, and his
stations are the most beautiful buildings in the suburbs in which
they occur.

like Pick, was from the north – Bolton in his case, although he'd moved to Welwyn Garden City, the model for Hampstead Garden Suburb, where Pick resided. Like Pick, he was a teetotaller from a nonconformist family. They had met in 1915, at the inaugural meeting of the Design and Industries Association, which promoted the doctrine of elegant utility: 'fitness for purpose'.

Christian Barman's description of Holden suggests another unworldly figure after the fashion of the calligrapher Johnston. He evokes

> a man of short stature with a calm, earnest face enlivened by the reflections from the round-rimmed gold spectacles he was never seen without. From each side of a lofty forehead, the forehead of a great chemist or mathematician, the hair hung down almost vertically; the little beard, meticulously trimmed, suggested an unimpressive chin.

Holden 'spoke little, in a soft, colourless voice'. The picture at Arnos Grove, being in black and white, spares the viewer the colour of that goatee beard: bright red. The fact that Holden's architectural practice had specialised in spartan and light-filled hospital interiors makes him seem more rather than less forbidding, but when it came to his work for the Underground, he always put the passenger first.

His first major commission was to design the stations on the Morden extension of the Northern Line. Pick wanted something more modern for this than the countrified stations on the northern extension of the same line. Whereas they were designed to fit in, Holden's stations to the south were designed to stand out. They are geometrically simple in grey Portland stone, with wide central windows into which is incorporated a stained-glass roundel. Further roundels were mounted on masts, like cherries on cocktail sticks, and overall the stations betokened a great confidence in the Underground's identity. The same theme would be pursued later in new station entrances for Knightsbridge and Leicester Square, and the latter (the entrance on the eastern side of Charing Cross Road) seems, in its purity, an antidote to the garish clutter of that part of the West End.

In 1928 Holden re-designed Piccadilly Circus station as part of the refurbishment of the central stations on that line. In fact, he created the Piccadilly Circus station we now know, with the subterranean concourse mimicking the Circus above, that focal point of the Empire. Whereas the Morden line stations may have seemed forbidding in their grey plainness, Piccadilly Circus is mellow and refulgent in luxurious marble and glass. There are retail booths around the perimeter of the circle, and in *Designed for London: 150 Years of Transport Design* (1995) Oliver Green describes the intended effect as that of 'a shopping street at night'. When rising up from the platforms today, on the escalators fitted in the Holden refurbishment, the traveller still feels himself to be at the centre of … something. Perhaps it is still the centre of the world, because there are always plenty of foreign visitors there, and there's always a concentration of them queuing at the Travel Information Centre to ask (and all these questions *have* been asked): 'How Do We Take the Tube to Piccadilly Circus?' or 'Can I Get a By-Pass?' or 'How do we get to Russell Crowe station?' or 'Do you sell Octopus cards?' (The last question is not as risible as it sounds, since the travel card of Hong Kong is called an Octopus.)

But if Piccadilly Circus really is still internationally significant, then the World Time Clock, which purports to show the time anywhere by some not immediately clear method involving a moving pointer and a flattened globe, would always be working. But it is not. In fact, it is always *not* working. So perhaps the effect of Piccadilly Circus is simply to transport that passenger back to the glamorous London invoked on the Underground posters of the inter-war years, where men in spats (Lord Ashfield loved to wear them) and cloche-hatted ladies 'touched the riches of the West End' – that is, went shopping before repairing to an Art Deco cocktail lounge.

Holden next designed what has been described as 'London's first skyscraper' – the headquarters of the Underground Group. 55 Broadway is a cruciform building in Portland stone, rising a dozen storeys high above St James's Park station. Just as one reads 'Morden' as 'modern' because of Holden's pioneering stations, so one reads '55' here as 'SS', or at least I do, because 55 Broadway reflects the Machine Age ethos behind the great liners being built at the time and, standing as it does on an acute corner, it seems to have a prow. Pick, who took up residence in a room on the seventh floor – north-facing for the steady light – had actually been consulted on the fixtures and fittings of the *Queen Mary*, and the interior of 55 is plushly carpeted and wood-panelled, as I would imagine the passenger quarters of a liner to be. Whenever Underground employees arrange to meet me there, they say, 'I'll meet you at 55 Broadway' in terms of reverence, never referring to it merely as 'the office'.

It was decorated with sculptures by such eminences of the day as Eric Gill, Henry Moore and Jacob Epstein, who had long been fingered as a rum cove by the British press for his many mistresses, his shabby sweaters, his preference for sculpting primitive-looking nude figures (some of his sculptures were destined to feature in a sort of peep show in Blackpool) and for generally being a Bohemian with a capital 'B'. In 1929 his first adornment of 55 Broadway was unveiled. The sculpture, *Night*, showed an enfeebled-looking man lying in the lap of a monumental female figure – a stylised version of Christ and Mary in the *Pietà* configuration, perhaps, but it provoked what the *Manchester Guardian* described as 'storms of criticism rising at times into terms of full-blooded abuse'. When a second Epstein sculpture called *Day* was revealed in July of 1929, the *Manchester Guardian* described the composition thus: 'A large father figure with a fierce face, flat and hard and round like the sun at noon, holds and presents a male child standing between his knees, while the child stretches up his arms towards the neck of the father, his face turning upwards in a gesture of reluctance to face his task.' The writer approved, concluding, 'Do we know that Epstein is bringing new beauty to our generation?' The answer was obviously 'No', because *Day* aroused fury in the press, and a jar of liquid tar was aimed at it. The trouble, in short, was that the child's member was too long.

Holden had commissioned Epstein, who was an old ally of his. But it was Frank Pick who had commissioned Holden, and so he offered his resignation. His future with the Underground Group – genuinely in the balance – was saved when Epstein took out his chisel and shortened the infant's member by 1½ inches, and I like to think that if he hadn't shortened the member, the Piccadilly Line might never have been *lengthened*, so important was Pick in that process.

It was the stations along that extension that would receive what are considered the masterpieces of Holden. He and Pick had made an architectural tour of northern Europe, and been impressed by the human-scale modernism of Dutch public buildings in particular. The Piccadilly stations used brick rather than Portland stone. There is Sudbury Town, a brick box with windows almost as tall as the building. There is the above-mentioned Arnos Grove, which is like a drum (and possibly modelled on Stockholm public library), and there is Southgate, which is quite clearly a flying saucer. My favourite is Boston Manor, which has a rectangular tower into which is slotted a slim, illuminated column, like a card being offered from a pack. All the stations acted as beacons at night, which seems poignantly over-ambitious. After all, how many people want to make *towards* a suburban Tube station at night? I once suggested to an architect that Holden's Tube stations were too superior to their surroundings, to the extent that they constituted an implied reproof. 'By that token,' he said dismissively, 'you could say that St Mark's was an implied reproof to Venice.'

CHAPTER TEN

1933 AND ALL THAT

THE LONDON PASSENGER TRANSPORT BOARD

The Underground Group was involved in the important business of government-sanctioned suburb-making, and yet it wasn't a public agency. It didn't even control all the public transport in London. It ran all the Underground lines except the Metropolitan, the Big Tube and the Waterloo & City. It ran some tram companies, but the LCC ran the trams of 'central' London (the very centre being off-limits to trams), and there were other municipal and private tram operators. The Underground Group ran most of the buses via the London General Omnibus Company, but its bus services were undercut by the independent bus operators – 'pirates' – who would swerve about the streets picking off bus queues.

There was a need for integration. Ashfield and Pick would have been only too delighted for the Underground Group to become a private monopoly, but the dapper and tactically shrewd Labour MP and London County Councillor Herbert Morrison (grandfather of the dapper and tactically shrewd Peter Mandelson) had campaigned throughout the 1920s for the municipalisation of transport in London. In 1929, when Morrison became Transport Minister in Ramsay MacDonald's second Labour administration, he modified his position. Transport in London would be run by a public corporation: a state-owned body with a commercial remit. It would run all the Underground railways, including the Met (but excluding the perennial stop-out the Waterloo & City); it would run all the buses and all the trams, but not the suburban overground railways.

Morrison worked on, and won over, Ashfield and Pick, and Ashfield sold the idea to Underground Group shareholders, who would receive stock in the new undertaking and a cash payment. Why did they cave in? Winston Churchill had called Morrison, the autodidact son of an alcoholic police constable, 'the New Man'; he was dangerous. Socialism might arrive in his wake, bringing outright nationalisation and worse compensation terms.

In the wake of the 1929 economic crash Labour lost the 1931 election, but Morrison's bill was taken up by the incoming National Government, with the further modification that the managing board would be selected by an independent committee rather than by the government. In *The Subterranean Railway* Christian Wolmar writes:

> … despite being separated from government in this way, London Transport would be able to benefit from the favourable borrowing terms which only state bodies, with their hundred per cent guarantee of solvency, can enjoy. London Transport was, therefore, one of the first big quangos – quasi-autonomous non-governmental organisations – long before the term was invented.

The London Passenger Transport Board (London Transport

for short) came into being on 1 July 1933. Ashfield was Chairman, Pick Vice-Chairman and Chief Executive.

It was deemed a successful organisation at the time and is fondly remembered as the very apex of British public service, partly because it continued the boldly expansionist policy and brilliant iconography of the Underground Group. Persistently high unemployment ensured that it would continue to receive 'cheap money', and in 1935 Ashfield and Pick took advantage to fund another programme of expansion, the Stalinist-sounding New Works Programme, to which we will turn after two brief diversions.

BY THE WAY: THE LOST PROPERTY OFFICE

The Lost Property Office was opened in 1933, an integrated operation for an integrated network. There used to be two 'shop windows' for the office at the north end of Baker Street. One said 'Lost Property', the other 'Enquiries'. 'Enquiries' has now become a Boots. In the remaining window, the last time I looked, some vinyl records were displayed: 'Have I the Right?', by the Honeycombs, 'Hello Dolly', by Kenny Ball and his Jazzmen, 'Downtown', by Petula Clark. There was also a primitive early mobile phone and a top hat. What was this clutter meant to suggest? Probably nothing more than the fact that this place houses things from the past, things that people used to have.

Until the late Nineties the reception was all dark wooden panels; now it's more like Barclays Bank. The 'losers', as they are somewhat pejoratively known, are reunited with their lost property, or it might be sent out by post. The charge for restitution varies from £1 to £20, depending on the value of the item. In deserving cases, the fee may be waived. In 2011 about 200,000 objects came into the office, a record number. Couriers constantly circulate the Tube stations and bus garages to collect the stuff.

The Lost Property Office, opened in 1933. Nothing is thrown away.
But uncollected items – including, on the author's latest visit,
a box of 144 condoms and a giant fluorescent orange synthetic
maggot – are sold off, given to charity, recycled, or retained 'to
illustrate the work of the office'. About 22 per cent of lost items
are returned to their owners.

Items left in taxis are also brought in, but they are viewed first by the police, which seems to me an implied insult to tube and bus users, as though a higher class of lost property – semi-automatic pistols or ministers' red boxes – is likely to be left in taxis.

Then again, the main part of the office is below ground, as though in solidarity with the Tubes. The lost property comes rumbling down a chute throughout the day, like prizes in a game show you wouldn't particularly want to win. Meanwhile, the staff of about forty are engaged in logging the items. On a recent visit, I looked over one clerk's shoulder as he entered the details of a suit. 'Type: casual. Colour: grey. Style: …', and here he hesitated for a while before selecting 'Other'. On the wall behind him, the office's mission statement was spelled out. 'Vision', it read, 'To reunite property with its rightful owner.' And it is very hard to argue with *that*. About 22 per cent of items are returned, but the figure is nearer to 40 per cent in the case of high-value items.

When I ventured beyond the receiving office into the subterranean antechambers and corridors in which most of the lost property is stored, I was immediately confronted by a giant orange maggot made of synthetic fur. On a shelf alongside it was a barrister's wig, two books – *The Writer's and Artist's Yearbook 1997* and *The Complete Book of Dreams* – and a traffic lollipop reading 'Stop: Children Crossing'. 'These items are "Miscellaneous"', a staff member told me, and they certainly were. Items uncollected after three months used to be sold off at Greasby's auctioneers in Tooting, which sounds just the kind of place that *would* sell off lost property. Now it's either sold off commercially to fund the office ('we are not in the business of making a profit,' I was assured) or given to a variety of charities or recycled. 'Nothing is chucked away.'

Some low-value items are kept, 'but only to illustrate the work of the office or as a snapshot of London at a particular time, not for the gratification of the staff'. One ante-room has a cockney theme, which is only fitting, given that this is a kind of plughole for the swirling debris of London lives. A photo on the wall is captioned: 'Arsenal's Peter Storey beats David Harvey of Leeds United from the penalty spot, Highbury, 11th September 1971'; there is also a West Ham shirt, a picture of Tommy Cooper, a placard reading 'Jack the Ripper Pub' and a box of 'Durex: 144 Ultra-fine Condoms'. Indicating this, my companion on the visit said, 'I bet losing *that* spoiled his weekend.'

For thirty-six years the Lost Property office was managed by Maureen Beaumont, and when I went there to interview her, back in the late Nineties, she told me people didn't seem embarrassed about what they'd lost. She'd known men collect stashes of porn, or blow-up dolls. 'And we had an American woman in here the other day, shouting about how she'd lost her vibrator.' She was telling me about some of the items that had come in during the previous days – a park bench, 2½ hundredweight of currants and sultanas – when one of her assistants came up to her carrying a polythene bag. 'Bit curious,' he said, passing it over. Inside were bones, possibly human. I asked if this could be the start of a murder inquiry, and Maureen sighed and said, 'Yes – I'll get the police to take a look.' But she wasn't in the least surprised.

I asked the current manager, Paul Cowan, whether he recalled the incident of the bones. 'Before my time,' he said, before adding rather beadily, 'you know there are a great many urban myths surrounding this office, don't you?' He relented somewhat, adding, 'We did have a person's ashes handed in.' These arrived at the office in 1999. The label said, 'W. Maile 5/10/98.' In 2007 there was an appeal for information on a television documentary about the Tube, and a member of the public began investigating. After genealogical research, he tracked down a Molly Schofield of Preston, Lancashire. The ashes were the remains of her father, William Maile, a veteran of the Normandy landings, who had been cremated in Preston in 1998 at the age of ninety-one.

Molly had spent happy times visiting London with him, and she decided to scatter his ashes under Westminster Bridge. She put the urn in a bag and put it on a luggage rack on a train that came into Euston – where the bag was stolen. It was then abandoned on a Tube line. The last that was heard from Molly Schofield, she was planning a return trip to London with her father. 'But I won't put the ashes on the luggage rack this time.'

When the office first opened, the most frequently lost items were umbrellas. Every white-collar professional carried one, but despite, or because of, that they were easily forgotten about. (The broadcaster Robin Day once said he lost an average of one umbrella a day.) In the 1930s, a quarter of a million umbrellas a year came into the office. Now it's more like 10,000.

A top ten of lost items in 2011 read:

1. Books
2. Bags
3. Clothes
4. Valuables (anything expensive – including wallets, cash, laptops, cameras, jewellery)
5. Telephones
6. Keys
7. Ops (i.e., 'opticals' – glasses)
8. Umbrellas
9. Jewellery
10. Pairs of gloves.

THE MAP

On the Embankment, on the outer wall of Temple station, there is a map of the Underground marked, 'This is an original London Passenger Transport Board map from 1932. It has been preserved for your interest.' But having once stood alongside it for half an hour on a fine summer's evening, I reckon about half the people who walk up to the map don't register the inscription and take it to be a depiction of the modern Tube. You can tell they're using it to plan their routes, even though the Bank branch of the Northern is still billed as the City & South London, and the Central Line is purple. Perhaps some of them walk straight up to the Temple ticket office and ask for a ticket to Southend, having read the little note on the map to the effect that District Line trains run regularly to that resort. (The service – beginning on the District before proceeding seawards by main-line tracks – ran from 1910 to 1939.) But to those of us familiar with the modern, straight-line Underground map – introduced a year after the Temple map, in 1933 – it's as though a disastrous sagging and melting of the lines has occurred.

The early Tube maps are, as David Leboff and Tim Demuth write in *No Need To Ask! Early Maps of London's Underground Railways* (1999), 'accidentally charming'. The first ones tended to show the lines superimposed on the streets. This implies modesty on the part of the lines: they were an adjunct to the streets, not an alternative to them. Then again, the individual lines showed little modesty in the face of their competitors. The maps of the Metropolitan would grudgingly show the District as a faint, threadbare thing, and vice versa. At the turn of the twentieth century, private companies might produce their own Tube maps, to advertise their businesses. For example, in 1900 the Public Benefit Boot Company produced its own map showing 'New Electric Railways', 'District Railways' (i.e., Met and District), a fairly arbitrary selection of 'Other Railways' and 'London Trams'. The map carried the giant-size suffix: 'Public Benefit Boot Company, 125 Edgware Road, W. For Good Boots.' The company premises were shown on the map by large red crosses that made them seem much more significant than mere Underground stations.

In 1908, as we have seen, Albert Stanley chaired the meeting at which the general managers of the lines agreed on a common map. The different lines acquired different colours but not, to modern eyes, always the 'right' ones. Yes, The Bakerloo was generally brown (although it had an interlude of being red), and the District was generally green. But up to the First World War and for some years afterwards the Central was almost always blue, for heaven's sake.

In the 1920s the man chiefly responsible for the Underground map was a certain F. H. Stingemore. Under him the background streets were comprehensively banished, stations became little circles, and exchange stations open circles. Good work, and had the pronunciation of Stingemore's name been evident from its spelling, he might be better remembered today. But I doubt it, because it was Stingemore's fate to be elbowed aside by a genius.

In 1931 Harry Beck first presented his first draft for a new type of Tube map to the Underground Group. Beck was an engineering draughtsman who had recently been laid off from a temporary position by that same Underground Group. His idea was to simplify what he characterised as not a plate of spaghetti but worse, 'vermicelli'. He proposed a map that stylised the system, so that all lines were shown as vertical, horizontal or diagonal, and the congested central area would be expanded for the sake of comprehensibility, as though, he later wrote, 'I was using a convex lens or mirror.' The idea was rejected.

In 1932, by which time he was back working for the Underground Group (but still only as a temporary), he tried again, and this time he was told that three-quarters of a million would be printed as pocket maps in January 1933. On both his first and second drafts, interchange stations were depicted as diamonds, but whereas on his first draft other stations were shown as blobs (as had become traditional on Underground maps), his second draft replaced the blobs with little horizontal marks called ticks. If, as has been suggested, Beck's map was influenced by electrical circuit diagrams, then the replacement of the blobs by the ticks was an important miniaturisation: a move, so to speak, from electricity to electronics. The ticks made an already clear map clearer still.

Later in 1933, by which time the Underground Group had become the London Transport Passenger Board, a poster version of the map was printed. Beck received 5 guineas for the printing of the pocket map, 10 for the printing of the poster, and this is all he would ever be paid – the equivalent of about £400 in today's money. Given the importance of the map in the corporate identity of the Underground, and its function as an alternative logo for the system, this does not seem enough.

Harry Beck didn't mind being paid so little, as long as he had control over the evolution of the map, and he maintained that he had been given that control, a point on which London Transport remained silent. The story of the next thirty years is well told in *Mr Beck's Underground Map* (1994), by Ken Garland. London Transport officials would either suggest, or just unilaterally inflict, crass changes on the map, and Beck might give way initially before trying to reassert his principles of angularity and elegance. Among the brainwaves from LT were: put a medieval-looking 'North' arrow on the map; write out the word 'station' after every interchange station; double the thickness of all lines within the Circle Line; show the Metropolitan and the District in the same colour; airbrush the outer stations in an insipid blue-green.

London Transport didn't appreciate Beck, even though his map was always popular with the public, and he seems to have existed in a blind spot even for the aesthetic Frank Pick. The top men were wary of the stylisation, and if you'd helped create the network, as these men had done, you might not want to see your creation caricatured for the benefit of people willing to pay it only scant attention. Certainly the map can be misleading. On some of the early Beck maps the distance between Wimbledon and

South Wimbledon on the Northern seemed to be about a third of the total width of London, when in fact they're less than a mile apart. The rule about compressing the distance between the outer stations also dictated that roughly a centimetre separated the four final stations on the east of the Central Line – Epping to Ongar – whereas that stretch is actually half the length of the entire Bakerloo.

Beck was described by one LT official as 'rather fretful', and you can see that from the photographs: a neat, balding, bespectacled man. He was obsessive about the map and slept with bits of paper under his pillow in case inspiration should strike about where to put Mornington Crescent. According to Ken Garland, Beck felt he'd 'never done justice' to Mornington Crescent. (While it is shown on the Tube maps as being a pimple on the Charing Cross side of the neck between Euston and Camden, it ought strictly speaking to be shown on the City side of the neck, even though City branch trains do not call at Mornington Crescent.)

But all Beck's ideas for his map were better than other people's ideas, and in 1960 he had an attractive shade of lilac in reserve for the Victoria Line, which was about to be constructed, and which he planned to represent as an elegant horizontal, reclining regally across the centre of London. But the Victoria Line would be kinked, and coloured a chilly and weak blue, because in 1960 Beck lost control of the map.

In that year a certain Harold F. Hutchison, Publicity Officer at London Transport, produced a version that might have been designed to give Beck a nervous breakdown, which it very nearly did. Hutchison put some station names in capitals and some in lower case, whereas Beck had always been required to capitalise them all, and write out the names in full. Hutchison wrote some names in full, some not: hence 'Edgware Road' and yet 'Bow Rd'. Most heinously of all, the word 'Aldgate' was split into 'Ald' and 'gate', cleaved in two by the Circle Line. Also Hutchison jettisoned the small curves by which Beck had softened his verticals, horizontals and diagonals at their intersecting points, so that his looks as if it was drawn on an Etch-a-Sketch. It was still a Beck map – just a very bad one. All the more galling, then, that Hutchison had the nerve to put 'Designed by Harold F. Hutchison' in the bottom left-hand corner. Beck's distressed letters to Hutchison are quoted in Ken Garland's book: 'In 1937, in return for my signature on a copyright form, I was given an undertaking that all future design work on the underground diagram would be given to me to do or edit, and that my name would always appear on it.' Hutchison replied with the deadest of dead bats. 'Thank you for your letter … I am not aware of any undertaking by my predecessors, but I shall be very happy to use your work again whenever a job arrives which would suit you.'

Beck remained embittered towards LT at his death in 1974. You might say he was another Tube martyr. In 1994 a reproduction of the first printed version of Beck's map was put up at Finchley Central station, with some details of his life, and the inscription 'A design classic – one man's vision.' Beck had lived in Finchley, and the plaque had been suggested by a letter to LT from Mrs Jean de Vries, who had friends who were friends of Harry Beck. A couple of years after the gratifying but unheralded appearance of the plaque, she thought it would be nice to have a proper, formal unveiling, and LT seemed keen on the idea. Further letters were exchanged, and suddenly they were less keen. No 'resources' were available for an unveiling, she was eventually told.

I met Mrs de Vries shortly after she had received this depressing communication. Over tea and cakes in her Finchley home she told me she had first met Beck in 1945, when she was fourteen. 'He looked old-fashioned even for the time. He was a typical English gentleman, always in tweeds – and always with a pen in his top pocket.' Also present at the tea was Joan Baker, Harry Beck's niece. She recalled: 'Whenever you went round to see Harry and his wife, Nora, Harry would be working on the map, which would be spread out on the floor. He'd be very polite. You could ask him any questions you liked about the map, but what you *didn't* have to do was stand on it.' When the discussion turned to why LT had gone cool on the idea of an unveiling, the cakes began to be passed with more urgency – agitation, almost. The suspicion was that lack of resources was a polite smokescreen, the true reason being that Mrs de Vries had proposed inviting Ken Garland, author of the above-mentioned *Mr Beck's Underground Map*. Mr Garland was also present at the tea party. He could not say for certain if he was persona non grata; nobody could. His book certainly makes Beck out to have been badly treated. Then again, the Beck plaque *was* put up, and it is still there today, on the southbound platform, and when I cycled to Finchley Central station recently, and asked if I could go through the barrier without paying, since I only wanted to look at the Beck memorial, the gateman smiled in approval and nodded me through. There is also a permanent exhibition devoted to Harry Beck in the London Transport Museum, and after years of the map appearing unsigned, his name has been restored: 'This diagram is an evolution of the original design conceived in 1931 by Harry Beck.'

If I may, I will add a personal footnote. As a journalist writing regularly about public transport, I scored two campaigning victories. The first was that I secured the removal of some plastic potted plants from the roof of the Burger King in Victoria Station. Their placement was consummately inept in that they: (a) made the Burger King look even viler than necessary; and (b) blocked the names of the stations appearing towards the bottom of the indicator boards. I admit that my 'campaign' – which involved one phone call to a press officer – was triggered by a letter from a reader, and that was also the case with my second victory.

On a version of the Tube map appearing in 1998 the Central Line was shown as going *over* the Metropolitan, Circle and Hammersmith & City at Liverpool Street, whereas it was traditional to show the Tube lines as going *under* the cut-and-cover ones (which reflects the true situation), and they were so shown in all other instances of the conjunction on that same map. I asked a Mr Lee Ginger, London Transport's Creative Service Manager, whether there was any good reason for the anomaly. 'No,' he said, disarmingly. 'It's a quirk. We'll change it next time we re-do the map.' And the Central Line has been back where it belongs ever since.

CHAPTER ELEVEN

NEW WORKS

THE NEW WORKS PROGRAMME

In June 1935 the New Works programme was announced. The most ambitious aspects involved extensions to the Northern and Central Lines. The first of these was called the Northern Heights programme, and this can be divided into what did happen as planned, and what didn't. What did happen was that in 1940 the Northern Line was extended, at first beneath and then along the lines of the London & North Eastern Railway from Archway to High Barnet, with a spur westerly over the Dollis Brook Viaduct (the highest point on the network, and therefore an opportunity for vertigo on the so-called Underground) to Mill Hill East.

What didn't happen was a series of other electrifications of other lines belonging to the London & North Eastern Railway, which would have further embellished – or complicated – the north of the Northern Line. The LNER line running south from Highgate via the pretty stations of Crouch End and Stroud Green to Finsbury Park was to have been electrified. This would have been a momentous connection, opening up the City to north Londoners, because in 1939 the plan for Finsbury Park overground station, as noted earlier, was to make it the northernmost point of the Big Tube. The overground line leading *north* from Highgate to Alexandra Palace via Cranley Gardens and Muswell Hill stations was also to be electrified; further electrifications would have created a connection between Mill Hill East and Edgware with a station on the way called, not – as would have been gratifyingly logical – Mill Hill West, but Mill Hill The Hale. A final electrification would have created a line probing north from Edgware to Bushey Heath.

This work was interrupted by the war, and there was no money to complete it afterwards. The success of the new High Barnet branch killed the prospective electrification of the Alexandra Palace branch, which continued to be operated by steam trains until 1954. The idea of an extension from Edgware to Bushey was killed by the coming of the Green Belt. Not only did Crouch End and Muswell Hill not get their electrified railways, they also lost their steam services, as those dwindled in the 1950s, and those places are now inhabited by a breed of bus users, doomed constantly to calculate how much more their already valuable houses would be worth if they were on the Underground. Just to rub it in, the signs of the abandoned electrification – remnants of power rails and conducting cables – are still mouldering in the shrubbery of what is now called the Parkland Walk, a nature reserve that follows the route of the old LNER tracks between Finsbury Park and Highgate. More than a hundred species of wild flower have been found along its length, if that's any compensation. Above Highgate Tube station, you can see the old Highgate London & North Eastern Railway station, looking both ghostly and very abandoned, but also strangely modern, since it had been prepared for the electrification that never came.

As for those people living west of Mill Hill East Northern Line station, they are permanently in mourning for Mill Hill The

Hale, the station so rudely snatched away from them (even if its name *is* a bit of a mouthful).

We now return to the Central, last seen in the early 1920s, by which time it had reached Ealing Broadway to the west, Liverpool Street to the east. During the 1940s, as part of the New Works programme, it was extended easterly to Stratford, from where it would run – as in the Northern Heights plan – over lines yielded up by the London & North Eastern Railway, these ones stretching out to Ongar. It would also extend westerly from North Acton over tracks of the Great Western Railway to West Ruislip.

The extension to the west is on the surface. The extension to the east – which is more interesting – comes above ground briefly at Stratford, then again at Leyton. After Leytonstone, it splits to go to either Snaresbrook or Wanstead. The latter branch is 'in Tube', as were the two following stops, Redbridge and Gants Hill, and these three were among the last designs for the Underground by Charles Holden. At Gants Hill he really let rip. If you want to get an idea of what the Moscow Underground looks like, you can go to Moscow, or you can take the cheaper option – for a Londoner – of going to Gants Hill. When it was being built, there was a department in London Transport called London Transport International. (*Somewhat* hubristic, you might have thought, but this was a time when Pick and Ashfield were at the top of their game.) The department had just been advising the man Stalin had appointed to oversee the creation of a prestigious Moscow Metro, Nikita Khrushchev, and some of the principles recommended had rubbed off in the building of Gants Hill. The station is beautiful, with pale orange tiling, and clocks with the roundel in place of numbers, but it is beautiful in a Muscovite way by virtue of the wide lower concourse with barrel-vaulted ceiling. There is a feeling, as with the Moscow Metro (I am told), of palatial proportion and no expense spared.

I was once shown around Gants Hill by the London Transport Museum curator, Oliver Green, who told me that the only giveaway from a subterranean perspective that you were in Gants Hill, a humble suburb, and not a place of more metropolitan grandeur, was the fact that there were only two escalators debouching into the concourse, both at the same end. 'Ideally,' said Oliver, 'there'd have been two at each end.' That's how they'd have done it in Moscow, for maximisation of 'passenger flow'.

Overall, the eastern end of the Central is a jumble of Victorian and 1940s' stylings. At Leytonstone the station was reconstructed to accommodate the arrival of the Central. Bending over backwards to find features of note in *London Underground Stations*, David Leboff comes up with 'curved, glazed skylights located in the canopy soffits'. But the preceding station, Leyton, remains 'largely as built' – in 1856, that is – hence 'valanced canopies supported by delicate iron pillars and brackets'. The lines on this stretch have the prettiest, most country-branch-like names of any on the network: Buckhurst Hill, Theydon Bois … and some of them really do look the part. In the late Nineties, I was told by an Underground press officer that a man patrolled the eastern end of the Central with a hawk trained to kill pigeons. At Fairlop, incidentally, you wouldn't be surprised to see coal bunkers. But just in case you might forget you're on the London Underground, there's a 'gap' at Hainault.

BY THE WAY: EPPING–ONGAR

I have said that the Central reached Ongar, 25 miles from central London, but that's less impressive when you consider that this ultimate stretch of the eastward extension of the Central Line – a project taking place under the heading *New* Works, remember – should have been operated by alternately pulling and pushing steam trains. Yes, I'm afraid the electric trains of 1949 went only as far as Epping. The single line beyond there would be taken over by the Underground from the London & North Eastern Railway, but it would be operated as a steam shuttle because there just weren't enough people at Ongar to justify electrification.

... Until 1957, that is, when the line was equipped with 'light' electrification, which sounds pleasant enough but meant only sufficient power to propel trains of two or three carriages. Passengers on those trains looked out on pretty fields in which sheep grazed, the development of the countryside roundabout having been inhibited by the Green Belt supported by the very man (Pick) who had been one of the drivers of the New Works programme. John Betjeman enjoyed riding on the line and said that, when he retired, he'd like to be the station master at Blake Hall, which was the stop before Ongar until it (Blake Hall) was closed permanently in 1981, its passenger footfall being down to six a day, or twelve, depending on whether you're counting passengers or feet.

Anyway, the Epping–Ongar had always been marginal. Even when it was part of the LNER its short trains had been emphatically 'Third Class Only'. By the early 1990s the shuttle was being used by about eighty people a day, and it was said – to me, by a man slightly inebriated in a pub in Leytonstone – that the line was only kept open so that, in the event of a nuclear attack, members of the Cabinet could be evacuated by rail to the nuclear bunker at Doddinghurst. The argument against this theory is that any government entrusting its fate to the Central Line would have to have been pretty naive. The argument in favour is that the Ministry of Defence did de-commission the bunker at about the same time that London Underground closed the Epping–Ongar line, which happened in 1994. In 1998 the line was sold to a private company who intended to operate a peak-hour commuter service, and did so for a while. (The nuclear bunker, meanwhile, was bought by a local farmer, who advertised it widely as

'The Secret Nuclear Bunker!') The line has since changed hands several times, and is now to re-open as a preserved railway (a railway for leisure only), running vintage diesels and electrics, but with the aim of restoring steam.

THE RED TRAINS (THE 38s)

Experts on the Underground abandon their normally pedagogic kindliness when it comes to rolling stock. It's for your own good, they'll tell you: the subject is too complicated. Stock may be designated by a date, or sometimes a letter. Today those who name stock are sometimes good enough to make the letter stand for something, as in 'S stock', to denote the sub-surface stock being introduced on the cut-and-cover lines, but in the past a letter might just represent a point reached in a wayward alphabetical progress, and some idea of the number of stocks that have existed is given by the fact that on the District Line alone, 'N stock' had been reached by 1935.

Even though the so-called Standard Stock built between 1923 and 1934 brought a measure of uniformity to the deep-level Tube stocks, it was not quite a single train type. In fact, a man who knows about these things once infuriatingly reflected in my presence, 'Each year brought new variations. In fact, the whole thing about the Standard Stock was that it was *not* standard.' But Standard Stock trains, as mentioned earlier, were the first to *look* like Tube trains. They dispensed with the end platforms and had automated air doors set into the carriage sides. The gatemen were thus out of a job, but guards survived, mainly to operate the doors and – it seemed – to prevent people from boarding via the guard's own door. (I would become tense, on trains with guards, as I watched another tourist lumbering up to the guard's door, knowing he'd just turned away three others in quick succession. This fourth idiot was really going to be in for it.) The days of the guards were numbered after the introduction of O.P.O. – that is 'one-person-operated' – trains on the Victoria Line from 1967, and the last of the breed were seen – usually looking suitably glum – on the 1959 stock on the Northern Line, until it was replaced, in a neat inversion, by the 1995 stock, which did not require guards.

It would be fair to say that seats have become smaller – and an Underground manager once told me that the ideal train would have no seats, and the whole platform-side of it would roll up and down like a venetian blind. It would be a cattle truck, in other words. It would also be fair to say that the only type of stock to have been universally loved is the 1938 Tube stock, introduced as part of the New Works programme. This stock was used on the Northern, Piccadilly and Bakerloo, on which latter line they lasted in regular service until the mid-1980s, although five 1938 stock trains also returned for a brief encore on the Northern Line in 1986–7. Whenever a picture of a 1938 stock train is shown at the meetings of the London Underground Railway Society, the ferociously technical analysis breaks down for a moment and someone utters, 'Ah … lovely little trains!' It is also the stock favoured by Tube modellers, as we shall see.

The 1938s were the first type of Electrical Multiple Units to have the motors secreted entirely below the carriage bodies, thus leaving more space for passenger seats. But that wasn't the reason people loved the '38s. No, they loved them because they were red. The cars were cherry-red with grey roofs which seemed to have eaves, making the trains reminiscent of a cosy little bungalow on the move. The interiors were of louche dark red, green and cream, and every carriage looked like the smoking carriage – an invitation to decadence. In short, the 1938 stock was the Routemaster of the Underground. Not that their colour (formally known as 'Train Red') was the same red as the Routemaster (Pantone 485), which is in turn not the same red as the pillar boxes and old telephone booths, which shared a colour originally, and exuberantly, designated Vermillion Giant. There is no 'London red', although the architect Jean Nouvel tried to imply there was when he created a temporary pavilion outside the Serpentine Gallery in 2008, the main point of which was its vibrant redness. It's just that London takes to redness in general, probably as an antidote to the greyness of the city.

The '38s were not the first Underground trains to be red. *Most* Underground trains before them had been red, or reddish. The Standard stock had been red, for example. The appeal of the '38s lay in the fact that they were the *last* trains to be red, and the new Tube trains that succeeded them over the next forty years would be grey – the colour of the aluminium from which they were made, steel being in short supply after the war. Aluminium also had the virtue of being lighter than steel, and it was 'Space Age'. The first aluminium Tube carriage, romantically named R49NDM23231, was exhibited at the Festival of Britain in 1951, and the first aluminium trains ran on the District in the following year. The last all-grey trains – London Underground prefers to say 'silver' – ran, also on the District, until February 2008. The novelty had worn off, and it was increasingly apparent that the tags of the graffiti artists did not do so. They left a ghostly trace when cleaned off. If only you could paint over them … and so red has crept back, together with white and blue. Patriotic, I suppose.

But why can't we still have warm red and green interiors? A couple of years ago I interviewed Mike Ashworth, Design and Heritage Manager of Transport for London. I told him how much I liked the mellow interiors of the '38s. 'Ah,' he said, 'tungsten lighting … beloved of women of a certain age.' I indignantly pointed out that *I* was not a woman of a certain age, and demanded to know why train interiors can't be cosy again. He conceded that there had been a reaction against the grey and pale blue that had predominated on the post-war Underground trains and stations, and bolder shades were making a return. He cited a seat moquette of mid-blue with an element of red that he himself had designed for the new Victoria Line trains. It is called Christian Barman, after the colleague and biographer of Frank Pick (a posthumous compliment of sorts, I suppose, to be sat on by millions of Londoners). But he added that 'a thirty-point colour contrast' was required by disability discrimination legislation – and that wouldn't be possible with moody hues I favoured. Also: 'The modern trains are so crowded that dark colours throughout would make them intolerably claustrophobic. Even you wouldn't like them,' he said, 'believe me.'

BY THE WAY: PASSENGER FLOW

There was warmth, humour and glamour in Frank Pick's underground publicity, but there was also a mechanistic aspect to the Underground, whose tunnels operated as giant pistons pushing the 'commuters' – the term was common by 1940 – inwards in the morning and outwards in the evening. In the stations and on the trains human beings were marshalled – streamlined – according to the new discipline: 'passenger flow'. It was the science of station design, exit placement, signage, train dispatching and announcements, and it is well expressed in the name, and concept, of the ticket booth called a passimeter.

Passengers were meant to flow past a passimeter on either side, as when the water of a fast-flowing river meets a rock. They usually had the choice of two queues, which must have been agonising because of course the one you pick is always the slowest. The queues were slowed down by the turnstiles that frequently operated in conjunction with the ticket booths, but these would give way to automatic ticket gates, first introduced on the Victoria Line from 1969, and refined in the 1980s. Automatic gates would speed flow, as did the growing prevalence of automatic ticket-dispensing machines, which had first been introduced in the 1930s, and the wrong placement of which in Holden stations caused Frank Pick to expend a lot of green ink.

But the raw material that the Underground had to work on – Londoners themselves – was possibly not of the best. In 1905 Charles Yerkes had said:

> Londoners are the worst people to get a move on I ever knew. To see them board and get off a train one thinks they had a thousand years to do it in; still they are doing better, and in the end I shall work them down to an allowance of thirty seconds.

In 1919 'hustlers' were employed on the District platforms at Victoria to co-ordinate the boarding of busy trains. After thirty seconds the hustler sounded a siren that dispatched the train no matter what the state of play on the platform. Unlike in Tokyo, there have never been platform guards whose job it was actually to push people onto crowded trains, but there is a cartoon from the 1930s in which a guard does push a fat bowler-hatted commuter through the end door of a crowded train, only to cause another one to pop out through the middle door.

It is unlikely that Londoners have sped up very much since Yerkes's day. There aren't many more trains per hour at peak times than there were then, so they haven't had to. Also, those trains are more crowded than ever, a situation that can be mitigated by 'letting them off first', but that practice is not universally observed. A poster of 1918 by George Morrow commanded, 'Passengers Off The Car First, Please', with the addition of the patronising rationale: 'First – when one gets out another can get in. Second – Those that would get in before block the way of those that would get out. So to secure room and save seconds there can be no other rule.'

In 1927 a poster by Lunt Roberts called *Behave Yourself* began to be displayed:

I entered the Tube station and took my place in the queue
I had the exact fare ready
I passed across the lift
I stood clear of the gates
I bewared of pick-pockets
I passed down to the other end of the platform
I let them off the car first …

And so on, down to:

I had my ticket ready
I emerged by the 'Exit Only'
I walked smartly to the office
Why?
Because I do it every day.
Why?
Because I'm, unfortunately, that sort of chap.

The 'unfortunately' was meant to draw the sting, but in *Underground Writing*, David Welsh chronicles the bad press that the inter-war Tube – the 'machine' – received from novelists, their reaction ranging 'from alienation to fear to anger and frustration'. The critic-in-chief was George Orwell. In *Keep the Aspidistra Flying* the social drop-out Gordon Comstock observes the Tube, that enabler of capitalism, with increasing bitterness: 'Something deep below made the stone street shiver. The tube-train, sliding through middle earth. He had a vision of London, of the western world; he saw a thousand million slaves toiling and grovelling about the throne of money.' Welsh makes the point that Comstock's girlfriend, Rosemary, can afford the Tube while he can't. She is liberated by the thing he rejects; the Tube is emasculating.

Comstock inhabits a London containing 'seven million people, sliding to and fro, avoiding contact'. He 'avoided and was avoided'. People attempted the same on the Tube. *The Tube Train*, a wood-cut of 1934 by Cyril Edward Power, shows a carriage packed with commuters, and every single one is reading the newspaper – apparently the same newspaper. And so the atomisation the novelists complained of is voluntarily reinforced. Today you can insulate yourself doubly, with newspaper *and* iPod.

And while more and more Tube riders are listening to their own soundtracks, London Underground is ever keener to make announcements.

For a long time the Underground communicated with its passengers largely by signage, or by occasional shouting – as in the case of the gatemen calling out the station names – and I liked it better like that because the shouts were intermittent. You could surrender your body to the machine but keep your mind independent. In 1938 loudspeakers were installed at 120 of the busiest stations, enabling news of delays to be broadcast to passengers from line control centres. The driver was given the ability to communicate with all his passengers when the first one-person-operated trains were introduced on the Victoria Line in the 1960s, and today the communications are incessant. This is partly determined by disability discrimination legisla-tion, partly because about 20 per cent of the Tube's customers are from outside London and genuinely don't know where to alight for London Zoo. Also, between 2003 and 2009 London Underground had a managing director – an otherwise charm-ing Irish-American called Tim O'Toole – who was messianic about 'passenger information', regardless of the consideration that the most beautiful thing about the off-peak Tube used to be its dreaminess. And so regular announcements are made 'in real time' by staff at particular stations, or recorded by them for regu-lar use. Announcements can also be made 'long line' – that is, from the control centre of the line. And the drivers have a menu of automated announcements that they can trigger. (I prefer the ones who address the passengers themselves, but in a low-key way, with the mumbling modesty of indie rockers: 'Right … this one's via Bank.')

The operation of the first escalators provided an early excuse for shouting at passengers. The very first escalator had been installed at Earl's Court in 1911, and may or may not have been demonstrated to the public by a one-legged man called Bumper Harris. In the early 1920s Charing Cross (now Embankment), where the Hampstead Tube, the Bakerloo and the District coincided, was the busiest station on the network, and its escalators operated in conjunction with a scratchy, wheedling voice endlessly saying 'Please keep moving. If you must stand, stand on the right. Some are in a hurry, don't impede them.' The voice came from a shellac disc played on a machine called a Stentorphone, which was a gramophone with a primitive amplifier. Note: (a) the use of the word 'impede', too rarefied for modern London; and (b) 'stand on the right.' Why on the right? Possibly because the early escalators ended in a diagonal, the stairway terminating sooner for the right foot than the left, and you'd better be ready for that, hence standing. A silent film of 1928 called *Underground* shows a drunken soldier frowning as he descends over signs reading 'Step off: right foot first', and he falls over at the bottom.

My dad once had a fist-fight at King's Cross with a man who was standing on the left and refused to move after polite requests. But in a way that man was correct. It would be better if we didn't walk on escalators; the swaying and bouncing motion is bad for them. This was explained to me in 1993 by a London Underground escalator engineer who had been part of a campaign called the Key Asset Plan, which had started in 1989, with the aim of fixing the hundred or so escalators on the system (about a third) that were then designated 'non-goers' – in other

The art of moving people in and out of stations is called 'passenger flow'. Yet walking on escalators damages them, as most of these passengers seem well aware (or perhaps they're just posing for the photographer). Hence the injunction: '*Stand* on the right'.

words, they were broken and had remained broken because of under-funding. The Underground escalators had been installed over the twenty years after that first one at Earl's Court, mostly by the American firm Otis ('escalator' was a trade name of Otis until 1949), and they were meant to last about thirty years. The majority worked with minimal maintenance until the mid-Eighties, when, rather in the same way that all your light bulbs go at once, lots of them stopped working. The ones fixed under the Key Asset Plan, or KAP, were said to have been 'Kapped', but this could take up to take six months, causing passenger flow to cease altogether at the stations concerned, an escalator being far more efficient than a lift (the rule of thumb is that one escalator does the work of five lifts).

We have two more passenger injunctions to deal with. First, 'Keep Feet Off Seats', a command introduced on notices from 1984, but now that most seats are longitudinal it is increasingly *impossible* to put your feet on the opposite seat. Secondly, there is 'Mind the Gap'.

Gaps occur because a train cannot be as curved as a curved platform. I once asked a London Underground official whether many people had been injured by stepping into the gap. 'Oh God yes,' he said, 'thousands.' The very charming Brian Hardy, who is now retired but used to be the Duty Manager of London Underground's Network Control Centre, has a sort of party piece wherein he names all the gaps on the system. He started doing this for me once, and after a while I intervened, asking, 'How long is this likely to take?' 'About twenty minutes,' he said, so I asked him just to confine himself to the Northern Line, which he did: '... Woodside Park has a very slight curvature, and West Finchley a bigger one, but I don't think there's a "Mind the Gap" announcement because the station's in a built-up area and it would annoy the neighbours. Kentish has a slight curve, so does Belsize and Chalk Farm. Euston on the Charing Cross branch has a very definite gap. Leicester Square has a slight one …' And so on.

I once interviewed the man who made the first 'Mind the Gap' announcement: the one that reverberated for about thirty years on the Central Line at Bank, on the Bakerloo at Waterloo and on the northbound Northern Line at Embankment. It was a stentorian command, with that patrician, 1950s' way of saying 'gap' – 'gep'. The speaker was Peter Lodge, who in the late Sixties was a sound engineer running his own recording studio in Bayswater, a too provincial location for Michael Winner, who complained 'it's practically in the country' after an arrangement had been made for one of his films to be dubbed there. So Mr Lodge was spared *that*, but he did work on soundtracks for *The Goodies*, *Emergency Ward 10* and much else. In 1968 or 1969 – Mr Lodge can't quite recall – he received a call from a Scotsman employed by Telefunken, who had been awarded the contract to provide the equipment for playing the first automated 'Mind the Gap' announcements. It was the advent of digital technology that had made these a workable proposition.

A professional actor had been recruited to say the words; he was willing to travel all the way to Bayswater, and the Scotsman brought him along to Mr Lodge's studio. He said the words to everyone's satisfaction, but a few days later his agent phoned the Scotsman. The actor wanted it understood that he was to be paid royalties; that every time 'Mind the Gap' was played he would receive money. According to Mr Lodge, the Scotsman said, '"Not likely!" with quite a few expletives along the way.' The warning would be re-recorded, with the Scotsman saying the words, but at the start of this second session Mr Lodge tested the levels by saying, 'Mind the gap!' at which the Scotsman said, 'That's fine, I'll take it!' Soon after the announcements went 'live', Mr Lodge took his children to Waterloo and watched their reaction as an incoming train triggered the warning. 'Daddy, it's you!' they exclaimed. It was the only feedback he ever had. Today there's a gentler male voice at Waterloo; on the Central at Bank it's an actual woman, and Mr Lodge only reigns at the northbound Northern Line at Embankment.

EXIT PICK

Early in 1938 Frank Pick said, 'There comes a point when the size of London could become its undoing. You cannot pile up people on one site and think they can live efficiently on it.' The statement was made during discussion of the plans for a Green Belt around London, and the words contain a note of despair. It was not the first time. In 1927 Pick had spoken of a 'Victorian flood tide. Rows and rows of mean houses in mean streets filled in all the gaps for which the suburban network of railways supplied a ready means of transport ... Cheap fares for the working classes produced the vast and dreary expanse of north-east London, a district without a redeeming feature in the way of plan or building or object of interest.' London was apparently uncontainable: the trains were faster, and beginning to operate in sinister alliance with cars, in the sense that commuters were willing to drive to and from stations. As Pick's biographer writes: 'The idea that the Outer Ring ... might be in danger of losing all its open spaces filled him with a sort of horror which cannot but have been chilled by a sense of personal involvement.'

The Green Belt (London and Home Counties) Act was passed in 1938. It enabled local authorities around London to purchase land for protection. It would be augmented by the Town and Country Planning Act of 1947, which allowed local authorities throughout Britain to designate areas as 'green belt' within their development plans.

At the beginning of the war the railways, including the Underground, were subsumed under the Railway Executive

Committee. Pick resigned from London Transport in May 1940. He had reached the end of the seven-year term to which he had been appointed in 1933; he had always been a neurotic workaholic, and now his health was failing. On leaving, he worked first for the Ministry of Transport, then the Ministry of Information, where, in late 1940, he came up against Winston Churchill.

Churchill had proposed that leaflets containing falsehoods should be dropped over enemy countries so as to lower morale, but Pick argued it was 'bad propaganda' to tell lies. Churchill said this was 'no time to be concerned with the niceties', and Pick responded, 'I have never told a lie in my life', in which remark we see the priggishness of that 1927 poster: 'I entered the Tube station and took my place in the queue/ I had the exact fare ready …'

Churchill – *not* the sort of man who made a point of having the exact fare ready – contemplated Pick for a moment, and said, 'Mr Pick, Dover was heavily shelled from the French coast yesterday. I shall be at Dover myself tomorrow, it is likely that the town will again be shelled, and it is quite possible that I myself may be killed by one of those shells. If that should happen to me, it would give me great comfort to know that a few hours before my death I had spoken to a man who had never told a lie.' As Pick left the room, Churchill turned to his secretary, John Colville, and said in a deliberately audible whisper, 'Never let me see that impeccable busman again.'

Pick, incidentally, *was* an 'impeccable busman', because buses were part of his remit, and he was impeccable in everything. He had pioneered the introduction of fixed bus stops (before then you could flag down a bus from anywhere on its route), and very elegant they were: a tapering concrete pole with an enamel flag on the top, featuring the roundel. He spent many of his weekends travelling on buses, note-pad and green-ink pen to hand, planning new routes and stops. And he was just as keen to educate bus passengers as he had been Tube riders. He arranged for notices to be posted in buses drawing attention to trade fairs, rugby games, the birth of an elephant in London Zoo and, in 1912, a 'Votes for Women' meeting at the London Pavilion Theatre.

Pick was dismissed from the Ministry of Information, and he died of a brain haemorrhage in 1941. In *London: The Unique City* (1934) Steen Eller Rasmussen wrote: 'The moment you enter the London Underground you feel, though you may not be able to explain exactly how you feel it, that you are moving in an environment of order, of culture.' You feel the same today, and it is the true memorial of Frank Pick.

CHAPTER TWELVE

THE WAR AND AFTER

THE WAR

In the Second World War the London Underground 'did its bit' and entered wartime mythology by providing sheltering space for Londoners, but these shelterers were an embarrassment to the authorities. The habit of taking shelter in the Underground had developed in the First World War, when the stations were made available from the time of the first Zeppelin raids on London in May 1915. There was far less bombing of London in the First World War than in the Second, and yet a higher peak of sheltering was achieved. As Stephen Halliday writes in *Underground to Everywhere*, 'A final sequence of raids in February 1918 prompted as many as 300,000 people to seek shelter in the Tubes on a single night – almost twice the number recorded in the much worse conditions of the Blitz twenty-two years later.'

There had been jingoistic criticism of the shelterers of the First World War – cowardice was alleged – whereas it would be nearer the mark to say that those of the next war were the objects of patrician distaste. They were like the guest at a party who won't leave. Also, they'd invited themselves. At the start of the war the authorities feared that, once people went down into the Tubes, they might not come out. And it was more important to keep the trains running than to provide shelter for the masses. Tube stations packed with snoring Londoners? Here was the very opposite of 'passenger flow', and so signs were put up outside the stations, announcing that they were not to be used as shelters. The Communist Party campaigned against the ban and so struck a chord. After all, for the previous thirty years Londoners been taught by Frank Pick to think of the Tubes as a civilised place of refuge – a home from home, 'Where it is Warm and Bright', as a poster of 1924 had put it.

When the Blitz began, in September 1940, the pressure mounted, and on the evening of 19 September there was a new kind of evening rush hour, with people besieging the stations and threatening to storm them. So the public were admitted to (as it would turn out) every one of the deep-level Tube stations. But men were encouraged to think it was beneath them to shelter in the Tubes. They were urged to 'Be a man and leave it to them' – meaning women, children and the infirm. To the patrician mind there was really no need for anyone to shelter in the Tubes. People ought to have their Anderson shelters in their gardens – named after the very politician, Sir John Anderson, who as Lord Privy Seal had originally determined that Underground stations were not to be used as shelters. But the shelterers usually didn't have gardens. Or they could use the indoor Morrison shelters, reinforced table-like arrangements named after our dapper friend Herbert Morrison. The Morrison shelter never caught on, perhaps because it would only come into play if the user's house were collapsing about his ears – a depressing scenario to have to envisage. But notwithstanding their snubbing of his shelter, Morrison, as Home Secretary in Churchill's government, became a champion of the troglodytes.

They were given some of the comforts of home – three-tier bunk beds, for example – and they were supplied with food and drink by catering trains: Tube Refreshment Specials. When I say 'food and drink', I mean food and tea, which was served in giant, two-gallon teapots or, as revealed by a photograph in *London Transport at War* (1978) by Charles Graves, a watering can. People also bought their own comestibles: bottles of ginger pop, jam rolls, meat pies. Graves writes:

> One old woman proudly announced that she had brought enough cheese and tea-cakes for a fortnight, and indeed it was noted that she did not leave the East End railway platform which she had chosen for fourteen days, except to get a ten-minutes breath of fresh air when there was no air-raid in progress.

The Tube stations offered warmth, camaraderie. You didn't pay for light or heat; there were, in fact, few overheads, except the one that really mattered. There were two peaks of sheltering: the first, and highest, was during the Blitz; the second during the rain of V1 and V2 rockets in 1944. A count taken one night early in the Blitz found 177,000 Londoners sheltering in the Tubes. It is said that about 4 per cent of Londoners took to the Tube at some point during the Blitz.

You could book your space in advance by acquiring a ticket (no charge was made, of course) that allocated you a space on a platform. The trains continued to run – as the slogan had it, 'London Transport Carried On' – and the late and early ones, which disturbed the sleepers, were much resented.

Let us ride the last train of the evening, as it rumbles past those crowded platforms. The windows of the trains were covered with mesh, to collect broken glass should a blast occur. But people would tear away this stuff, even though – or perhaps

Wartime sheltering in Underground stations was at first permitted only with the greatest reluctance. It was feared that once the working classes went underground, they'd never come up again. Yet, for years beforehand, Londoners had been encouraged to think of the Underground as a place of cosiness and security, 'Where it is always warm and bright'.

because – they were counselled against doing so by 'Billy Brown of London Town', a small bowler-hatted prig depicted on public information posters, and a successor to that earlier, un-named paragon, 'The Man Who Always Took His Place In The Queue' etc. And the subterranean platforms *were* lit (sometimes too brightly for the sleepers, so they would tie bits of cloth around the shades); therefore we ought to see *something*.

We might, for instance, see shelterers sleeping on deckchairs on the platforms. We might see one shelterer not sleeping but scratching him- or herself, because the humid Underground ('It's warmer down below', remember) harboured a type of flea, *culex molestus*, which must have thought that all its Christmases had come at once when the shelterers moved in. We might see a shelterer spitting, and one of the paid wardens (there was one at every station, working alongside volunteers) reproving him. We might see card schools or chess games in progress, because most of the shelterers knew each other … or we might see somebody sitting up in one of the three-tier bunks and reading one of the journals specially produced by and for the shelterers. We might see Henry Moore – although he wasn't famous then – drawing the shelterers, creating the *Shelter Sketchbooks* that *made* him famous. He said the holes through which the trains disappeared reminded him of the holes in his sculptures. There might be a piano on the platform, and a singalong taking place. Then again, members of the Council for the Encouragement of Music and Arts might be playing gramophone records of classical music, seeking to better their captive audience, but apparently their efforts were not always appreciated. (I am reminded of a late night conversation I had with a ticket gate attendant at Charing Cross. Classical music was being played on the tannoy. I asked him why, and he said, 'It's because people don't like it. So they leave the station quicker.')

The cut-and-cover lines were no good for sheltering – not deep enough, as proved in November 1940, when the newly rebuilt station at Sloane Square was directly hit. Seventy-nine people were killed on a departing train. But the Tube shelterers faced other hazards besides bombs. At Balham on the night of 14 October 1940 a bomb blew open a water main and sewer, killing sixty-eight shelterers. At Bank on 11 January 1941 fifty-six died when a bomb penetrated the upper layer of the station. The worst was at Bethnal Green, in the new station built on that westerly extension of the Central, and not yet open as a Tube station, but open as a shelter.

At 8.27 p.m. on 3 March 1943 a new, deafening and unfamiliar sort of anti-aircraft gun began to be fired at nearby Victoria Park just as three buses disgorged their passengers at a stop near the entrance to the shelter. According to Sandra Scotting, honorary secretary of the Stairway to Heaven Memorial Trust, 'We'd bombed Berlin two nights earlier, so people were expecting reprisals. They thought the guns they heard were bombs. So it was ... "Into the shelter, quick." There should have been a warden on duty; there should have been a policeman.' And there should have been a handrail running down the middle of the nineteen stairs that led to the first level of the Tube station. There is such a handrail at Bethnal Green now – as there generally is on Tube station staircases because of what happened next.

A young woman carrying a baby tripped at the bottom of the stairs. Three hundred people fell on top of her, becoming trapped between the bottom of the stairs and the roof of the station corridor into which the stairs descended. If you look at that 11 foot by 15 foot aperture today, it looks completely innocuous. 'But it became blocked with a wall of people,' says Sandra, 'all intertwined.' One hundred and seventy-three people died, including sixty-two children, and ninety were injured. It was worse than Hillsborough, worse than Aberfan. There is a small brass plaque inside the station. It reads, 'From Great Things to Greater ... Site of the worst civilian disaster of the Second World War. 173

men, women and children lost their lives descending these steps to Bethnal Green Air Raid Shelter.'

Sandra's grandmother, her mother (then a young girl), and her cousin were in that wall of people. Her grandmother and her cousin died in it. In later years her mother would say, 'They died at Bethnal Green,' without supplying further details; she'd then change the subject. 'The memory – they just buried it,' says Sandra. 'The authorities had told them not to talk about it.' An inquiry was held soon after, but its conclusion (fiercely rejected in Bethnal Green) – namely that there had been a mass panic – was suppressed until after the war in the name of morale. In common with many residents of Bethnal Green, Sandra's mother never used the station after it opened *as a station* in 1949. And there are still people in Bethnal Green who boycott the station.

Enough money has been raised – partly from collections at Bethnal Green Tube – for the first stages of a monument that will eventually comprise an inverted duplication of the original staircase. It will be built in a small public garden next to the fatal entrance. London Underground has given every assistance.

It was Herbert Morrison's decision to open the station as a shelter. In November 1940 he announced on the radio that a new system of tunnels would be built under the Underground, and the implication was that these would be made available to the public. These fabled deep-level shelters were finished in 1942. Each took the form of twin concrete tunnels. There are eight of them. One is under the Chancery Lane, the others are under Northern Line stations at Clapham South, Clapham Common, Clapham North, Stockwell, Goodge Street, Camden Town and Belsize Park. They found a variety of uses during the war. The one at Goodge Street – signified today by its sinister, utilitarian surface building, ruining what would otherwise have been an elegant crescent off Chenies Street – was General Eisenhower's base in 1942, and from there the D-Day landings were planned.

The public were admitted to some of the deep shelters during the raids of 1944, but they are basically eight white elephants, mainly used today for storage of things such as architectural drawings, which have to be kept for a long time. London Underground has 'given up its option' on the shelters.

Another subterranean command centre was at Down Street, the under-used Piccadilly Line station in Mayfair that closed in 1932, having been caught in a pincer movement between a new westerly entrance for Dover Street station (which would be renamed Green Park), and a new easterly one for Hyde Park Corner. It is said that in 1938 Frank Pick led a candle-lit tour through the corridors of Down Street for officials of the Railway Executive, which controlled the railways in the Second World War. 'It's just what we're looking for,' they told Pick, 'we'll take it.'

A bombproof steel cap was placed over the top of the station, which was adapted to accommodate not only the Railway Executive: Winston Churchill would also put up there in 1940, when the cabinet's underground lair off Whitehall was being strengthened. He later recorded that he ate some very good dinners in Down Street, and others have speculated that the smell of his roast fowls, his cigar smoke and brandy vapours may have drifted along the tunnels, affecting the dreams of the shelterers uneasily replete on meat pies and jam rolls at, say, Hyde Park Corner.

I was given a tour of Down Street a few years ago. You could still see the remains of the flock wallpaper that had made the executive feel at home. My guide, an Underground employee called Geoff, pointed out the remains of what he thought was a breeze-block runnel or channel. 'It's just wide enough to have accommodated a tea trolley,' he said. Some members of the Executive lived in Down Street around the clock, and you could see where their bunks had been fixed to the walls. The ones who did come and go would venture down to the platforms, most of which were – and are – bricked off from the eyes of any spies that might have been riding the Piccadilly Line. But there was an access point to the tracks, from where a red lantern could be dangled, bringing any approaching trains to a stop. Departing members of the Executive would then board the train via the driver's door. At the end of the tour Geoff led us to this alcove, and we watched the faces of the passengers on the trains going by – stared directly at them – but none seemed to see us. It was like being a ghost, unable to communicate with the world of the living. But then we did make contact. Geoff hung out his own red light; a train stopped, and we departed by that privileged means. (You can never really hate the Underground after that sort of experience.)

But let us go back to our wartime ride through the shelter stations.

We might see a bride and groom on a platform. In 1940 Peggy and Jack Birmingham dashed into Edgware Road Bakerloo station when the sirens wailed, minutes after they'd been married. Their guests came with them, and the party continued on the platform. For their wedding night the station manager, a Mr Palmer, offered Mr and Mrs Birmingham the privacy of a lift with the doors jammed shut.

We might notice George Orwell on the platform. Fag in mouth (because smoking was permitted on the shelter platforms), he is gently prising a scrubbing brush out of the grasp of a two-year-old girl shelterer who had been scrubbing the filthy platform with it and then sucking the bristles. Orwell recounted this in his 'London Letter' to the *Partisan Review* dated 24 July 1944. It was one of many 'disgusting scenes' he had observed in the station shelters, where 'sordid piles of bedding cluttered up the passageways at night'. Orwell hated the Tube, but the sheltering phenomenon did seem to make snobs of even liberal writers, including Vera Brittain, who in *England's Hour* (1941) wrote: 'Soon, I reflect, London's poorer population, like melancholy troglodytes, will spend its whole life in the Underground, emerging only for half an hour after the morning "All Clear" to purchase its loaves and its fish-and-chips.' The saving grace of the Underground had been that the people you met upon it were transient; now it meant tawdry stasis. We saw off Hitler, but the Underground had been allied to a kind of defeat. Pick was dead, and it had lost its inter-war sheen of success.

It would be a long time before it came back.

AFTER

In the later stages of the war, with the arrival of US soldiers, the system became unprecedentedly packed: a cartoon by W. A. Sillince, a *Punch* regular, shows civilians fighting to board a crowded Tube train. It's called 'The Home Front'.

London Transport did manage to 'carry on' during the war, and was not judged in need of high-priority first aid afterwards, the 'big' railways being in a worse state. So far, this had been a story of geographical expansion, but in the late Forties and Fifties that stopped. Yes, the New Works extensions of the Central would be completed in 1949 (whereas those for the north of the Northern would be curtailed); yes, the Metropolitan would be electrified beyond Rickmansworth in 1961. But essentially we are looking at twenty years of austerity and under-investment, a climate that would eventually produce one rather etiolated, pale blue flower: the Victoria Line. In the process our story ceases to be about railways, and becomes a matter of mutating bureaucracies: the politicisation of the Underground.

In January 1948 London Transport was nationalised by the Labour government of Clement Attlee. A body called the London Transport Executive would be overseen by the British Transport Commission, which had also taken over the overground railway companies, which might otherwise have gone bankrupt. Lord Ashfield was not on the Executive; instead, he was on the Commission, but not for long. He died on 4 November 1948. There is a blue plaque on what had been his house at 43 South Street Mayfair, a fittingly dashing address. Ashfield had pioneered the harmonisation of transport with social needs, and it is a tribute to him that the first logo of British Railways (created in 1948) was essentially a London Transport bull's-eye, albeit with a lion on top.

The government now had London Transport at its disposal but did little more than keep a tight rein on the policy and expenditure of the Executive. Yet the Executive was not entirely cowed, and from the early 1950s it was campaigning for a new Tube line connecting north-east London, and its great bulge of railway-made suburbs, with Victoria via the West End. Here was another attempt to ease that old bugbear, the Finsbury Park logjam, but this time with the aim of bringing passengers into what had long been the growth area of central London, the West End, rather than the City. An early working title for the line was KingVic, a Bakerloo-type concatenation, indicating a connection between King's Cross and Victoria, but carrying an unfortunate implication of cross-dressing. ('ViKing' was also bandied about.)

Never mind Kingvic, the Fifties and early Sixties were the era when the car was beginning to be king. It was also an era of Conservative governments, who were more likely to favour private transport than Labour ones. But there were two isolated instances of pro-rail thinking at this time. The first was the modernisation plan for British Railways, which was published in 1955 and enabled by rising prosperity. But it only diverted investment that might have gone to the Underground into the national network. The second came in the form of a paper presented to the Royal Statistical Society by two Oxford academics in 1962, and making an argument for building what was now being called the Victoria Line. The paper acknowledged that the fares earned by a Tube line would not repay the capital cost of building the line. It argued for the line not in nebulous terms of social benefits but in terms of the specific transport benefits to be gained elsewhere. Other Tube lines would operate more quickly and comfortably if relieved of overcrowding by the Victoria, and the argument – very characteristic of its time – was made that motorists would benefit, as a result of a decrease in congestion on the roads. Furthermore, the boom of the 1950s was fading; Britain had lower growth than its competitors and higher unemployment. As before, the lever marked 'economic boost' was reached for, an action that by now might have been described as Keynesian. London would have its new Tube line, funded by government loan and a fares increase, but it would be built on the cheap.

THE VICTORIA LINE
(OR THE RAILWAY IN A BATHROOM)

The line opened between Walthamstow and Highbury on 1 September 1968; it was then extended to Warren Street, then Victoria, at which suitably regal moment the Queen declared it open. The Victoria was the first line to use automatic ticket barriers. (They were fed by tickets of yellow card with oxidised backs that made them seem sinister, as though they were half-coated in lead.) Accordingly, on 7 March 1969 the Queen bought a 5d. ticket in order to access the platform and 'drive' the train from Green Park to Oxford Circus. The word 'drive' has inverted commas because: (a) Her Majesty had assistance in the cab; and (b) Victoria Line trains were powered and signalled automatically. The drivers just opened the doors – this being the first line without guards – and pressed the start button, and it was rumoured early on that they were waxworks. Since any passing

idiot could press that start button, or since it might be pressed
by accident, the train cabs did not have side-doors, which might
have allowed unauthorised ingress from the platform; instead,
the driver entered the cab from the door dividing it from the
front carriage – the 'J' door – and the train wouldn't start until he
had performed certain rituals in the cab, including opening and
closing the side-window.

In *The Victoria Line: A Short History* (1968) M. A. C. Horne
writes: 'At 3pm, the public gained access to London's latest tube.
They liked it, and have flocked to it ever since.' They certainly
have flocked to it. In its first year it carried a third more passengers than had been expected. Victoria was, and is, the busiest station on the network, and Oxford Circus and King's Cross were
not – and are not – far behind. In recent years Victoria Line staff
have periodically had to stop access to the Victoria Line ticket
hall, since it becomes too packed; hence the current expansion
of the station, which is one of the biggest projects of the Tube
Upgrade. Access to Oxford Circus is also often restricted. The
staff make desperate pleas over the tannoy for order and patience
which echo out into Oxford Street so that the uninvolved passer-
by feels he is intruding on private grief, as when a domestic argument is overheard.

For most of my time in London the Victoria Line has been
the most efficient way of crossing London, with its stations sufficiently far apart for its frequent trains to reach 50 miles an hour,
and numerous connections. In fact, Pimlico looks oddly bereft
on the line diagrams, since it is the only station without a connection to either national rail or another Tube line. In about 1989
someone tipped me off that the best way of accessing the West
End from north London, is to change onto the southbound Victoria Line from the southbound Northern Line (Bank branch)
at Euston. It's a very quick change. The two platforms are adjacent, since they occupy a single wide-bore tunnel that used to

accommodate both the southbound and northbound lines of the Northern Line City branch. (The northbound one was diverted to make way for the Victoria.)

But did passengers like the line?

On its opening, the *Observer* called it 'extraordinarily bleak', and the line has all the charm of a Sixties' tower block. It would have seemed lonely: the absence of guards; fewer ticket staff because of the barriers; and the first 'passenger information points' allowing passengers to speak to the control room at Euston rather than a platform guard (all these novelties determined in part by the fact that this was a time of labour shortage). There was a new, clinical style of lighting – fluorescent tube – and the too narrow passageways were lined with drab, grey and pale blue, 6-inch square tiles. They're bathroom tiles, basically.

The stations featured tile panels in the platform seat recesses, and these were decorated with images of local significance, but the designers seem to have been hard-pressed to find any. The one at Warren Street shows a maze – a type of warren, you see. The one at Stockwell shows a swan, the name of a nearby pub, evidently. The one at Euston shows the Euston Arch, which had just been knocked down.

Also there is a shortage of natural light, since the line is entirely underground. So is the Waterloo & City, but whereas that's only a mile or so of unnaturalness, the Victoria is 13½ miles of it. Because the Victoria was fitted in below existing stations (requiring, incidentally, the complete reconstruction of Oxford Circus), there are few surface buildings, and certainly few of any note, and it has been suggested that the most beautiful above-ground manifestation of the line is the little neo-classical structure by Quinlan Terry that surmounts a ventilation shaft in Gibson Square, Islington.

M. A. C. Horne writes that the automatic barriers 'faded away gradually'. It was too expensive to roll them out system-wide, but the barriers would be back. At the time of writing the line is losing its position at the top of the class, owing to the introduction – again as part of the Upgrade – of the new trains, which are afflicted with teething troubles. The *Evening Standard* enjoys pointing out that they are 'twenty-three times less reliable' than their predecessors. But the line will settle back into its efficient, if unlovable, groove.

CHAPTER THIRTEEN

THE MODERN TUBE
(OR LIVINGSTONE'S WARS)

ENTER LIVINGSTONE

In 1962 the British Transport Commission was replaced by a London Transport Board, answerable directly to the government. A further politicisation of the Tube occurred in 1970, when London Transport became the responsibility of the Greater London Council, which had been created in 1965. The transfer was made by Harold Wilson's dynamic transport minister, Barbara Castle. At last the municipalisation advocated by Herbert Morrison had occurred. Transport in London – along with the police – became the main business of London politicians. It also became their battleground. Transport policy in the metropolis became, as Christian Wolmar has observed, a 'blame game'. One side attacked the policies of the other, and the side that was supposed to be running the London Underground frequently attacked its executives, which was a bit like blaming themselves, because they had set the policy, and they had the power to appoint or remove those executives. One way or another, the good name of the London Underground tended to be dragged through the dirt.

At the same time, the population of central London was falling, offices rather than houses having risen up on the bomb sites – and the population of the suburbs was continuing to rise. The Tube was therefore ever more associated with the grim business of getting to and from work; it was no longer the Londoner's ally in pleasure-seeking, or its avuncular cultural guide, as in the days of Frank Pick and 'It's a Bank Holiday, Go Out!' If the Londoner did go out on a Bank Holiday (and he might just stay in and watch television, thank you very much), there was a good chance he'd do so as a proud first-time car owner.

Rising car ownership helped to keep Underground use static or in slow decline from the mid-Fifties to the early Eighties, and the Tube train was compared with the greater comfort if not necessarily speed, of the family motor. The Tube was a second-class form of transport, commonly to be spoken of in intemperate terms.

Municipalisation was financially beneficial to the Underground, since its debts had been written off by the government so as to sweeten the deal for the GLC. And in 1971, when the Jubilee Line was authorised under the working title 'Fleet Line', the government agreed to provide three-quarters of the capital cost, the GLC providing the rest. The Jubilee was not at first very much of a new line. It would open in 1979 between Stanmore and Charing Cross, but most of that distance (Baker Street to Stanmore) was accounted for by its having taken over the Stanmore branch of the Bakerloo. (Where the Jubilee Line is concerned, the big news was its glamorous appendage, namely its Extension, which opened in 1999.)

The Seventies was a bleak decade for the Underground, what with the high cost of oil (affecting electricity generation), inflation, high wage settlements, ticket price rises and an overall decline in the population of London. The spirit of Thatcherism was on the rise, and from 1977 a Conservative head of the GLC, a bow-tied egomaniac called Horace Cutler, castigated London Transport as over-unionised, inefficient and lacking in direction. In 1981 Labour took control of the GLC, and an assault from the right upon the London Transport Board was now succeeded by an assault from the left.

The assailant was Ken Livingstone, who has done more for public transport in London than anyone since Frank Pick, or at any rate since that earlier embodiment of municipalisation, Herbert Morrison. Like Morrison, Livingstone was born into a working-class family in Lambeth. His father was a merchant seaman, his rather beautiful mother a music-hall performer, an acrobatic dancer who performed in music halls – also in circuses, where she would balance on elephants. When Livingstone took power at the GLC in 1981, a journalist wrote that Herbert Morrison 'would be turning in his grave'. By then Morrison was being looked back on as the embodiment of Old Labour pragmatism, but in his time he, like Livingstone, had been the frightening 'New Man'.

Livingstone the firebrand is slowly becoming the patrician elder statesman. Such contradictions are his stock in trade. Livingstone is the phlegmatic controversialist, the self-deprecating self-publicist. When he first came to prominence, this former lab technician and breeder of newts and other amphibians was depicted as an ascetic loner and nerd. It later became apparent that he liked a glass of wine, that he was quite the ladies' man and that he appreciated good food. The earliest pictures of the boy Livingstone in *Citizen Ken* (1984) by John Carvel show him riding bikes, but he was never a transport romantic. Unlike Frank Pick, he does not combine an aesthetic appreciation of transport with his desire to use it for the social good. For Livingstone, transport is *all* about the social good – and the aggrandisation of

Ken Livingstone, of course. (So he would phase out the beautiful Routemaster bus in favour of the sinister but supposedly more user-friendly 'Bendy Bus' in 2005, which may in turn have been a factor in his defeat by Boris Johnson in the mayoral election of 2008. Johnson *is* a transport romantic, albeit with a romanticism not confined to public transport – the last time I looked, he was the motoring correspondent of GQ magazine – and he has commissioned a new Routemaster for the twenty-first century. But he is not steeped in transport, as Livingstone is.)

London politics is very largely concerned with public transport, so any aspirant in that arena had better become interested in it, and Livingstone has been engaged right from the start of his career.

In the early Seventies the Conservative administration of the GLC campaigned for four orbital motorways to be built in London: the London ringways. The scheme was at first supported by the Labour grouping on the council, but in 1973 Labour won the GLC election on a platform that included opposition to the ringways, which were already partially built: hence, for example, the lovely Westway. Stephen Joseph, the director of the Campaign for Better Transport, told me, 'I say that's a turning point. If London had had the ringways, it would have looked much more like Los Angeles than it does now.' That vision had real momentum behind it in the early Sixties. In her novel *The Heart of London* (1961) Monica Dickens paints a portrait of a community called Cottingham Park – actually Notting Hill – that is becoming excited about rumours of a 'Transurban Expressway'. One character asks, 'Don't you think it's time somebody did something about getting traffic in and out of London?' and the new road is seen by some as likely to bring an end to the shabby parochialism of the area. The building of the ringways would have been the fulfilment of the vision of the Buchanan Report, which was published in 1963 and set out a plan for the civilised accommodation of cars in city centres by means of flyovers, underpasses and pedestrianised zones. According to Stephen Joseph, the Barbican gives us a taste of it. 'That was the look: walkways with cars underneath. The lower level is for the cars, the upper level is the pedestrian.'

Ken Livingstone was elected to the GLC in 1973, representing Norwood in south London. He opposed the ringways and was perhaps elected because of the plan to build them. As he writes in his memoir, *If Voting Changed Anything, They'd Abolish It* (1988): 'My own campaign in Norwood was greatly helped when the Tory GLC member made the mistake of voting in favour of a last-minute change in the motorway plans, which would have re-routed them through the middle of the constituency he was asking to return him to County Hall.' In allying himself against the road-builders, his even more left-wing colleague 'Red' Ted Knight suggested to Livingstone that he was consorting with 'middle-class environmentalists', but then 'Red Ted' attended a number of meetings with 'Red Ken', and he saw the popularity of the anti-car cause. In 1977 they would both disrupt the inquiry into the plans for widening the Archway Road, a proposal strongly opposed by Red Ted, who had become Parliamentary candidate for Hornsey.

You can't win votes on a road-building platform in London. Too many houses have to be knocked down. In the late Seventies it was clear that, as Stephen Joseph says, 'the focus had to go back to public transport', and it would do so when Labour won the GLC again in 1981 and Livingstone replaced Horace Cutler as its leader.

Livingstone introduced the policy on which Labour had campaigned: 'Fares Fair'. Bus and Tube fares were cut by a third, with the aim of increasing the use of public transport from its static level, and of counteracting the fares increases of previous years. It was partly paid for by an increase in the surcharge levied by the

GLC on the London boroughs, but the Conservative-controlled borough of Bromley, where there was no Tube station (Bromley-by-Bow on the District Line is not in Bromley), objected all the way to the House of Lords, which ruled in their favour. In March 1982 the GLC was obliged to double fares, and whereas the reduction had increased use of buses and Tubes by half a million, the fare increase reduced it by a million. In 1982 a compromise was reached, resulting in a net fare reduction of 25 per cent, and this together with the emergence of the economy from recession and London's increasing attractiveness as a tourist destination marks the point at which Tube use ceased gently declining and became a steeply rising curve.

London Underground managers were wary of another part of the Livingstone package: the system of zoning that would allow the introduction of the Travelcard for use on bus, tube and main line – a 'coarsening' as they saw it, of the existing and more numerous fare gradations, and one that would simply lead to a reduction in revenue. They were wrong. According to Stephen Joseph, 'The argument that simplification drives growth was not accepted by the Underground people, and when Livingstone was proved right, he became sceptical of transport models that extrapolated past trends into the future.' In other words, Livingstone's tremendous boldness – his cockiness, you might say – comes from that victory. Are we to blame Livingstone for Tube overcrowding? In part, yes, but as Sir John Eliot had observed in 1955, while Chairman of the London Transport Executive: 'They're not crammed in. They cram themselves in.'

The system of zoning would lead logically to the introduction of the modern ticket barriers from 1987 (the Underground Ticketing System, or UTS), in that it allowed the software in the ticket gates to be relatively simple. Although the widespread introduction of automatic barriers was an innovation, Underground stations have always been screened off by some sort of gate where tickets are checked. You have never been able to just saunter onto the platforms and look at the trains, or meet someone off a train. That's a shame, but at least the determining logic is infallible: you can't check passengers' tickets on an Underground train. But now barriers are being introduced on main-line inter-city stations, and Richard Malins, a consultant in railway revenue protection, campaigns against this. 'It is extending an urban railway principle into inter-urban railways, and it's not necessary,' he says. Automatic barriers are not civilised, and there is always a moment of tension when you approach, although if you push the paddles (as the ticket gates are called) they will open as easily as a curtain.

To continue with barriers for a moment ... at first, the ones on the Underground were only in Zone 1, where most journeys start or end. Gradually they spread to those places where manual ticket checks were being evaded, and if you found ticket barriers in your local suburban station soon after 1987, then, yes, an aspersion was being cast on your area. The barriers were in turn a necessary precondition of electronic payment; in other words the Oyster Card, which was introduced in 2003, when my son was nine. He immediately insisted I start using the Oyster, but I didn't trust it. With typical boldness, however, Livingstone bullied middle-aged technophobes like me into using Oysters by making the cash fares sometimes twice as expensive, with the result that Oysters are now used on 85 per cent of public transport journeys in the capital.

Fares Fair was a popular policy with Londoners, but Livingstone barely had time to take a bow before Mrs Thatcher brought the curtain down on him. She had fought the General Election of 1983 promising to abolish the GLC – in other words, to abolish Ken Livingstone – and she duly won, whereupon the functions of the GLC were distributed across a range of obscure and undemocratic bodies. In 1984 something called London Regional Transport was established as a quango, with something

called London Underground Limited a quango within it. As a
result of the policies of Livingstone, passenger numbers continued to rise, paradoxically enabling reforms more to the liking of
a Conservative mindset. Staffing levels were reduced, through
the extension of one-man operation of trains and the contracting
out of aspects of the business. The next set of modifications were
caused by disaster.

On 18 November 1987 a fire that started underneath an escalator at King's Cross killed thirty-one people. It was caused by
a dropped match, probably by someone gasping for a fag, having endured the penance of not being able to smoke on any of
the trains, and many of the platforms. (I have often wondered
whether the person who dropped that match knew that they
had dropped it.) After the fire, the smoking ban was made total.
The wood was stripped from escalators, and wooden fixtures
generally were taken out of the system. Where they survive, as
with the wooden benches on the otherwise charmless Victoria
Line platforms, they seem like a touch of old world luxury. The
management structure was also rationalised – it has been said
that the Underground had been run by 'baronies of engineers'
– and a culture of 'safety first' was implemented. The frequently
heard and ungrammatical mantra reporting that any given station is closed 'because of the London Fire Brigade in attendance'
is a legacy of the King's Cross fire. In previous years any suspi-
cious smouldering would have been investigated by station staff.
Another legacy of the fire.

Between the late Eighties and the late Nineties the Underground received fitful bursts of proper funding from the government, in part to make the changes required by the Fennell Report
into the King's Cross fire. Meanwhile rising passenger numbers
and increasing traffic congestion made the Underground a
deserving case for sustained investment, preferably from the private sector. And so the scene was set for another of Livingstone's

wars. But first the story of a line whose Extension represented an early idea of what private money might do for the Tube …

THE JUBILEE LINE

The Jubilee is, to adapt the footballer's phrase, a line of two halves. The first part opened in 1979, comprising the route it inherited from the Bakerloo: Baker Street to Stanmore. There was also a new tunnel from Baker Street to Charing Cross. The second part comprises the extension to Stratford, opened in 1999. The line is like a man who wears a scruffy tweed jacket, but with expensive trousers and shoes by Armani, because the Extension is determinedly glitzy. It was well funded and ran through an area where there was room to build, so the stations are 'future-proofed': that is to say, big.

The older half has its charms, mainly left over from the 1930s: the lovely, lambent station at St John's Wood, with its cosy, recessed wooden benches, and the forest of uplighters on the escalators. (It was not designed by Holden, but is in the manner of Holden.) Beyond Finchley Road there's a pleasant sleepiness about it: the creepers growing over the backs of the houses at Dollis Hill, the overgrown embankments leading up to Kingsbury, the cottage-like charm of the stations at Stanmore and Queensbury.

Baker Street and Green Park feature experimental decoration characteristic of the late Seventies and early Eighties, in which some stations were given motifs reflecting their particular locations: at Baker Street, scenes from the Sherlock Holmes stories appear; Green Park has vivid orange tiles on which black leaves are superimposed. Charing Cross Jubilee platform had images of Nelson's Column. I say 'had' because when the Jubilee was extended, Charing Cross was not invited. The new line would run directly from Green Park to Westminster, before proceeding

The opening of the Jubilee Line in 1979 coincided with a rather indeterminate, or experimental, period in Underground station decoration. The coming of the line to Baker Street was celebrated with a Sherlock Holmes theme at the station. The tiling here is actually from a Bakerloo platform, but it photographs better than the wispy (if charming) illustrations from the Holmes stories that feature on the Jubilee platforms themselves. The author suggests (tentatively) that nowhere in the stories are Holmes and Watson described as arriving at or departing from Baker Street station.

to Waterloo and points east. When it became clear in the late Nineties that this would happen, I received anxious letters to my 'Tube Talk' column from Charing Cross Jubilee users, and I raised the matter with a press officer. 'It's not possible to run new tunnels between Charing Cross and Waterloo,' she said. 'Why?' I asked. 'There's just too much stuff below the ground,' she replied, not completely convincingly. So the Jubilee Line platforms at Charing Cross were closed to passengers and opened to film-makers, including those responsible for the above-mentioned horror film *Creep*, in which a lot of blood is spilled on those platforms, a very fitting metaphor. Christian Wolmar has described the abandonment of the Jubilee Charing Cross as 'a shocking waste of money', given that it had been opened only a decade before.

It had long been acknowledged that south-east London was badly served by public transport, and it was always the idea that the Jubilee should head in that direction. The particular route it ended up taking – through Docklands – was a result of the fact that the regeneration of that area by private capital was a major project of Thatcherism. Olympia & York, the developers of Canary Wharf, did contribute to the costs of building the line, but not nearly as much as had been envisaged. British Gas also contributed towards the building of North Greenwich station, which would serve their aim of redeveloping the land on which the East Greenwich Gasworks had stood. North Greenwich is today the station for the O2 Centre, a fact announced on every train passing through. But in 1999 the O2 was the emerging Millennium Dome, that vast symbol of ... something or other that became the second magnet for the extension after the Canary Wharf development had been completed. And by now Tony Blair's ego was on the line (so to speak) just as Margaret Thatcher's had been.

It was essential that the guests at the opening of the Dome be taken there by Tube, and so it was also essential the line be completed by the end of 1999, which it was (just), the effort adding considerably to the expense of construction. The extension opened along its entire length on 22 December 1999, at a cost of £3.5 billion pounds, £2 billion over-budget.

I rode the extension in its first week, carrying an Underground press release so emboldened by the positive reviews of the station architecture that it was headed 'What's *Your* Favourite Station?' I interviewed some passengers, and a man at Canada Water said, 'Why all this grey? What's wrong with a bit of colour … Some red here and there? Tell you what,' he added confidentially, 'a bit of *green* wouldn't go amiss.' At Canning Town a woman whispered, awestruck, 'It's so clean, isn't it?' The line remains pristine, and the scale of the stations is still striking; the passengers within, riding the banks of escalators, descending through the multi-levels, resemble the numerous extras in Fritz Lang's *Metropolis*. You could fit the whole of Canary Wharf Tower into Canary Wharf station; you almost need a Tube train to get from one end of it to the other. But North Greenwich is even bigger. You could fit the QE2 into *that* … And North Greenwich is *not* grey. There the moulded concrete and polished steel that characterises the extension gives way to giant ovoid pillars clad in mosaic tiles of dark blue, the melancholic but reassuring shade of an old-fashioned police lamp.

The ride comes above ground after North Greenwich. Next comes sprawling West Ham station, followed by even more sprawling Stratford, where the Jubilee, the Central, the Dockland Light Railway, London Overground and two national railway lines coincide beneath an over-sailing glass roof. This is the Olympic station, and the last time I was there, when I wanted to have a look at the new stadium, I found myself directed towards it by signs leading me through part of that reverberating hangar the Westfield Stratford City Shipping Centre, and I didn't approve. Not that anyone gives a stuff because I am just another of the extras on the set, but I mean … talk about 'exit through the gift shop'.

Compare the other end of the Jubilee. In the small but pretty ticket hall at Stanmore local information is displayed behind glass panels, and it has been the same local information for years, if not decades. Alongside notices about Stanmore Choral Society and Stanmore Bowls Club is the following: 'The Bird Walk of Canons Park meets during autumn, winter and spring on the first Sunday of every month at the Donnefield Avenue entrance to Canons Park. The walk is led by Robin, an RSPB member who has an encyclopaedic knowledge of ornithology.'

The Jubilee Line extension has played its part – albeit slowly – in making Canary Wharf an easterly rival to the City. Whereas its working population was only 15,000 when the extension opened, it is now 90,000, and predicted to double by 2020. At the time of writing, the Jubilee is receiving a bad press because of the disruption caused by the implementation of 'moving block' signalling. But all of that will be forgotten about when the system is fully working. Then again, the sheer inaccessibility of southeast London before the extension was built may also be forgotten about. During the opening week it was still fresh in the memory of one woman I spoke to at Canary Wharf. She said, 'I love this station.' I asked why, and she said, 'Do you know how many buses it used to take me to get to the West End? Four.'

LIVINGSTONE RETURNS

Ken Livingstone became the MP for Brent East in 1987 and set about irritating the Labour leadership just as he had irritated Mrs Thatcher. He had no time for the triangulations of Tony Blair, and didn't care for Blair's idea of returning a limited measure of local democracy to London by means of a mere 'strategic' body (it would set policy and run services through proxies, not directly), to be called the Greater London Authority. It would be mainly concerned with policing and transport, something called Transport for London (with that ingratiating lower-case f in 'for') replacing London Regional Transport. But there was a vacancy for a star, since the Authority would be headed by an elected mayor, who would be rather lightly overseen by an elected twenty-five-member Greater London Assembly. Livingstone wanted the job, to the annoyance of Blair, whose idea of a London mayor was a benign elder statesman who had outgrown political squabbling.

Frank Dobson was selected as the official Labour candidate for mayor, but in the election of 2000 Livingstone stood against him as an independent, and won. Here he was in charge of transport again. He had the power to set fares and to introduce road pricing for London, and this he did, by his introduction of the central London Congestion Charge, with the money raised going into public transport. The Tube being 'at capacity', he improved the bus network so as to accommodate as many as possible of the motorists who would now leave their cars at home. (London buses now provide a de luxe service – they're regular and well maintained – and almost half the people using them pay nothing to do so, being under eighteen or of pensionable age. So the buses are not as cheap to operate as they once were, and they no longer subsidise the Underground.)

Livingstone was empowered to appoint a Commissioner for Transport to run TfL (of which London Underground Limited was a wholly owned subsidiary), and he chose an American, which ought not to surprise us by now: Robert Kiley, a man with a tough-guy persona who'd revitalised the New York Subway, the money raised by the issue of bonds backed by the guaranteed fare income of the system. Bond issues have long been favoured by Livingstone as the cheapest method of raising funds for the Underground, and a transport expert recently suggested to me that, because of its 'rock solid' fare income, London Underground had a better credit-worthiness than most European governments. But built in to the legislation that had created the Greater London Authority Act of 1999 was a new scheme of funding that took the principle of contracting out to bizarre lengths of complication: the Public Private Partnership (or PPP).

The PPP was not privatisation, which the Conservatives had been proposing, but it was the next best, or worst, thing. London Underground would operate the lines, but two consortia of engineers, or 'infracos' – Metronet and Tube Lines – would be contracted to maintain them over a period of thirty years, during which an Upgrade would be implemented that would compensate for the thirty years of neglect after the war.

The infracos would be financially rewarded or penalised, according to extremely abstruse mathematical formulae that were supposed to characterise good or bad customer experience. In essence – and I am not disguising the desperation with which I reach for that phrase – the consortia won or lost according to how much time they saved the customers. One problem was that the contracts did not sufficiently motivate the consortia to make improvements; another was the cost of creating a contract for every Underground relationship. What had been an organic entity became a stiffly working machine built by lawyers charging hundreds of pounds an hour. Another problem was the demoralisation of Underground managers, caused by the implied statement 'Only the private sector can be trusted to modernise the Tube.' Oh, and the PPP was never meant to fund the entire Upgrade; it would provide only about a quarter of the money, and the rest would come from government. Livingstone and Kiley fought the plan all the way to its implementation in 2003.

In 2007, three years into Livingstone's second term as mayor (this time he had been the official Labour candidate), Metronet found that it could not afford to meet its obligations under the PPP. It went into administration, and London Underground bought most of the debt, with assistance from the Department of Transport. In 2010 Tube Lines and London Underground were in dispute over funding, and this ended with London Underground buying out Tube Lines and the collapse of the PPP. The responsibility for the Upgrade has now been taken 'in house' – that is, London Underground itself commissions private companies to 'deliver' it, by means of 'simple contracts for achievable jobs'.

Livingstone had been right all along. But a prophet is without honour etc., and in 2008 he was swept from office on an anti-Labour tide. Will he go down as another of our Tube martyrs? He doesn't seem the martyred type, but it is too early to say.

THE UPGRADE

We are stuck with that word 'Upgrade', although other, subsidiary designations have been used on the posters that have been half-boasting, half-apologising for it (because it does bring the dreaded 'weekend closures') in the decade since it began. Sometimes the posters have read 'Transforming Your Tube'; the expression 'PPP Upgrade' is long gone and now not even to be mentioned. I like the ones that say, in Johnston typeface, 'We have a plan', concluding with that winking-eye, the diamond-shaped full stop. Apparently the Upgrade is referred to in-house at London Underground as 'The New, New Works', and being a traditionalist, I like that as well.

The theme of the publicity is that the Tube is 'at capacity', with the latest, record-breaking figure being 1.1 billion passenger journeys a year. So the aim is to increase capacity by 30 per cent, by means of bigger stations, longer, more capacious trains and new signalling systems allowing a faster throughput of trains. Many aspects of this effort have already been touched on, to which I will add mention of the expansion of both Tottenham Court Road (the new station will be six times bigger than the old one) and Farringdon to accommodate Crossrail, and the redevelopment of King's Cross St Pancras, where the circulating areas are now wonderfully airy spaces in white and dark blue.

The scale of the changes continues to seem extravagant, even though the Upgrade was cut back after the collapse of the PPP. The aspect that has been curtailed is the aesthetic improvement of the stations. Fortunately, this programme has already touched most of the stations, and it extends well beyond the central area. In charge of the Customer Environment Design Team (as you might be able to tell from the nattiness of his suits) is Mike Ashworth, the man who made the connection between the '38 trains and 'women of a certain age'. He is from Rochdale; another 'Man from the North' who, like Frank Pick, became entranced by the Underground on boyhood visits to London: 'We would visit relatives in Kensal Green, and I was more interested in the journey along the Bakerloo line than I was in the relatives. My parents were mortified when they discovered I'd started writing off to London Underground asking for leaflets.'

His job title, 'Design and Heritage Manager', is attested to by the regard the new decor has for the old decor. For instance, at Bethnal Green he implemented a couple of years ago a 'complete replication' of its original New Works appearance, with concourse tiles of the colour known as 'biscuit', while the ones on the platforms are yellow, with orange and black trim – all as first prescribed by Charles Holden. When the wraps came off, a woman who had used the station all her life said to Mike, 'Well, you've just cleaned it haven't you?' All the departures from the original colour scheme that had eroded the identity of a station since her girlhood had been instantly forgotten. Further along the easterly extension of the Central Line are the stations once served by overground steam trains. These had subsequently 'gone everywhere' in their colour scheme, and Ashworth and his team had proposed redecorating them in the colours of the Great Eastern Railway that had built them. 'But that turned out to be two shades of brown.' Instead, three shades of green were chosen for Woodford, Fairlop and Snaresbrook, in accordance with the colour scheme of the Great Eastern's successor, the London & North Eastern Railway.

But Mike Ashworth admits that, 'If people can go from A to B without trouble, they don't pay much attention to the look of the station.' Or if they do, they might disapprove, suspecting that money spent on what may seem mere cosmetic changes is money wasted. Hence this letter, which appeared in the *Evening Standard* in March 2011:

> It seems billions can be spent on public transport without any discernible improvement in the service. The Tubes I have used have got no more reliable in the past two years, but the Victorian wall tiles have been replaced. I don't mind if stations look 120 years old. It adds character.

By way of reply, Mike Ashworth hit me with some of the jargon: 'The customer-facing ambience is important for pragmatic and operational reasons. If customers enter a thoughtful and well-organised environment, they have the impression of an organisation that knows what it's doing.' 'So they move quicker?' I suggested. 'That's it,' he said.

Doubtless the Tube will be 'beyond capacity' again in thirty years' time. The restored stations should still look handsome, given good maintenance. It would be a shame if there were too many people in the way for the ordinary Tube rider to appreciate them.

CHAPTER FOURTEEN

LONDONERS AND THE TUBE

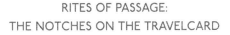

RITES OF PASSAGE: THE NOTCHES ON THE TRAVELCARD

In *The Subterranean Railway* Christian Wolmar writes: 'There is a paradox about the Underground. The miraculous system created by the pioneers is largely disliked and reviled by today's regular users.' He cites overcrowding as one reason for this. The Underground also reminds Londoners of going to work, and whereas the commuting life once generated semi-affectionate satire – think of Tony Hancock in *The Rebel*, taking his seat on his morning train and sighing, 'Journey number 6,833' – even that has now gone. The novelty has worn off.

But since Londoners are locked into Tube use, they accumulate experiences, and they share those experiences. When I was writing my column, a man called Mr Cross, from east London, wrote to me on the subject of the Tube user's rites of passage, the 'notches on the Travelcard', as he put it, that signify the seasoned passenger. Mr Cross wrote that he had witnessed a 'one under' (a suicide); he had been led along the tracks (with the current switched off) from a train broken down in a tunnel; he had, from sheer high spirits when younger, run down the up escalator; he had left an umbrella on a train.

What Mr Cross had never done was pull the passenger safety alarm until, that is, the week before, and this was the reason for his writing. He had been on a Northern Line train at Camden, due to head south on the City branch. A drunk boarded the train and began abusing passengers. 'Eventually,' wrote Mr Cross, 'the drunk recorded his disapproval of the company he was keeping by being comprehensively incontinent on his seat just as the train entered King's Cross station.' Unable to bear the thought of any other passenger taking that seat, Mr Cross pulled the passenger alarm. A station attendant appeared ('It was like rubbing a lamp'), closely followed by a British Transport Policeman. The drunk was led away; everyone was turned out of the car, and its doors were locked. Mr Cross settled into the car next to the one that had been sealed, only to be joined by another abusive drunk at Angel. This character roared expletives at everyone present, and then used the communicating doors to enter the car that had been sealed at King's Cross. 'It was with a deep sense of satisfaction,' wrote Mr Cross, 'that I watched him squelch down in the seat recently vacated by his colleague.'

I would add to Mr Cross's Travelcard notches the first time an attractive stranger speaks to you on the Tube. I don't know whether to lament or boast about the fact that this happened to me only a few weeks ago. Her opening gambit (she was drunk, of course) was: 'You seem to be older than me.'

'For Valentine's Day,' an editor once instructed me, 'I want you to write about love on the Underground', but I couldn't dig up much. I read in *Underground News* that on 30 April 1986 at Bank station a woman hit her eighty-year-old husband with a handbag, which sent him tumbling down an escalator. Just before Christmas in 1989, an Underground labourer who had consumed ten pints of bitter had an unorthodox interaction with a cat on a Tube train. Then he fell into a stupor, and his first remark on being awakened by an appalled fellow passenger was, 'What cat?' He was later fined £500. For many years the dating agency Dateline placed posters throughout the Underground that showed a man and a woman crossing on adjoining escalators. 'A hidden glance, a forgotten smile', ran the copy. 'Have you ever looked and wondered what might have been?' That drove me mad, because if you'd forgotten the smile then you wouldn't wonder what might have happened as a result of it. Even so, when the fashion designer Bella Freud (who launched one of her collections on a Tube train) said, 'There's a strange tension on the Tube, a moodiness, a sexiness', I think she was right.

You're entitled to carve a notch the first time you see a celebrity on the Underground. My wife saw Tony Blair on a Tube train just before the election of 1996: 'He was reading about himself in the *Observer*.' I have never seen a senior Conservative on the Tube. I do not read much into this, but they are reputed not to be familiar with public transport. I grew up on the story of the newly installed Conservative Transport minister who was being shown about the Tube by Underground officials. On boarding one train, he says, 'I'm rather thirsty. Which one's the dining car?' In May 2010 a Mark Redhead wrote to the *Guardian* telling this story, describing it as 'almost certainly true' and naming Nicholas Ridley (Transport Secretary 1983–6) as the minister in question, but I didn't believe Mr Redhead. I saw Anthony Hopkins asleep on the Piccadilly Line at Russell Square. I've seen Jonathan Miller twice on the Northern Line, and I saw Julian Barnes reading the *TLS* on an escalator at Euston.

Noticing a pigeon boarding a Tube train can also be a punctuation point in one's life. They do this commonly, especially on the cut-and-cover lines. They let the passengers off first, then hop onto the trains, alighting one or more stops later, and the question is: do they know where they're going? Because pigeons do have highly developed navigational skills. They certainly look as though they know what they're doing, but then they always do; I mean … can a pigeon look confused? In 1995 this question of Tube travelling by pigeons was debated in the letter columns of *New Scientist* until a man from the RSPB authoritatively pronounced, 'A pigeon's only incentive to step on a train is to look for food.' He meant any food that might be on the train, not at the next stop along the line.

Then there is the first time you are pickpocketed on a Tube train. This has yet to happen to me, but I am regularly warned against pickpockets by more or less deafening announcements. (There is also the more general announcement. 'This is a message from the British Transport Police. Thieves will lose no opportunity to steal your personal belongings', which reminds me of Peter Cook playing a thick policeman in a sketch, and declaring, 'We believe this robbery to be the work of thieves.') Pickpocketing accounts for half of all Underground crime, and the leading pickpocket in London, so to speak, is Keith 'The Thief' Charmley, a stage pickpocket, who used to be a Tube train driver. He told me that, when riding on the Tube, he will often see 'blokes who look like they're at it. The dipper might be scratching his eyelid to show the stall that he's just eyeballed the mark.' To translate: the dipper is the pickpocket; the stall is his accomplice – a person who might collide with the victim, or 'mark', distracting him at the crucial moment. Keith worked on the Metropolitan Line and became fascinated by a certain bin at Whitechapel station where local pickpockets used to leave 'skinned' (empty) wallets. He told me that if you see a man scrunching pieces of paper into a ball, and throwing them on the track – a common sight, he insists – then that might be a pickpocket, destroying the evidence.

THE MORBID INTEREST

There is an overlap between the notches of Mr Cross and the folklore of the Underground that expresses a truth about our relationship with the Underground, namely that it's all right to take an interest in it as long as it's a *morbid* interest.

Was a man with a wooden leg, Bumper Harris, employed to demonstrate that first escalator at Earl's Court in October 1911, the idea – perhaps – being to show that, if he could use an escalator, then how much more easily could a person with the full complement of legs? Of our leading Tube authorities, Jackson and Croome assert it as bald fact, Christian Wolmar describes it as 'a myth'; Stephen Halliday describes it as 'a semi-myth'. *Underground News*, the journal of the London Underground Railway Society, believes in Bumper Harris and has asserted that he was an Underground employee who had lost his leg on the job, and that he eventually retired to Gloucestershire, where – a clinching detail, surely – 'he made violins and cider'.

There is also the 'secret tunnel' genre. Does a secret passageway link Buckingham Palace to the Victoria Line in order to facilitate the emergency evacuation of the Queen? I once phoned the Palace to ask whether such a tunnel existed. 'No,' said a woman, who sounded very *like* the Queen, 'it does not.' 'Are you sure?' I said, and she put the phone down.(There used to be a not-so-secret tunnel allowing MPs to access the District Line platforms at Westminster station.)

There are the books full of Underground ghost stories. An invisible runner pounds along the platforms at Elephant & Castle; children scream in the basement of what used to be the surface building of Hyde Park Corner, and which became Pizza on the Park. (They continued to scream it was said, even while the Four Seasons and Margheritas were being rolled out.) William Terris, an actor murdered in 1897, manifests in Covent Garden station. The best one I know of was sent to me in a letter a few

Francis Bacon on the Piccadilly Line. The Tube is a relatively upmarket way to travel, and the rich and famous are frequently to be seen upon it. The author has logged sightings of, amongst others, Julian Barnes, Jonathan Miller, and somebody who might have been Anthony Hopkins. He (the author) once asked a man had written books about the New York Subway whether Woody Allen used the Subway. 'Of course, he does', came the reply. 'He's not a schmuck.'

years ago. Late one night a Piccadilly Line driver was running his empty train into the depot at Northfields when he heard a knock on his cab's connecting door into the carriage. He turned and opened the door, saw no one there but noticed that all the connecting doors of the carriages were open, as though someone had walked along the length of the train. The driver refused to continue, so another man was brought in to close the doors and take the train into the depot. Shortly after he started the train he heard a knock … and all the doors were open again.

There is a great fascination with the closed-down stations, which are sometimes called 'ghost stations'. A businessman, the somehow fittingly named Ajit Chambers, has set up the Old London Underground Company to provide 'tourist adventures' in the abandoned stations and to offer them as venues for parties and corporate events. Mr Chambers believes the appeal of the closed-down stations lies in their 'ghostliness'. It's an association clinched at the old British Museum station on the Central, which was supposed to be haunted by one or more Ancient Egyptians whose mummified remains were in the British Museum – a 'farcical suggestion', according to *London's Disused Underground Stations* (2001), by J. E. Connor. Just before the closure of the station in 1933 (when the Central Line platforms at nearby Holborn were opened), a newspaper offered a reward to anyone who would spend a night there, and I do not believe there were any takers.

In the archive of Theobald's Road Library, I once came across a photograph of two Edwardian shops on Kentish Town Road. The first was called Henderson's Hygienic British Bakery, the window advertising Hovis Rusks ('As supplied to His Majesty The King') and 'Artistic High Class Wedding Cakes'. The shop next door was 'H. Ritchie, Beef and Pork Butcher', and there was a notice in the window: 'These premises have been acquired for the building of the Tube Railway.' In fact, the Tube railway – Yerkes's Hampstead Railway – would do for both shops, and I wonder: was it worth it? Because the station built on the site was South Kentish Town, which I cycle past half a dozen times a week, and which was opened in 1907 and closed in 1924. You see, it was too close to Kentish Town station. In his short story 'South Kentish Town' (1951) John Betjeman described the station as being 'like a comma in the wrong place in a sentence or an uncalled-for remark in the middle of an interesting story'. In his own story a Pooterish chap called Basil Green is so engrossed in the *Evening Standard* that when the doors of his train accidentally open at South Kentish Town he gets off and spends a hairy night on the dark platform. Today retail has reasserted itself, since the Leslie Green surface building houses a Cash Converter (and also the enticing-sounding Omega Massage Parlour). The manager of the Cash Converter told me he doesn't often think about the closed-down station below, except that 'Sometimes the blokes from the Underground come round. They open a trapdoor in the floor, and they go down and kill all the rats.'

About a mile away, and also on the Northern Line, is another station that is part of the folklore, and one with a jollier, if still bathetic, resonance: Mornington Crescent. It too is under-used and once was closed down, between 1992 and 1995, but the closure only enhanced its status as the joker in the pack. Mornington Crescent exists in a kind of ellipsis. It's not on Mornington Crescent; it's only near that charming if shambolic street. (The painter Frank Auerbach referred admiringly to its 'seedy curve'; there used to be a Hotel Splendid on Mornington Crescent, only the '-did' had fallen off, coming to a rest at an angle in the balcony below.) Mornington Crescent station is on ... well, Camden High Street, Eversholt Street and Hampstead Road, since it occupies a corner site. The station is separated from Mornington Crescent by what used to be the Carreras cigarette factory (now thoroughly rehabilitated as the home of the British Heart

Foundation), which sits on Hampstead Road and no other, and whose workers used to supply most of the station's customers. Essentially, Mornington Crescent station is called Mornington Crescent because to have called it Hampstead Road would have risked confusion with Hampstead station.

There isn't much *around* Mornington Crescent, and the station was Monday–Friday only for a long time before its temporary closure. I recall from my early days in London that it did its best business on Wednesday nights, when trainloads of Draculas rolled up there: Goth Night at the Camden Palais. The actual closure was triggered by 'seepage on the staircase', and the station was re-opened, extensively and handsomely refurbished, after it was decided the seepage could be 'managed'.

Mornington Crescent was declared re-opened by some or all of the regulars from the Radio 4 'antidote to panel games', *I'm Sorry I Haven't a Clue*, and there is today a plaque commemorating the life of one of those regulars, Willie Rushton, alongside the notice warning you that the staircase has eighty-six steps. That the *Clue* men should have called their best and strangest game Mornington Crescent is entirely fitting in view of the station's anomalous status. The many listeners writing in to say they are baffled by the rules are referred to N. F. Stovold's *Mornington Crescent: Rules and Origins*, which they are also told is, and always has been, out of print.

PROPER FANS

These people prove their fandom by expenditure of time and money. They might join the London Underground Railway Society, which celebrated its fiftieth anniversary in 2011 but didn't go out of its way to court journalistic interest. The members have been turned over as 'trainspotters' too often. There are monthly meetings, at which learned speakers give lectures on the

Underground, and there is a journal, *Underground News*, containing news of more or less everything that happened on the network in the previous month – 'A smell of burning from an escalator at Wood Green kept the station closed until 6.50 on Bank Holiday Monday' – along with essays, clearly and very elegantly written but with daunting levels of detail ('District Electric Trains, Part 13, Segregation and Disappointment'); members correspond with one another, bandying incredible arcania: 'In *Underground News* No. 581, there is a query whether trains reversing at Loughton depart westbound empty while platform resurfacing is under way. The short answer is "apparently not" but some explanation might be of interest.' Some 500 words follow.

The style is old-fashioned, the voice passive, and a phlegmatic dry humour is the hallmark of the journal. The July 2010 number reported that four model owls were installed near the stairs at Wembley Park station to deter pigeons. 'It was thought this was due to staff complaints and illness from the resulting "crappage". Sadly, it hasn't worked as the pigeons they are supposed to scare off now perch next to them. The next move is to place the owls on springs so they move in the wind, thereby scaring the pigeons.'

Membership – about a thousand – has remained steady in recent years, which is an achievement when other railway societies are dying off. The Society is independent of London Underground, but a third of the members are LU staff.

… Or these proper fans might join *Subterranea Britannica*, which has a website at subbrit.org.uk. The organisation is devoted to, in alphabetical order and among many other underground phenomena: air-raid shelters, coal-mines, dungeons, grottoes, ossuaries, priest holes and … underground railways. An official of the society, a town planner in the surface world, once attempted to explain to me the appeal of underground travel: 'There's just something nice about the idea that you can move without being seen – that you can go down *there* and come up *here.* I grew up in a stately home, he continued without a trace of boastfulness, 'and there actually was a secret passage. I think that's what started me off. But I also read a lot of Rupert books, and he's always finding trapdoors in lawns that lead to interesting places.'

The proper fans might also expend time – about twenty hours – trying to visit every Tube station as quickly as possible. Plenty of people have visited every Tube station. I myself have visited *almost* every Tube station. I had a friend who had visited every one and had the photographs to prove it: 'Here's me at Willesden Green' etc. John Betjeman visited every Tube station as an adolescent, in company with a man called Ronald Wright, who went on to become a monk. But to visit every station *in record time* – which people have been attempting since at least 1960 – requires real fortitude. You must get up before dawn; you must drink and eat almost nothing during the attempt, so niggardly is the Underground with toilet provision. You must know your Tube system. In the years when Olympia on the District line was open for exhibitions only, you had to choose an exhibition day.

A man called Robert Robinson – not the late quizmaster – dominated this field in the Eighties and Nineties. He has made almost fifty attempts on this record, often with a friend called 'Mr McLaughlin of East Wokingham'. In 1994 the two established a time of 18 hours, 18 minutes and 9 seconds, which was not beaten until 2000, and it was Mr Robinson who beat it. 'You've got to be able to interpret the signals,' he told me. 'For example, if there's a red light at Hyde Park, it probably just means a train is being held because it's early, but a red light at Knightsbridge … chances are there's a problem.'

The rules are arcane. You must arrive at and depart from each station on a train. You can travel between the end points of lines on foot or by bus. It has been ruled that you cannot do so on a Spacehopper. You must keep a log of times, train numbers and carriage numbers, and these must accord with the detailed records of train movements that London Underground keeps for six weeks. The start and end-points are up to you. In 2004 Geoff Marshall and Neil Blake set the record by starting at Amersham on the Met at 5.29 a.m. and finishing at Upminster on the District at 12.05, a slower time than Mr Robinson's, but the Jubilee Line Extension had been built since then. Every time the network is modified, the challenge is 're-set' – for example, when Heathrow Terminal 5 station was opened in 2008. A recent holder of the record was Marc Gawley of Manchester, and it was no coincidence that he was a marathon runner. When I asked Mr Robinson why he'd made his own attempts, he said, 'It gets to be a bug. And I suppose I'm a nutter.'

… Or the proper fan might make a model of the Underground. Probably the leading Underground modeller is John Polley, who used to be a Tube train driver. The layout that he tours around model railway exhibitions is called Abbey Road. It's not named after the Beatles album, or the street in St John's Wood that inspired that name. It's just that, as he says, 'Abbey Road sounds like the name of a Tube station.' John has a gift for such names, and he is working on a new layout to be called 'something like Bishop's Park'. The Abbey Road layout shows an above-ground suburban station on a Tube line, and surrounding premises. For the buildings John uses plastic sheeting employed in the window banners of a particular ladies' clothing chain. 'It used to be called Evans Outsizes because it's for the larger lady, but now it's just Evans. I think it's a politically correct thing.' I asked John if the sales assistants in those shops thought he was odd, walking in and asking for bits of plastic. 'What you've got to remember,' he said, 'is that they get a lot of cross-dressers going in there, so I'm not that weird in comparison.' Not many people model Underground trains: 'It's a niche thing', and it always has been.

Among John's peers are men who have built and exhibited

layouts called London Road, Willesden Green, Dora Park (named in honour of the maker's wife) and Scrub's Lane.

You can't just walk into a model shop and buy little Tube trains, although you could for a brief period in the Fifties, when Eveready made a model Underground train, to advertise the battery that powered it. So Underground modellers work from 'scratch' – that is, they make their own stuff, or adapt. John runs a business whereby he imports from China brass static models of Underground trains; he then fits a motor and bogies, and a great deal of fine detailing. He does the '38 stock, of course; also the '59 stock. In 1999 John was exhibiting an Underground layout called Mill Ridge (another completely plausible name) at Chesham when he noticed a man looking on with acute interest. This was the late Mark Adlington, a former bus conductor who spent most of his time caring for his wheelchair-bound mother and so seldom left his home. At Chesham Mark asked John if he had time to come and see his own model. When, a few hours later, John was shown into a modest bedroom, he 'felt like Howard Carter when he opened Tutankhamen's tomb in 1922'. The room contained a model of an entire wing of 55 Broadway in card and plastic, and brilliantly detailed models of Pick- and Holden-era Tube stations, trains and buses, all done from memory, the detail extending to the tax discs on the buses. Before his death Mark asked John if he could find a home for his models, and they are now part of the collection of the London Transport Museum, to which we now turn our own steps, it being a likely destination of the Proper Fan with money to spend.

The London Transport Museum was established, from disparate collections, at Covent Garden in 1980. Its role, says Mike Walton, Head of Trading at the Museum, is 'to preserve, interpret, educate'. The role of the adjacent shop is to make money. Three hundred thousand people visit the Museum annually, three times more than when it was established, and the sales at the shop are up 'hugely' since then. In the shop, postcards and posters are the big sellers. And the image 'that really punches above its weight' is Harry Beck's Tube map. You can buy a bag made out of Tube or bus seat moquette, or commission a sofa made in that moquette, so you can be sitting watching television on the same stuff you rode home from work on … except that historical moquettes are what interest most people. 'Ah,' I said to Mr Walton, 'then we must be talking about the green and red of the 1938 stock.' 'That appeals to the older generation,' he said, deflatingly, 'but the biggest seller is the mainly orange and black one, designed by Misha Black, that went onto the District trains from 1978, and the Jubilee from 1983. It was also on most London buses from the late Seventies to the early Eighties. That's the "old" moquette to the younger generation.' Mike Walton suggests, 'The Underground branding is iconic: the roundel, the typeface, the map. It is the language of the city, whether for Londoners or visitors.'

The proper fans are certainly not confined to this country. I told Mr Walton that a friend of mine had been out with a Swedish girl, and she'd said there were two extraordinary things about London. One: the houses had drainpipes on the outside (which they apparently don't in Sweden, because the water will freeze). Two: the smell of the Underground. She thought they should bottle it and sell it.

Underground News regularly publishes photographs taken by its readers of the Tube roundel as it has been employed around the world. (And I'm sure all users have applied for permission, because the roundel is a registered trademark.) A recent number showed a photograph of a health centre in Vancouver with 'Care-station' written on the blue bar; and a jeans shop in Hazeyview, South Africa, with 'Blue Junction' written in the bar. A deli in New York called The London Underground Gourmet features the roundel prominently on its menus. The fare is named after

Tube stops, so a 'Wood Green' is a salad containing eggplant (or aubergine), zucchini (courgette), red peppers and mushrooms, served with mixed salad. A 'Queensway' features smoked turkey and brie and salad. Another salad is called 'Parsons Green'. There is also a sandwich called a 'Nottingham', which might cause the experienced Tube user to raise an eyebrow. Not that it doesn't sound absolutely delicious, comprising fresh mozzarella with grilled red peppers, pesto sauce and, of course, salad ... but when I visited New York, I wondered whether there might have been some confusion with Notting Hill. I spoke to the manager of the deli, a man called John, who said it had been named by its owner, Amy, after she'd returned from an enjoyable trip to London. John said, 'We get two or three English people in here every day, and they all think it's cute that that the food is named after Underground stations.'

'But what about the Nottingham?' I asked. 'What do you mean?' said John. 'Well,' I persisted sadistically, 'Nottingham is not an Underground station.' John paused thoughtfully for a while: 'Well I'll tell you something,' he said. 'It's quite a great sandwich.'

The difference between a foreigner and a Londoner is that a foreigner isn't stuck with the system. He doesn't regard the dot matrix message, 'High Barnet ... 8 mins' as another nail in his coffin. Why do Londoners want to buy into the iconography of a system that can cause them so much grief? An assistant in the Museum shop once told me, 'Let's face it, when your train's late you've got the hump. But when you stand back and look at the system it's something incredible isn't it?' And there does seem to be this duality. The Museum shop really began to take off in 1990, when the centenary of the City & South London – nascent Bank branch of the Northern Line – was being celebrated. The Northern Line was then being denigrated every week in the *Evening Standard*, but that didn't stop sales of the associated memorabilia. I am reminded of a trenchant sentiment from *Parallel Lines* (2004), by Ian Marchant. He wrote that in Britain there are two railways: the railway of reality and the railway of romance. The former, he said, was 'largely shit'. That is not usually true of the Underground, but even if it were, it might not matter, because the iconography trumps the service provision.

MODERN WONDERS

While my father was working on British Rail in the 1970s, we had a neighbour who was a travelling salesman – a man who practically lived in his car and loved his car. He believed that trains were uneconomic, inefficient and somehow (even though we'd invented trains) anti-British. He said that, if he were running the country, he'd scrap the railway lines and replace them with fleets of buses running along an improved network of roads. 'And would they be long buses with comfortable seats?' my father asked. 'They would,' he said; 'they'd be longer and wider than normal buses and much more comfortable – also faster.' 'And would they run in quick succession?' inquired my father. 'Yes,' said our neighbour, 'they'd follow each other almost continuously.' 'Then that would be called a *train*,' said my father, scoring a rhetorical coup only slightly tarnished by his constant re-telling of the story over subsequent years.

My father retained his commitment to rail travel in the years when the motor car was in the ascendant. Today the motor car is not taken seriously as a solution to the problems of mass transport, and the transport planners of south-east England – and the mayor of London himself, judging by his Transport Plan – think in terms of trains and underground trains in particular with all the burrowing fervour (if less of the social idealism) of Charles Pearson himself. Or you might say the planners are echoing the words of that head of the post-war railway executive John Elliot, who on 1 June 1958 said, 'We must get people underground … Our policy is to get more and more people underground.'

The Underground itself will not be much increased, although it seems as though the Northern Line will be extended from Kennington to Battersea. Another course, so to speak, will be added to the dog's dinner … because the Northern Line is already over-complicated. (Then again, TfL is also considering prising it apart at Camden, allowing a simplified, and therefore more frequent, service to the trains north of there, which would require the complete rebuilding of Camden Town station – and therefore of much of Camden Town itself – in order to allow changing en masse between the branches.)

The Big Dig, however (it's only a matter of time before it's called that), will be Crossrail: 73 miles from Heathrow and Maidenhead in the west to Shenfield and Abbey Wood in the east. Crossrail, its spokespeople want to make clear, is definitely not 'a Tube'. They don't think the term does justice to a line with full-size trains, only 13 of whose 73 miles will be 'in tunnel'. But those 13 miles go through central London, and where the Underground interchanges with Crossrail, its own stations will be boosted and glamorised, especially at Bond Street and Tottenham Court Road. The tunnelling shields for Crossrail will incorporate a canteen and toilets, and there is to be a tunnelling academy at Ilford, to train the thousands of employees in mole-like arts. That other half-underground line, Thameslink, is to have a capacity increase; and Crossrail will probably be followed by Crossrail 2 (a tunnel from Chelsea to Hackney), just as High

Speed 1, through Kent (which starts and ends in a tunnel), will be followed by High Speed 2, heading north (which will also start in a tunnel).

Crossrail (Crossrail 1, that is – let's keep our feet on the ground) will apparently alleviate congestion on the Central, Jubilee, Bakerloo and District Lines by 'between 20 and 60 per cent', which is just as well. The Tube Upgrade, which will be completed about when Crossrail opens in 2018, will provide a 30 per cent increase in capacity to a system that is unfortunately 50 per cent over capacity. And the population of London is expected to rise by nearly 20 per cent by 2030. The Tube, in other words, will continue to be crowded ... at which point I take off my London bowler hat and put on my northern flat cap, and say that the only answer is to make the whole of the neglected rest of the country into a giant Enterprise Zone. Get everyone who hasn't got a good excuse for being in London out of it. The Tube made the city too big, and it remains too big. In these moods I look at London through my northern filter. In London people will think nothing of going (by Tube) from Finchley to Wimbledon, a journey that might easily take two hours, in which time you could travel so much more bracingly from London to York, but Londoners are blinded to the comparison because their journey is 'all within the same city'.

How is that city to be regarded in the twenty-first century? A centre for the elite, and the suburbs for the ... less elite? It is clear that suburban living has its appeal, hence the middle-class flight from the centre of London which only began to be reversed with the loft-living movement of the Eighties. But it is hard to find a defence of suburban living in literature. I wonder how many residents of suburban London – I'm one of them myself – feel a sense of alienation from the city in which they live owing to their apparently marginal status. It is said that Crossrail will bring 1.5 million people within a 'one-hour commute' of central London, which sounds like no fun at all.

Philip Ross is an author, a transport consultant and CEO of Unwork.com, which 'challenges the way we work'. His research has discovered that the length of commute considered ideal by Londoners is ten minutes. Ross therefore proposes alternatives to the great respiration of London, by which we are sucked into the centre in the morning and exhaled in the evening. He favours 'polycentric working', so people are not tied to the central offices of their corporations, where, apparently, their desks are in use for less than half the day. Technology enables people to work remotely from their desks, why not also remotely from their offices? Philip Ross does not mean working from home. His research shows that people don't want to do that. They go stir crazy. Rather, they might work in an annexe of the company's main office, and that annexe might be in Finchley, or Wimbledon … or Surbiton. The biggest single starting point of commuters working in Canary Wharf is Surbiton. So why don't they just stay in Surbiton? At least for some days of the week, or until midday, getting the work that can be done in Surbiton out of the way before coming into HQ for meetings and the face-to-face stuff. This way journeys would be staggered, which has long been the aim of the Underground. (Remember the command designed to stop everyone going home at the same time: 'Play Between Six and Twelve.') Staggering could also be promoted, Philip Hall cunningly suggests, by Tube customers receiving a top-up to their Oysters in return for not travelling in the peak times.

This polycentric approach would boost the suburbs. The annexe-office workers would buy their coffees and sandwiches, and perhaps much else, there rather than in the middle of town, and ideally from an independent retailer. It would help raise morale in the outlying places, and London might truly become the collection of villages it is often romantically said to be … and the Tubes might become tolerable.

The needle is likely to lurch further towards 'intolerable' when mobile phones become usable on the network. On the plus side, the new 'S' stock trains that will eventually be running on all the cut-and-cover lines will be air-conditioned. That is good news because the earth around the tunnels on all the Underground lines gets hotter every year. It is hard to make deep-level Tube trains air-conditioned, because there isn't the space for the equipment, but there has been a general 'cooling programme' in place across the network since 2006. The new trains will also be fully 'walk-through', with no carriage end-doors. Travelling on them is like riding on a sinuous, moving corridor. It's less claustrophobic than the old arrangement, but now you can no longer choose the carriage not occupied by the declaiming loony.

Will Underground trains be completely driverless? The new signalling being installed as part of the Upgrade will allow this, and the development, allowing a faster throughput of trains, might arise from, or be stopped by, a battle with the unions. Mike Brown, Managing Director of London Underground, envisages driverless trains within twenty years. There might be a 'train captain' on board, as on the Docklands Light Railway (DLR), but this would be an unenviable role on our packed Tube: the train captain would be condemned to live in a permanent rush hour. Or the train might be completely unattended. Either way, lasar sensors detecting any movement on the tracks (but disregarding the movement of, say, pigeons or mice), and platform edge doors, as in the Jubilee Line extension stations, could make Tube suicide rarer. One benefit of driverless trains is that you can sit right at the front and have that privileged, hypnotic, driver's-eye view of a ride through the tunnels. On the DLR, or on the driverless Line 14 on the Paris Metro, I always try to sit at the front. (It's usually just a matter of elbowing aside some ten-year-old boys; I can then get on with pretending to drive the train.)

It's likely that ticket offices will also be closed, as ticketless

One of the new 'S' Stock trains that will be coming to all the cut-and-cover lines. It is walk-through, a moving hotel corridor (there are no end-doors to the cars). It is also air-conditioned, but the residual seating points to an over-crowded future.

travel comes in. (The barriers will effectively pickpocket you, by debiting the bank card in your wallet rather than your proffered Oyster.) It is my understanding that the vast majority of the stations on the Underground, unlike those on the Paris Metro, will continue to be staffed because of safety worries formulated after the King's Cross fire, but with the constant pressure for 'productivity increases', such speculation is dangerous. In fact, all speculation about the future of the Underground is dangerous …

Before me is the edition of *Modern Wonder* comic for 20 August 1938. It shows a streamlined Tube train racing through a tunnel in cross-section: 'There are four of these trains now in service on the Piccadilly Line.' The strong implication is that they are the future of Tube travel. The trains were a subdivision of the famous '38 stock, but the fashionable streamlinings brought a speed increase of precisely nothing (Tube trains didn't go fast enough to feel the benefit) and some passengers – older ones especially – thought they looked ridiculous, just as I think cyclists wearing Lycra look ridiculous. Those trains had been taken out of service by the time the war started, and some of the carriages came to a bathetic end as air-raid shelters at Northfields and Cockfosters.

I once interviewed a German businessman who tried to interest London Underground in technology that would project images onto tunnel walls so that, as the train moved, passengers would see a lateral film. The idea was that it might be used for advertising, or to show, say, the Yorkshire Dales on a sunny day, making for a less stressful ride. A friend of mine says that, in a future, more civilised London, there will be mattresses in the suicide pits – to provide a soft landing for those who survive the attempt. I'm sure Charles Pearson would have approved of that, while lamenting the necessity for the suicide pits in the first place. What would he have made of the way his creation has unfolded? You'd have to sit him down and give him a stiff drink before unveiling the whole story. The real 'facer' (a word he might have used to denote a shock) would be the realisation that, in creating the Metropolitan, he had created the modern Metro-*polis*. But I wonder what detail would have horrified him, or tick-led his fancy the most? Here is the writer with whom we began, Arnold Bennett, in a work called *How To Live on 24 Hours A Day*: 'There was a congestion of traffic in Oxford Street; to avoid the congestion people actually began to travel under the cellars and drains, and the result was a rise of rents in Shepherd's Bush! And you say that isn't picturesque!'

ACKNOWLEDGEMENTS

This has not been an official history of the London Underground, but the press office of Transport for London has been most helpful, especially Ann Laker. Several senior Underground people have given me interviews, and Mike Ashworth has given me more than one. I should also mention that every time I have asked a question of a member of staff on the Undergound they have tried to help me without first asking 'Who are you?' and 'Why do you want to know?' (Perhaps they *should* be asking those questions, but I am glad they are not.)

I am grateful to Brian Hardy and Piers Connor of the London Underground Railway Society, and to John Scott-Morgan, railway author. Each of these men, it seems to me, knows everything about the Underground – or at least, they answered every question I put to them straight off the top of their heads. Piers Connor, incidentally, runs one of the most comprehensive and clearly written websites about the Underground in all its aspects, at www.tubeprune.com. (The name stands for Tube Professionals' Rumour Network.)

I would like to thank Niall Devitt, of the London Transport Museum, and Peter Saxton and Peter Best for invaluable assistance with the text, and Wendy Neville, also of the Museum, for letting me in free. On Underground electricity I am grateful to Bob Gwynne and Eddie Wearing; on Underground gas lighting, Chris Sugg (see website on gas lighting www.williamsugghistory.co.uk); on Underground Steam, Oliver Densham of the Southwold Railway Trust; on general London history, Lisa Freedman and David Secombe (his elegant website is at thelondoncolumn.com); on Brunel's tunnel, Robert Hulse, Director of the Brunel Museum. Finally, I would like to thank Adam Edwards, who first commissioned me to write journalism about the Underground.

PICTURE CREDITS

The author and publisher would like to thank the following for permission to reproduce the illustrations: © akg-images, p. 227; © Bloomberg via Getty Images, p. 278; © Bob Krist/ CORBIS, p. 248; © David Secombe, p. 107; © Getty Images, p. 53; © Johnny Stiletto, p. 262; © TfL from the London Transport Museum, pp. 7, 8, 32, 74, 96, 140, 164, 185, 218.

SELECT BIBLIOGRAPHY

BOOKS

Peter Ackroyd, *London: The Biography* (2000)

T. C. Barker and M. Robbins, *A History of London Transport: Passenger Travel and the Development of the Metropolis*, vols 1 and 2 (1974)

Jeremy Black, *London: A History* (2009)

Michael Freeman, *Railways and the Victorian Imagination* (1999)

Ken Garland, *Mr Beck's Underground Map: A History* (1994)

Oliver Green, *Underground Art: London Transport Posters 1908 to the Present* (2001)

Stephen Halliday, *Underground to Everywhere: London's Underground Railway in the Life of the Capital* (2004)

Alan A. Jackson and Desmond F. Croome, *Rails through the Clay: A History of London's Tube Railways* (1962; 2nd edn 1993)

Simon Jenkins, *Landlords to London: The Story of a Capital and Its Growth* (1975)

David Leboff, *London Underground Stations* (1994)

John Scott-Morgan, *Red Panniers: Last Steam on the Underground* (2010)

David Welsh, *Underground Writing: The London Tube from George Gissing to Virginia Woolf* (2009)

Christian Wolmar, *The Subterranean Railway: How the London Underground Was Built, and How It Changed the City Forever* (2004)

DVD

John Betjeman, *Metroland* (1973)

INDEX